THE
LOBBYISTS

Also by Jeffrey H. Birnbaum

Showdown at Gucci Gulch
(with Alan S. Murray)

THE
LOBBYISTS

How Influence Peddlers

Work Their Way in

Washington

JEFFREY H. BIRNBAUM

TIMES BOOKS

RANDOM HOUSE

To the people with real influence:
my beloved parents and family

Book design by M. Kristen Bearse

Library of Congress Cataloging-in-Publication Data

Birnbaum, Jeffrey H.
    The lobbyists : how influence peddlers work their way in
Washington /
    Jeffrey H. Birnbaum. — 1st ed.
        p.   cm.
    ISBN 0-8129-2314-6
        1. Lobbyists—United States.   2. Lobbying—United States.
    3. Business and politics—United States.   4. Corporations—United
    States—Political activity.   I. Title.
    JK1118.B47   1992
    324'.4'0973—dc20   92-53673

Manufactured in the United States of America
9 8 7 6 5 4 3 2
First Paperback Edition

Introduction

Public awareness of—and disdain for—lobbyists reached a new height with the presidential campaign of 1992. Ross Perot never tired of bashing "alligator-shoed" lobbyists. And Bill Clinton quickly copied him with his own brand of populism. In his acceptance speech at the Democratic National Convention, candidate Clinton said of President Bush, he "won't break the stranglehold the special interests have on our elections and the lobbyists have on our government. But I will." Influence peddlers, and the special interests they represented, came to symbolize everything that was wrong with Washington, and Clinton's election confirmed that the public wanted the system to change.

This book was written to convey a sense of how lobbyists worked in 1989 and 1990. But in every significant case, they are still working the same way. The party in power may change the laws governing lobbying a bit, but the methods of this ancient vocation remain constant.

Even the vilification of lobbyists in 1992 was not completely new. Presidents Wilson, Truman, and Kennedy were masters of it, and President Reagan exploited the same sentiment to help pass his historic Tax Reform Act of 1986. Still, there was something extra this time around. Clinton made clear he would not rest until the rules of the game were altered.

As one of his first acts as president, he put his campaign rhetoric into action. He barred his top appointees from becoming lobbyists at their own agencies for five years after they left government and forbade them from lobbying for foreign governments for life. He also proposed to eliminate the tax deduction for lobbying expenditures, a measure that Congress went on to pass with little dissent.

But he did not stop there. He proposed, and Congress was poised to pass, legislation that required lobbyists to disclose more about who they were working for and how much they were paid. He even put campaign-finance reform on the table, a long overdue measure designed to reduce the clout of special-interest money in Washington.

Each move was widely hailed, and for good reason—especially the additional disclosure requirements. The lobbying-registration laws already on the books were toothless and allowed lobbyists to ply their trade free of serious scrutiny. Almost no one defended that system; it was clearly in the public's interest to know more about lobbyists. An awareness of what they wanted and fought to get was often central to understanding how laws were made and implemented.

Even lobbyists supported additional disclosure. "Lobbying ought to be regulated—it ought to be regulated more effectively—if for no other reason than to help to increase public confidence and understanding of our representative form of government," said Howard Marlowe, a former president of the American League of Lobbyists. "People have a right to know who is trying to influence what in the policy-making process and how much they are being paid."

It seemed it would not be long until the American people could glimpse into the secret world of lobbying and, with that new vision, fight more effectively for control of their own government.

But nothing under discussion in 1993 threatened to end the influence of lobbying. The repeal of the lobbying deduction would simply make it somewhat more expensive. Disclosure would make it more open. Campaign-finance reform would diminish the persuasiveness of campaign cash. And the Clinton lobbying bans were riddled with loopholes and affected few people. Experts agreed that lobbying would remain a potent force. The "stranglehold" of lobbyists would not be broken by President Clinton or anyone else.

"I don't think these things will have a major impact on lobbying. Lobbyists get used to things pretty fast," said James Thurber, director for the Center for Congressional and Presidential Studies at American University. "All of these reforms are good for the system; lobbyists will have to clean up their ethics a bit. But they won't go away. Lobbying may even grow a little to help keep track of the new changes."

The best proof of this was the great budget battle of 1993. Despite public disapproval of their vocation, lobbyists worked furiously to influence President Clinton's massive deficit-reduction bill that year. And, as usual, their efforts bore fruit. Massive letter-writing stirred by the senior citizens lobby limited the size of cutbacks to Medicare and Social Security. Drug company lobbyists kept alive a huge tax subsidy for their Puerto Rican operations, despite President Clinton's opposition. And a million-dollar campaign bankrolled by oil companies killed Clinton's large tax increase proposal, a broad-based energy tax.

Each of these squabbles was remarkably similar to the ones detailed in this book, which is about the budget fight three years earlier. The unavoidable conclusion is that lobbying is perennial and predictable. There is little doubt that the great budget battle of 1997 or of 1999 or of 2003 will have many of the same components. Only perhaps more so.

What, then, is ahead for lobbying? More growth and diversification, for certain. Activist presidents lead to an even even more active lobbying business. And President Clinton seemed allergic to sitting still. Indeed, his determination to overhaul the nation's health care system promised to produce the biggest explosion in lobbying since the tax bill of 1986.

And despite the president's populist rhetoric and legislation, he continued to work closely with lobbyists. One of the most important functions in the White House was to coordinate the support of lobbyists and their clients on behalf of the Clinton policies. There was a whole department devoted to the purpose. Clinton himself reached into the ranks of lobbyists to populate his administration. The top White House lobbyist, Howard Paster, was once a top corporate lobbyist; and several members of the cabinet, including Commerce Secretary Ronald Brown and Trade Representative Mickey Kantor, were also professional lobbyists.

In the years to come, some of the more subtle forms of the profession will likely grow in importance—especially "grass-roots lobbying," which entails generating letters and telephone calls from back home to convince decision-makers that real voters want what lobbyists are promoting. In addition, the cast of characters will change over time, and younger, even more sophisticated and well-informed lobbyists will become more prominent.

But without doubt, lobbying is here to stay.

Jeffrey H. Birnbaum
Washington, D.C.
October 1993

Contents

Prologue

The
Bag of
Tricks
Is Opened

"Okay," the President says. "Let's talk."

.   .   .

It is the bright, clear morning of Tuesday, June 26, 1990, and President George Bush is meeting in the White House with his economic advisers and the congressional leaders of both parties. Together, over steaming coffee in the private quarters, they face a crisis. The federal budget deficit is careening out of control, and efforts to negotiate a solution are getting nowhere. At around 8:30 A.M., after an hour of fruitless talk, the Democrats finally assert that the President has run out of choices. He must renounce his "no new taxes" pledge—the oath that was instrumental in getting him elected. He must make a public statement, they say, about the need to raise taxes.

The room grows silent.

Then the President utters those fateful words.

Not long thereafter, a short statement is tacked to a bulletin board in the White House press room. "It is clear to me that both the size of the deficit problem and the need for a package that can be enacted require all of the following," it reads, including the real shocker: "tax revenue increases."

The announcement hits Washington like an explosion.

One person who feels the impact is Thomas Donohue, the white-haired president and chief lobbyist for the American Trucking Associations. This morning, he is dashing from meeting to meeting in Washington's Grand Hyatt Hotel. Scattered there in conference rooms around a glass-and-marble atrium are dozens of truck-company executives on one of their regular pilgrimages to the nation's capital. Donohue, who is paid more than $300,000 a year, is going over legislation that might affect them.

But Donohue's prognostications come to an abrupt halt with a telephone call from Sam Chilcote, Jr., president of the Tobacco Institute. He is alarmed by a wire-service story that says the President is reversing himself on taxes. "He what?" Donohue demands. "I'll find out more and get back to you." Donohue's first move is to locate Kenneth Simonson, one of his top aides. Simonson looks like Groucho Marx, but at times like these he is a deadly serious fellow. At Donohue's request, Simonson rushes to the truckers' command center at the hotel, a room ringed with telephones and word processors, and sends out a barrage of calls. He soon reaches Lawrence Lindsey, a White House economist, and several other people just as highly placed. The news is not good. "I'm concerned," Simonson reports grimly back to Donohue. The federal tax on diesel fuel, so important to the trucking industry, is probably about to rise.

Later that morning in another part of town, the phones start ringing at Concord Associates, a small lobbyists-for-hire company that overlooks the Treasury Department in the Willard Office Building. Wayne Thevenot, a balding former staffer in the Senate, gets a call from his wife, Laura, who is also a lobbyist. And James Rock, a bearded former aide in the House, hears from his wife, Sue, who works inside the government on the staff of the Senate's budget committee. Both women bring the same news about the President's announcement, and both men confess embarrassment. "How could I not have known?" they each wonder. As lobbyists, they are no longer part of the government, but they know enough high officials in Washington to hear about most significant things before they are announced.

This time, as usual, they had plenty of opportunity to know in advance. Four days earlier, Rock had attended a lobbyists' breakfast where Robert C. Byrd, the powerful chairman of the Senate Appropriations Committee, was the featured speaker. And just the day before, Thevenot had been among a small group of lobbyists who paid Senate Minority Leader Robert Dole to have lunch with them at the 116 Club, an exclusive haunt for lobbyists on Capitol Hill. If anyone in Washington had known what the President was going to do, these two would have. But apparently they knew nothing; neither had breathed a word about the momentous change.

Thevenot and Rock are surprised about the turn of events, but they are not disappointed. Far from it. This is just the kind of news lobbyists love; it gives them something to act on. As a result, their expensively decorated offices now hum with excitement. Unlike Donohue and Simonson, who work only for the truckers, Thevenot and Rock are freelance lobbyists. They sell their services to almost anyone who is willing to pay their fees. That means that bad news for corporate America is good news for them. Crisis is their stock-in-trade, and that is precisely what the President's statement has created. His words have greatly enhanced the prospect for a big tax increase and that probably will mean more clients for Thevenot and Rock—if they are able to act quickly. So Rock parks himself in a chair across from Thevenot, who sits behind his oversized partner's desk, and they begin to plot and plan. They decide to contact the liquor distributors with whom they had once met; surely they will fear a tax increase now and will want to hire more lobbyists. Maybe there is reason to talk to securities firms too, they speculate; and some extra retainers from the real estate industry ought to be easy to find. "It's time to go to work," Rock concludes. "Now!"

In the meantime, on Capitol Hill, lobbyist Robert Juliano has nothing to do. He has already made his usual visit to the office of his hometown buddy, Democratic Representative Marty Russo of Chicago. But Russo was not in. So the rough-talking Juliano has ambled over to H-154, better known as "The Doorkeeper's Office," one of the main lobbyists' roosts in the Capitol. There, one floor below the House chamber in a dingy green side room that reeks of dust and cigar smoke, Juliano discovers that Congress is in joint session, listening to Nelson Mandela, South Africa's recently freed anti-apartheid hero. To most people, the address is a remarkable, even awe-inspiring event. But to Juliano it is merely another impediment to his business. Lawmakers cannot be lobbied if they are intent on watching a speech. "The whole place is paralyzed," Juliano grumbles, and tries to make some telephone calls.

A few minutes later, the House's deputy doorkeeper does for Juliano what the winner of the Nobel Peace Prize cannot. He arouses his interest. "You heard?" Robert O'Malley asks Juliano, and then tells him about the President's startling reversal. The lobbyist can only moan. "It's a terrible process, this budget-summit shit," he says, and sets out to learn more. Eventually he scrounges a copy of the statement from another congressional office and reads it with a sigh. His most important clients are now obviously in dreadful danger. Juliano represents a wide range of interests that have in common a single desire—to preserve the tax deduction for business meals and entertainment, better known as the "three-martini lunch." Whenever Washington policymakers want to raise revenue, they always consider cutting Juliano's three-martini subsidy. "One might think these people could look at some other issues too sometimes," he says as he roams down another familiar corridor. But he knows they never will.

For most of the day, another lobbyist, Mark Bloomfield, is out of touch with current events. He is in Hershey, Pennsylvania, a city fragrant with the smell of chocolate and with streetlights shaped like Hershey Kisses. It is a fitting venue. As president of the American Council for Capital Formation, a Washington-based "think tank," the dapper Bloomfield promotes ideas that corporate bigwigs crave almost as much as children like Hershey's candy. And this day he is the guest of the Hershey Foods Corporation, a dues-paying member of his group's research arm. He lectures the company's executives about the fiscal outlook.

In midafternoon Bloomfield returns to his office on K Street, the lobbyists' main boulevard, to find a thick stack of telephone messages and a fax. The fax is his copy of the President's statement, sent to him by a fellow lobbyist. The messages are mostly from wealthy individuals who know Bloomfield as "Mr. Capital Gains," the resident guru on the tax on gains from the sale of stocks, bonds and real estate. Today they all want to know: Does the President's statement help or harm their crusade to reduce the levy?

Clutching his suspenders, Bloomfield sits next to a picture window that overlooks the bustling avenue, and returns phone calls in rapid succession. "I don't see the big deal in it," he tells one person. To another he says: "It doesn't look like anything new." Indeed, Bloomfield thinks that the President's words have as little consequence as the breeze that is gently stirring the summer air. In fact, the statement will prove to be a political hurricane both for him and for the President.

One other lobbyist who overlooks the gale warnings—at least initially—is Stuart Eizenstat, a former senior adviser to President Carter. For most of the day he is busy with other matters, and is barely aware of the new development. But when he steps out of the front door of his suburban home the next morning at 6 A.M. to retrieve his *Washington Post*, a story about the announcement jumps off the front page at him. Unlike Bloomfield, Eizenstat immediately realizes that the chance for enacting the big-business benefits that he is paid so well to advocate is now greatly improved.

Eizenstat lobbies for a coalition of groups that includes some of the most profitable corporations in the nation. Their goal: to make a temporary tax credit for research-and-development expenditures a permanent part of federal law. The cost: billions and billions of dollars. But the hefty price tag is no longer as large an obstacle. In the perverse way of Washington, he knows, bitter medicine is rarely taken undiluted, even if the antidote aids the already rich. "Elated," then, is how the usually dour Eizenstat describes his mood, as he prepares to reach deeply into his lobbyist bag of tricks. Meetings must be arranged on Capitol Hill and constituents must be contacted to write letters to their lawmakers. Ah yes, he says, there is still so much to do.

Not every event in Washington has the weightiness of a presidential decision. But change, both big and small, is the city's only real constant. So reaction is a way of life, especially for the lobbyists. For them there is no right or wrong, only winners and losers. And with each new turn of the screw, they all must spring into action and work to get the job done.

THE
LOBBYISTS

1

The

Usual

Retainers

Washington has become a club in which the line between those inside and those outside the government is not clearly drawn. Corporate lobbyists have so suffused the culture of the city that at times they seem to be part of the government itself. One result is that corporate America, once a perennial sacrificial lamb when it came to government crackdowns, has become something of a sacred cow. Not only are lawmakers and policymakers reluctant to make changes that would hurt businesses, they even have a tendency to try to help them, as long as budgetary pressures do not interfere. In 1990, Congress passed, and President Bush signed, the biggest deficit-reduction bill ever. But of its approximately $140 billion in tax increases over five years, only 11 percent came from corporations. The rest came from individual, taxpaying families.

Most people outside of Washington see the world of corporate lobbyists in caricature: fat, cigar-smoking men who wine and dine the nation's lawmakers while shoving dollar bills into their pockets. If lobbyists were always so crass, surely they would be easier to understand. If they were so blatant, they would not be nearly as effective as they often are. And they are effective, at least on the margins. But it is there, in relatively small changes to larger pieces of legislation, that big money is made and lost. Careful investment in a Washington lobbyist can yield enormous returns in the form of taxes avoided or regulations curbed—an odd, negative sort of calculation, but one that forms the basis of the economics of lobbying.

The lobbyists' trade bears close similarity to the ancient board game Go, the object of which is to surround the enemy completely, cut him off from any avenue of escape, and thus defeat him. Blocking the decision-maker at every turn is the object of any successful lobbying campaign. Equally important is not to allow the decision-maker to know that he or she is being entrapped. That makes lobbying both high-powered and discreet, a dangerous combination.

Over time, the sheer pervasiveness of corporate lobbyists has had a major impact on government policy, beyond just the lucrative margin of legislation. The fact that lobbyists are everywhere, all the time, has led official Washington to become increasingly sympathetic to the corporate cause. This is true among Democrats as well as among Republicans.

Lawmakers' workdays are filled with meetings with lobbyists, many of whom represent giant corporations. And their weekends are stocked with similar encounters. When lawmakers travel to give speeches, they rarely address groups of poor people. The big-money lobbies often pick up the tab, and their representatives fill the audiences, ask the questions, and occupy the luncheon tables and throng the cocktail parties that accompany such events. "That's the bigger issue," contends one congressional aide. "Who do these guys hang out with? Rich people. If you spend your time with millionaires, you begin to think like them." Lobbyists provide the prism through which government officials often make their decisions.

This book tells the story of the modern-day corporate lobbyist. It is a look behind the scenes at the sometimes subtle and other times stunning ways in which lobbyists bend the political process on behalf of the richest business interests in the country. Some of the lobbyists' techniques are as old as the republic. But their influence these days is wielded with a precision and consistency that are purely high-tech.

The lobbying process will be viewed through the eyes and the actions of a handful of Washington's top corporate lobbyists during the 101st Congress in 1989 and 1990. These lobbyists will be seen during encounters with members of Congress, with officials of the Bush administration, and sometimes with one another. Their efforts will peak in 1990, at the end of the Congress, when a major tax-increase and spending-restraint bill becomes the law of the land. In that legislation, some of the lobbyists do well, some do less well. All of them survive to fight another day.

This, therefore, is an insider's glimpse at a process that is usually cloaked in the darkest secrecy. It will attempt to shed light on the trials and triumphs, the foibles and failings of a little understood but increasingly important group. It lays bare the brazen manipulation of both lawmakers and the public by the entire lobbying industry, which, by some estimates, has doubled in size in just the past ten years.

Most lobbyists in Washington represent corporate interests, and this book will focus on them. At the same time, anticorporate and labor lobbyists will play a vital role as well; their actions are integral to the daily lives of corporate lobbyists. In addition, lobbyists will be seen clashing with their newest and most challenging opponent: the federal budget deficit. Wherever they turned in 1989 and 1990, lobbyists were thwarted by a lack of government funds. The need to deal with the ever-burgeoning deficit is one reason that lobbyists have become so much more sophisticated than most people imagine they are.

Still, through it all, lobbyists sometimes behave like caricatures of themselves. There are still plenty of glad-handers and fundraisers. But right behind those classic types of lobbyists are people with more targeted and potentially more potent skills: economists, lawyers, direct-mail and telephone salespeople, public-relations experts, pollsters, and even accountants. All these skills and professions play a role in information gathering, which has itself become a thriving business. The best lobbyists not only know the most people, they are also the best informed about everything from the timing of legislative action to the inclinations of individual policymakers.

Every lawmaker's chief interest is getting reelected. So lobbyists see it as their job to persuade lawmakers that voters are on the lobbyists' side. To that end, Washington has become a major marketing center, in which issues are created by interest groups and then sold like toothpaste to voters from Portland, Maine, to Portland, Oregon. Thanks to Washington-based direct-mail and telemarketing wizardry, corporations can solicit letters and phone calls from voters in any district in the nation. And clever Washington-based lobbyists know that the best way to guarantee that their point of view will be heard is to take constituents with them when they go to speak to members of Congress.

Lobbyists also function as unpaid staff to the decision-makers, who often don't have enough people on their own payrolls. Lobbyists contribute the money that lawmakers need to get reelected. And, more important, lobbyists provide information about both policy and process that government officials often cannot get from their own, often underfunded, government agencies. Lobbyists are the foot soldiers and the friends of the people who run the government.

Sometimes corporate lobbyists are adversaries of the men and women who wield the federal government's enormous power. In every battle, there are winners and losers. And, sometimes, the lobbyists are the losers. Lobbyists also fight among themselves, because the corporate world is far from monolithic. As in any industry, there are also plenty of bad lobbyists. Money is wasted; campaigns can be sloppy and ham-handed. Sometimes corporate lobbyists seem to succeed despite themselves. They are the gang that couldn't shoot straight, but they manage to hit their target often enough to make a difference.

Despite their key role in the world of government, lobbyists are almost always the junior players, because, ultimately, they do not make the decisions. Taken as a group, they are a kind of underclass in the nation's capital, a lower caste that is highly compensated, in part, to make up for their relatively low stature in the city's severely stratified culture. At the top of the hierarchy are members of Congress and Cabinet secretaries. Next come con-

gressional and Cabinet staffs. And then, at the bottom, come lobbyists. Lobbyists chafe at this. But their status is readily apparent.
Frequently they suffer the indignity of standing in hallways or
reception areas for hours at a time. Theirs are the first appoint-
ments canceled or postponed when other business calls. They do
not even like to be called "lobbyists." They prefer "consultants"
or "lawyers." They also use euphemisms like "When I left the
Hill . . ." to describe the moment they left the congressional payroll to take a lobbying job.

One lobbyist put his predicament succinctly: "My mother has
never introduced me to her friends as 'my son, the lobbyist.' My
son, the Washington representative, maybe. Or the legislative consultant. Or the government-relations counsel. But never as the
lobbyist. I can't say I blame her. Being a lobbyist has long been
synonymous in the minds of many Americans with being a glorified pimp."

Still, lobbying has flourished. As the 1980s came to a close,
there were nearly three thousand trade-association offices in
Washington, most of which represented businesses of some sort.
They ranged in size from the 125,000-member National Association
of Home Builders and the thirteen-thousand-member American
Bankers Association, with annual budgets of more than $10 mil-
lion, to the Bow Tie Manufacturers Association and the Post Card
Manufacturers Association, each with fewer than ten member
companies and budgets of less than $10,000 a year. In addition,
hundreds of new individual lobbyists and lobbying shops opened,
ready to accept business.

Spurred in large part by the ever-expanding business of lobbying, Washington became a modern, prosperous city during the
1970s and 1980s. The Main Street of lobbying is K Street, a short
stretch through the heart of the sleek downtown. Spanking-new
office buildings, filled with law firms, lobbying firms, and the
allied services of the influence industry, sprang up everywhere
in the city, eventually forming an almost unbroken corridor that
stretched from Georgetown at one end of the city to Capitol Hill
at the other. When even more office space was needed, metal and
stone edifices were built on the Virginia side of the Potomac River.
By the 1990s, Washington was home to about eighty thousand
lobbyists of one kind or another, and the number was still growing.

. . .

Among English-speaking nations, the concept of lobbying goes back to A.D. 1215, when King John granted the barons of England the right to petition him to protest any violation of their new rights under the Magna Carta. More than five hundred years later, American colonists felt so snubbed by King George III that they rose up in revolt, and reaffirmed this right in both their Declaration of Independence from the motherland and in the First Amendment to the fledgling nation's constitution. The right "to petition the government for a redress of grievances" remains the basis for lobbying in the United States today.

In the beginning, lobbying did not entail a great deal of finesse. The first attempt at mass pressure on the U.S. government was accomplished with fixed bayonets during a meeting of the First Continental Congress in Philadelphia. Several hundred soldiers of a local garrison believed they were due extra compensation, and in 1783 threatened the assembled legislators with rifles shouldered. The Congress disagreed with them and boldly adjourned to meet again—at a safe distance, in Princeton, New Jersey.

Less threatening—and more successful—lobbying tactics were used by business interests, which even then were trying to win the upper hand in influencing the nation's leaders. After each legislative day, hogsheads of wine and port poured freely at sumptuous meals of mutton, pork, duck, and turkey. The dinner linens were snowy white, the cutlery was burnished and English, and the check was paid by the wealthy merchants of the day.

Another pattern also fell quickly into place: bribery. One of the first issues facing the new Congress when it met in New York in 1789 was whether to fund the national debt and to assume the debts of the states. The proposal produced a close and contentious fight. It is widely believed that the money changers who stood to profit most from the action bought Delaware Representative John Vining's deciding vote on the issue. Rumor had it that the bribe was a thousand guineas, but Senator William Maclay of Pennsylvania doubted it. He wrote in his journal that Vining's vote was probably purchased "for a tenth part of the sum."

The word "lobbyist" was first used in Britain to refer to journalists who stood in lobbies at the House of Commons, waiting to interview newsmakers. Its initial modern usage in America came in 1829. According to the essayist H. L. Mencken, privilege seekers in New York's capital, Albany, were referred to as lobby-agents. Three years later, the term was abbreviated to "lobbyist" and was heard frequently in Washington, mostly as an expression of disdain.

In 1833, during his second term, President Andrew Jackson sought to deflate the powerful financier Nicholas Biddle by withdrawing federal deposits from the Bank of the United States, of which Biddle was president. But Biddle was not without his supporters, notably Daniel Webster, who was then a senator from Massachusetts. The ardency of Webster's convictions on the issue was fueled not so much by principle as by cash. On December 21, 1833, Webster, a titan of the Senate, who would later go on to become a much-storied secretary of state, wrote to Biddle: "If it is wished that my relation to the bank should be continued, it may be well to send me the usual retainers." After an especially eloquent speech by Webster in the Senate on the bank's behalf, Biddle paid him $10,000. In all, Webster got $32,000 in what today would be seen as bribes, but was then business as usual.

As America grew as an industrial power, so did lobbying. By 1852, Washington was swarming with so many big-business lobbyists that future President James Buchanan wrote to his friend future President Franklin Pierce that "the host of contractors, speculators, stockjobbers, and lobby members which haunt the halls of Congress . . . are sufficient to alarm every friend of this country. Their progress must be arrested." The influence of business was so strong then that, at the close of one congressional session, Senator J. S. Morrill sarcastically noted the presence in the outer lobby of the president of the Pennsylvania Railroad. He then moved to appoint a committee to wait on him and inquire if he wanted any further legislation before adjournment.

One of the most heavy-handed corporate advocates at the time was Samuel Colt of the famous gun-manufacturing company. He paid a "contingent fee" of $10,000 to one congressman, and probably to many others, for refraining from attacking a patent-extension bill that would have helped his company's sales. To supplement his effort, Colt hired the high-living lobbyist Alexander Hay, who distributed beautifully decorated revolvers to lawmakers. Colt also dispensed other, more attractive gratuities: to wit, three young women known as Spiritualists, who, according to one account, were very active in "moving with the members" of Congress. Other women of less spiritual natures, called chicks, were also available upon request.

In the wake of the financial panic of 1857, Washington was flooded with even more lobbyists. And "everywhere," wrote one historian, "there was importunity." The most underhanded lobbying battle raged between railroad and steamship companies. Lobbyists for each side fought bitterly to reduce government subsidies for the other. Commodore Cornelius Vanderbilt led the steamship companies' campaign, often from the gaming tables of a night spot called Pendleton's Gambling House. Hapless lawmakers would fall into debt there and be forced to surrender their votes to Vanderbilt under threat of exposure or demand for payment. Other times lawmakers would be allowed to win—as long as they agreed to vote the right way.

The 1850s' most powerful lobbyist was Thurlow Weed. He was a tall, imposing man with an impressively diverse background that included working as a newspaper editor who crusaded against the perfidy of corporate power. For the price of $5,000, however, he switched allegiances and began to lobby on behalf of Bay State Mills of Lawrence, Massachusetts, as an advocate for lower duties on wool. The lobbyist who had preceded Weed at Bay State Mills came to Washington armed only with facts and figures and was laughed out of town. Weed brought cold cash. He hired, among others, David M. Stone, a reporter from New York's *Journal of Commerce*, to help spread the word for lower levies. Although in the end he failed, he did get a thorough hearing, which was better than getting nothing at all.

The first "King of the Lobby" was Samuel Ward, who reigned in Washington for fifteen years after the Civil War. He was the undisputed master of dinner-table deceitfulness. "The way to a man's 'Aye' is through his stomach," Ward said. He was the great-great-grandson of Richard Ward, a colonial governor of Rhode Island; the great-grandson of Samuel Ward, one of the framers of the Constitution; and the great-nephew on his mother's side of General Francis Marion, the famous "Swamp Fox" of the Revolutionary War. His father headed the New York banking firm of

Prime, Ward & King, and his sister, Julia Ward Howe, wrote "The Battle Hymn of the Republic." His cousin, Ward McAllister, coined the term "the Four Hundred" to describe New York's high society.

Ward was a mathematical prodigy, a scholar of languages, a poet of some note, a musician, a gourmet cook, and a renowned wit. In his adventurous life, he had been a banker and gone bankrupt, had traveled widely in Latin America, had prospected for gold in California, and had lived among the Indians. He finally settled in Washington, where he could use his penchant for living well and his ability to charm the natives to the most profit. With his balding pate, sweeping mustache, and diamond-studded shirts, he was famous for hosting vast dinners at the fashionable Chamberlain's restaurant and for cooking lavish breakfasts of ham boiled in champagne and seasoned with wisps of newly mown hay.

Sometime later a congressional committee questioned Ward about his activities. As always, he deflected their inquiries with erudition and humor. "Talleyrand says that diplomacy is assisted by good dinners," he responded. "At good dinners people do not talk shop, but they give people a right, perhaps, to ask a gentleman a civil question and get a civil answer."

Ward justified his vocation by saying he refused to take on issues that were meritless. But he also conceded that "the profession of lobbying is not commendable." He died in Italy in 1884, at the age of seventy, with a copy of Horace under his pillow and the *Rubáiyát of Omar Khayyám* at his side. Among those who put a tombstone over his head was Archibald Philip Primrose, a future prime minister of Britain.

Woodrow Wilson was the first of many U.S. presidents to mount a challenge to the authority of the business lobby; he made its villainy an important part of his campaign in 1912. When he was a professor, Wilson had studied lobbyists' impact in Washington and concluded that it was overbearing and dangerous. In one of his scholarly papers, he noted that special interests could not buy an entire legislature, but could purchase individual committees, which was where the real power resided anyway. Such observations became grist for his presidential campaign.

When Wilson took office in 1913, he in effect told the lobbyists to leave town, and for the most part they did. But they did not stay away for long. During the 1920s, special interests again began winning in Washington, raising hackles anew. Groups of World War I veterans, led by the American Legion, won passage of a costly bonus bill over the veto of President Calvin Coolidge. As a result, in 1927 a congressional inquiry was commenced under Senator Thaddeus H. Caraway, an Arkansas Democrat.

The Caraway Committee uncovered a variety of lobbying practices, including the revelation that most lobbying was simply fraud. Fully 90 percent of the nearly four hundred lobbying groups listed in the Washington telephone directory were "fakes," the committee said, whose primary aim was not to affect legislation but to bilk clients. "Every activity of the human mind has been capitalized by some grafter," the panel asserted. Caraway disclosed that one enterprising lobbyist had collected $60,000 in one year from business executives by doing nothing more than writing letters to them every time a bill passed that they might favor, and claiming sole credit for its passage. At the end of the investigation, Caraway recommended the enactment of a lobbyist-registration bill. The Senate passed the stringent measure without dissent, but it died in the House—thanks to the pressure of lobbyists.

One of the big legislative fights of the 1930s involved the so-called Wheeler-Rayburn Bill, a reform measure that was meant to stem the power of public-utility holding companies by placing them under federal regulation. The utilities hired almost every well-connected lobbyist in town and worked their ways outside of Washington as well. Their most spectacular effort was uncovered by a congressional committee chaired by Senator Hugo L. Black, a Democrat of Alabama and a future Supreme Court justice. It involved a nineteen-year-old Western Union messenger from Warren, Pennsylvania, named Elmer Danielson. According to the committee, the utilities paid Danielson and other messengers three cents for each telegram they were able to solicit in opposition to the Wheeler-Rayburn Bill. The telegrams were then sent free to the local congressman, Representative D. J. Driscoll, who in a two-day span received eighty-six of them. In all, thousands of telegrams were sent to Washington, at a rate of four thousand an hour, sometimes signed with names taken randomly from telephone directories.

Outraged by the effort, Black introduced yet another bill to register and regulate lobbyists, which passed both chambers of

Congress. But thanks to the efforts of hundreds of lobbyists, it too died, in a House-Senate conference committee. Utility lobbyists, however, were nicked a little. They were required to make limited disclosures of their activities under terms of the final Public Utilities Holding Company Act.

Congress finally got around to regulating lobbying in 1936. The Merchant Marine Act of that year required anyone employed by firms affected by certain shipping laws to file disclosures with the Commerce Department before working to influence legislation or administrative decisions. Two years later, amid reports of fascist and Nazi propaganda circulating in the United States, the Foreign Agents Registration Act was enacted. It required anyone who represented a foreign government or individual to register with the Justice Department. And then finally, in 1946, Congress passed the Federal Regulation of Lobbying Act as part of the Legislative Reorganization Act.

Under the law, lobbyists were required to register in Congress and report the amount and sources of their income from lobbying. There was no attempt to limit lobbying; that would violate the First Amendment right to petition the government. But the law defined a lobbyist as a person or organization whose job was to influence the passage or defeat of legislation, and who received money for that purpose. As enacted, the lobbying law covered both direct lobbying and indirect, grass-roots-style lobbying, which involved stirring up of contacts from actual voters back home. From the start, however, the law was largely ignored.

In 1950 a committee headed by Representative Frank M. Buchanan, Democrat of Pennsylvania, investigated a wide range of lobbying activities. Buchanan disclosed that even under the weak new disclosure law the number of registered lobbyists had more than doubled in just two years, to 2,074. "I firmly believe," he concluded, "that the business of influencing legislation is a billion-dollar industry."

He also noted that lobbying had undergone a transformation that made lobbying hard to track. "In the 1870s and 1880s, lobbying meant direct, individual solicitation of legislators, with a strong presumption of corruption attached," he stated. "[But] modern pressure on legislative bodies is rarely corrupt. . . . It is increasingly indirect, and [it is] largely the product of group rather than individual effort. . . . The printed word is much more extensively used by organizations as a means of pursuing legislative aims than personal contact with legislators by individual lobbyists."

In the wide-open days of the late 1940s and 1950s, it was "often hard to tell where the legislator leaves off and the lobbyist begins," according to a journalist and lobbying expert of that era, James Deakin. As an example, he wrote, fourteen lawmakers once delivered speeches on Portuguese policy in Angola that were written by the public-relations firm of Selvage and Lee Incorporated, which represented companies there. One of the lawmakers involved was Representative Joseph Martin, Jr., the former Speaker of the House. Selvage and Lee boasted that Martin "used [our] stuff without change, apart from abbreviation."

This period was also the heyday of Thomas "Tommy the Cork" Corcoran, former law clerk to Oliver Wendell Holmes and chief legislative operative for President Franklin Roosevelt for five years. The brilliant and brash Corcoran helped write much of the New Deal legislation, including the Securities and Exchange Act. He also gave Roosevelt the line "This generation of Americans has a rendezvous with destiny." But he made enemies when he tried to help Roosevelt pack the Supreme Court, and was blocked from becoming the U.S. Solicitor General, the government job he most wanted. So instead, he became a high-priced lobbyist for corporate interests, blazing what has since become a well-trod route from White House adviser to Washington lobbyist.

In the early 1950s, a congressional committee again recommended strengthening the lobbying law, but no action was taken. Instead, in 1954, the Supreme Court opened more loopholes in the already porous statute. In U.S. v. Harriss, the court narrowed the law's coverage by exempting many types of lobbyists from its disclosure requirements. The court decided that the law did not require all interests that spent money on lobbying to register— only those that solicited and collected money specifically with lobbying in mind. It also underscored that organizations were required to register only if they had lobbying as their "principal purpose" when they collected the funds. What's more, only direct contacts with legislators were considered lobbying; indirect pressure, such as the growing practice of grass-roots lobbying, was excluded. Robert Drinan, former dean of the Boston College Law

School and later a member of Congress, described the lobbying act as a "judicial shambles." And that, thanks to lobbyists, is where it remains.

During the 1960s, senior executives of corporations increasingly were used as lobbyists, but always under the strict guidance of their Washington consultants. E. I. Du Pont de Nemours dispatched its president, Crawford H. Greenewalt, to Washington to lobby for a law that would have allowed Du Pont shareholders to pay a lower-than-usual capital-gains tax on General Motors stock they received under a court divestiture order. He did so under the guidance of top Washington lobbyist Clark Clifford. Thanks to Clifford, Greenewalt visited more than fifty members of Congress and top government officers, including Speaker Sam Rayburn, Senate Majority Leader Mike Mansfield, House Ways and Means Committee Chairman Wilbur Mills, Attorney General Robert F. Kennedy, and Deputy Attorney General Byron R. White. The measure was enacted into law.

Clark McAdams Clifford was the very picture of corporate influence in the 1960s. Tall and patrician, he had been President Truman's special counsel from 1946 to 1950. But later, as a lobbyist, he wielded equal if not greater power. In 1960, he coordinated President Kennedy's transition to office, and acted as a trusted adviser to him, especially on intelligence matters. Few were better qualified; it was Clifford who, years earlier, had helped write the law that created the Central Intelligence Agency. During the Kennedy years, Clifford also played an important behind-the-scenes role in ending the nation's steel strike, when he went with Labor Secretary Arthur Goldberg to New York for a crucial meeting with Roger M. Blough, chairman of U.S. Steel Corporation.

Big-money lobbyists wooed not only lawmakers, but also their staffs during the 1960s, often flying them for weekend retreats to their farms in Virginia and their duck blinds on the Eastern Shore of Maryland. The most famous victim of this temptation for fancy living was Robert G. (Bobby) Baker, whose troubles hit the headlines in 1963. His travail is a case study in how public officials can be ensnared by private interests. Baker was secretary to the Democratic majority in the Senate. With a salary of $19,600 a year, he managed to accumulate assets of $2,166,886 in less than nine years. His route from Pickens, South Carolina, to riches on the banks of the Potomac River was eased by members of the Quorum Club, who numbered two hundred and were mostly lobbyists. In its exclusive rooms in the Carroll Arms Hotel, across the street from a Senate office building, Baker fed at the trough of the club's small but elegant bar, which was accessorized with three telephones and with paintings of bare-breasted West Indian women.

Improper contacts with lobbyists were also part of the Watergate scandal, which brought down the presidency of Richard M. Nixon. Investigations revealed that a number of American corporations violated the federal law that prohibited them from contributing to the campaigns of federal office-seekers. Some of those funds—in cash—found their way into the hands of the Republican operatives who broke into Democratic party headquarters in Washington's Watergate Hotel complex in 1972.

In recent years, foreign interests have increasingly hired Washington lobbyists. This foreign money led to scandal in 1976, when *The Washington Post* reported that South Korean agents gave between $500,000 and $1 million a year in cash and gifts to members of Congress to help maintain "a favorable legislative climate" for South Korea. The Koreans, led by businessman and socialite Tongsun Park, sought to bribe U.S. officials and buy influence among journalists, and succeeded in funneling illegal gifts to as many as 115 lawmakers. In 1978 the House voted to reprimand three California Democrats for their part in the scandal, and Richard T. Hanna, a former California congressman, went to prison for his actions.

During the 1980s, lobbying was rarely so heavy-handed. At the same time, it became astonishingly effective, as its techniques reached new heights of sophistication and complexity. When Congress was considering increasing milk-price supports in 1980, for example, lawmakers heard not just from lobbyists for the dairy farmers who wanted the subsidy hiked, but also from thousands of worried managers of fast-food restaurants who opposed an increase because it would raise food prices. The managers were responding to a newsletter, called an "action alert," sent to them by the fast-food industry's trade association.

Over the years, many politicians have campaigned effectively against Washington and its lobbyists. President Truman said he wanted to be remembered as "the people's President." "There are a great many organizations with lots of money who maintain lobbyists in Washington. I'd say 15 million people in the United States are represented by lobbyists," he said. "The other 150 million have only one man who is elected at large to represent them—that is the President of the United States." President Kennedy also bashed lobbyists, telling an audience at Ohio's Wittenberg College in 1960: "The consumer is the only man in our economy without a high-powered lobbyist in Washington. I intend to be that lobbyist." And President Reagan won one of history's biggest legislative victories against special interests when he backed the Tax Reform Act of 1986.

Nevertheless, lobbyists remained an integral part of the Washington establishment, by some accounts its Fifth Estate. In *Presidential Power: The Politics of Leadership*, Richard E. Neustadt, a Truman aide and Kennedy adviser, coined the phrase "the Washington community" to describe "the men who share in governing this country." The Washington community, Neustadt wrote, consisted of the expected: top policymaking and career officials of the executive branch, and the most influential members of Congress. But other stalwarts, he was quick to add, included military commanders, foreign diplomats, veteran journalists—and lobbyists.

· · ·

Corporate lobbyists have always had adversaries: muckraking reporters, public-interest advocates, and even other lobbyists from competing industries. But by the start of the 101st Congress in 1989—when our story begins—the biggest adversary was more overarching, amorphous and, indeed, more difficult to defeat. The enemy was the federal budget deficit, an untamed monster that threatened to devour not only the federal government, but the economy of the entire country as well.

Lobbyists and the deficit were always clashing. Every time a lobbyist wanted to get some goodie for a client, whether it was a tax break, a federal grant, or a deferred regulation, lawmakers demanded to know, "How are you going to pay for it?" And that was one question that most lobbyists were reluctant to answer, since it usually meant taking money away from somebody else's client. That made a lobbyist's job a hard sell, even under the best of circumstances.

Worse yet, the deficit meant that no matter how noble a lobbyist was able to make his clients appear, they were never completely out of danger. They, too, were liable to become victims of what seemed a never-ending stream of deficit-reduction measures flowing out of Washington. And no matter how hard federal officials tried, they could not cut the deficit enough. Lobbyists therefore were always checking over their shoulders to see when the next, inevitable attack would come. The deficit was constantly making lobbyists' lives miserable.

Without question, the deficit was an enormous problem crying out for solution. The annual deficit reached $221 billion in fiscal 1986; that year, the government spent $990 billion but took in only $769 billion. By fiscal 1989, the deficit was still massive—$152 billion. And for at least the next few years, the annual shortfall was expected to hover between $120 billion and $140 billion. But even that proved to be a low estimate.

Such sizable deficits were a relatively new phenomenon, spawned during the just-ended administration of President Reagan. At his urging in 1981, Congress had simultaneously cut taxes and increased military spending in the belief that reduced tax rates would *raise* federal revenue rather than deplete it. Instead, the deficit, which had been $16.4 billion, or 1.2 percent of the gross national product, between 1946 and 1981, ballooned thereafter to an average of $176 billion, or 4.5 percent of the gross national product. Under Reagan and Bush, the total accumulated federal debt nearly tripled, going from nearly $1 trillion at the end of 1981 to $2.9 trillion at the end of 1989.

Few economists doubted that these high deficits, and the huge and ever-growing federal debt they created, were doing serious, long-term damage to the U.S. economy. Charles L. Schultze, former chairman of President Carter's Council of Economic Advisers, said the deficits were not so much like the "wolf at the door," but like "termites in the basement," eating away gradually at the economy and at American living standards. President Bush thought the problem was even worse. In his own budget message to Congress at the beginning of 1989, he stated, "No other single measure open to the federal government is more likely to raise the national savings rate, and promote productivity growth, than a substantial reduction in the budget deficit." Still, he stuck unswervingly to his campaign promise of "Read my lips: no new taxes"—a pledge that made significant deficit-cutting difficult at best.

Amid all this talk, Washington lobbyists prepared for the on-going battle of the budget—whichever way it might go. They knew that, no matter what anybody said, they and their clients could get whacked at any moment. "Everybody thinks there is going to be a tax bill. The only disagreement is over the extent and breadth of the bill," Nicholas Calio, a lobbyist for the National Association of Wholesalers-Distributors, told *The Wall Street Journal*. As a result, lobbyists were hustling, trying to round up business. One Washington law firm, Verner, Liipfert, Bernhard, McPherson & Hand, negotiated with corporate clients for retainers that topped $500,000 a year. "It's not unusual for a client to pay our firm a retainer of more than a half million dollars to work on a tax provision," Berl Bernhard, the firm's chairman, told the *Journal*.

The entire first rank of the lobbying hierarchy, including Stuart Eizenstat and Charls E. Walker, girded for the battle. Eizenstat had been the chief domestic-policy adviser to President Carter and afterward became a top lobbyist, representing, among others, high-technology companies that wanted to extend the tax credit for research and development. Walker, a Republican, was a deputy Treasury secretary under President Nixon, and went on to become, as a lobbyist, the embodiment of big business in the nation's capital. One of Walker's pet lobbying projects was to cut the tax on capital gains, which are profits from the sale of assets such as real estate and securities. Eizenstat, a Democrat, did not much like that idea, and had many run-ins with Walker and his cohorts over the issue.

Much of the labor of lobbying was done by lobbyists who were less well known than these two, but who were no less important to their causes. On the research-and-development tax-credit issue, Eizenstat's partner was Kenneth Kay, a Washington lawyer who was a former aide to Democratic Senator Max Baucus of Montana. Kay coordinated an entire coalition of lobbyists who advocated the R&D credit. Walker also had a helper, Mark Bloomfield, who served as president of a self-styled think tank, chaired by Walker, called the American Council for Capital Formation. It was Kay and Bloomfield, both still in their thirties, who actually did much of the lobbying that was more closely associated with their elder colleagues.

Thousands of trade associations in Washington existed to help their members understand what government was doing to—and for—them. But they also were there to influence both legislation and regulation before they took effect. The American Trucking Associations was typical of these trade groups. At its helm was Thomas Donohue, a partisan Republican who tried to serve as much as ambassador for the ill-famed trucking industry as its chief lobbyist. And behind Donohue was a large staff of professionals, including Kenneth Simonson, an economist and budgetary expert who provided the facts and figures that Donohue used to make trucking seem benign to skeptical decision-makers on Capitol Hill and at the White House. The Donohue-Simonson coupling of flash and substance was increasingly common among lobbying groups of the time.

Another sort of lobbyist now becoming prominent was the gun-for-hire. Guns-for-hire were lobbyists who sold their services to almost anyone who was willing to pay their fees. What they did in return was provide entrée for their clients into the network of people, both inside and outside of government, who were able to get things done. Wayne Thevenot (pronounced *TEH* ven oh) and James Rock were former congressional staffers with close ties to the real estate industry, but who were willing—indeed eager—to find clients in almost any industry. Their specialty was gaining access to influential lawmakers whom they had known for many years both socially and professionally. Robert Juliano also had plenty of access to lawmakers, having worked as a lobbyist for a labor union. But, in addition to his labor client, he also helped heavyweight corporate clients such as American Express steer their way around Congress and the Bush administration. For a while these three lobbyists ended up on different sides of a major row over how to tax life-insurance companies.

Eizenstat and Walker; Kay and Bloomfield; Donohue and Simonson; and Thevenot, Rock, and Juliano allowed themselves to be followed for all or part of the two years of the 101st Congress—1989 and 1990. Thanks to their unprecedented assistance, this book will attempt to illustrate the work of all lobbyists through their colorful stories. It also will try to convey a sense of the enormous diversity of skills that mark what is no longer merely a profession—lobbying—but an entire industry.

The backdrop for all of this is one of the most scandal-ridden periods in recent history. During the 101st Congress, the number-one and number-three Democrats in the House, Speaker James Wright of Texas and Representative Tony Coelho of California, resigned under clouds of scandal; a Republican senator, David Durenberger of Minnesota, was denounced; and a former GOP senator, John Tower of Texas, was rejected as secretary of defense—in large part because of their too-close-for-comfort ties to business interests. On top of that, the entire Department of Housing and Urban Development was investigated for rampant influence-peddling.

Rarely has there been a more propitious moment to look deeply into the world of lobbying.

2

The

Greenbrier

and the

Pisces Club

On the drizzly Friday morning of February 3, 1989, a private nineteen-car train with a helicopter escort pulled slowly out of Washington's Union Station, carrying 142 Democratic members of the House of Representatives, their families, and several dozen lobbyists and reporters. They were bound for a weekend of bowling, ice skating, skeet shooting, and unrestrained 1950s-style dancing at the posh Greenbrier resort in White Sulphur Springs, West Virginia. The $250,000 event, called an issues conference, was bankrolled mostly by the lobbyists on board.

The weekend, which had become the House Democrats' annual retreat, could not have been more poorly timed. The new 101st Congress had just begun its two-year run. But for the first few weeks of the session, the lawmakers had been beaten up by radio talk-show hosts across the nation for trying to win a pay increase. A big one. Too big, it turned out. A presidential commission had proposed that the lawmakers get paid $135,000 a year instead of their current salaries of $89,500. That would have been a whopping 51 percent—$45,500—increase, which was about

$10,000 more than the average family of four made a year at the time.

Still, there was hope. Congressional leaders carefully plotted to get the raise without having to take the politically perilous step of voting for it. Under the odd rules of the presidential commission, the raise would automatically go into effect on Wednesday, February 8, which was just five days away, as long as Congress did not act to block it. The day before the train pulled out, the Senate voted overwhelmingly, 95–5, against the hike. But that had been expected. The plan all along had been to delay a similar vote in the House, where leaders have more control over what legislation gets to the floor and when.

But a few hours before the Senate cast its vote, the House Democrats' leader, Speaker James Wright, got cold feet. Without consulting anyone, the bushy-eyebrowed Texan yielded to home-state pressures and scheduled a vote on the pay raise for the following week. Many lawmakers on the train considered this an act of betrayal. Many of them saw Wright's rash action as incredibly self-destructive: The Speaker already had plenty of his own troubles.

Since June of the previous year, his personal finances—and his dealings with lobbyists and lobbying groups—had been under investigation by the House Ethics Committee. If the panel's report turned out to be negative, Wright would need all the friends he could get. And jeopardizing his colleagues' pay raise was no way to build friendships, especially on the eve of a festive weekend. Still, Wright set a vote to roll back the raise to 30 percent for Thursday, the day after the full 51 percent rise would have gone into effect automatically.

The Greenbrier sojourn itself was no help to the lawmakers' cause. They were greeted at Union Station by anti-pay-raise hecklers. Three dozen protesters waved placards reading MONEY FOR THE NEEDY, NOT FOR THE GREEDY and chanted a rap song that repeated the line "You dirty little member." Newscasts that night depicted the members of Congress as living luxuriously off big-business lobbyists. And much of the conversation on board the silver train amounted to little more than grumbling. "I'll talk about anything but the pay raise," Representative Floyd Flake, a new member from New York, told reporters.

Amid the contretemps, though, there was an underlying tranquillity to the trip. As the Amtrak special rocked gently through river valleys and mountain passes, life went on as usual. Lawmakers milled freely through the train, taking time to greet old friends. Among their closest companions during the hours-long journey were the lobbyists. Few, if any, of the lawmakers blamed the lobbyists for the pay-raise problems they faced. Instead, the lobbyists were considered allies in the struggle.

Indeed, the train itself, and the weekend that lay ahead, were a microcosm of Washington: lawmakers and lobbyists moving together in a largely closed and isolated system, discussing decisions that affect millions of other Americans. The retreat illustrated the earliest stage of what lobbyists do: gather information and develop contacts. Lobbyists on board that day—and at their jobs elsewhere in Washington—were relaxed, yet always persistent. There was much to learn, and many new people to meet. The lobbyists also knew that more difficult work was ahead of them as the congressional session unfolded.

For their part, lawmakers were at ease with this process, too. Some even welcomed it. "The lobbyists provide a bridge between the professional politicians and the real world," said Representative Jim Slattery of Kansas as the train neared the Greenbrier. "That's very important."

"Our sources of information are so limited," agreed Representative Jim Cooper of Tennessee. "Sometimes we have to play them off against each other to get things done."

• • •

The weekend retreat was underwritten, like so much in Washington, by a self-selected group of lobbyists. The group behind this trip was the National Legislative Education Foundation, a nonprofit organization headed by, among others, John McEvoy, a former chief of staff of the Senate Budget Committee who then became a lobbyist for financial institutions; Wayne Thevenot, a former top aide to Senator Russell Long and currently a representative for some of the nation's biggest real estate developers; and Debbie Dingell, an executive with the General Motors Corporation who was better known as the wife of Chairman John D. Dingell of the House Energy and Commerce Committee.

For room and board at the sprawling resort, each lawmaker was asked to chip in $500—though not from his or her own pocket. Two years earlier a lawyer-lobbyist associated with the foundation suggested that the money could come instead from the lawmakers' campaign coffers. In any case, the lawmakers' contribution only began to cover the $250,000 that went into the lavish weekend festivities, which besides a sock hop on Saturday night included the singing talents of a second-tier Hollywood starlet. Each of the sixty or so sponsors—read "lobbyists"—contributed $6,000 for the singular honor of helping House members discuss the issues of the day, and to be able to come along personally for the ride. For any lobbyist worth his cellular telephone, $6,000 was a small price to pay for such intimate and extensive contact with the lawmakers they wanted to influence.

The lobbyists vigorously denied that they did any lobbying at the event. And some lawmakers maintained that they were not even aware who the sponsors of the weekend were. But few people believed either assertion, and no one really seemed to care. Only the smallest part of lobbying, at the very end of the process, entails directly asking members of Congress for specific favors. The Greenbrier event, with its socializing and camaraderie, was more what lobbying is about most of the time: becoming part of the Washington network and, through it, learning the lay of the legislative landscape.

"It does put you in proximity with some members of Congress—the major players," Thevenot, the real estate lobbyist, said at the Greenbrier. "They get to know who you are. [And you] get to know who they are, something about them personally. Their likes, their dislikes, their family. Getting to develop a personal relationship with them. . . . This government, I'm becoming more and more convinced, is driven by human beings, not laws or institutions."

The white-columned Greenbrier resort hotel is perched on a mountain, four hours by train—and longer by car—from the city of Washington. It is the picture of Southern gentility, the kind of place where the men wear green pants and plaid sweaters, and everyone dresses up for dinner. Among its featured attractions are the luxurious baths in supposedly medicinal spring water that help make it a favorite preserve of corporate executives and lobbyists alike. During the lawmakers' visit there, it was always wise to make a reservation well in advance for a bath and accompanying massage. Part of each lawmaker's day at the Greenbrier was spent in seminars. Topics ranged from "Progress for All Americans: Reversing Growing Inequities" to "Progress or Decay: Deficits, Investment and Growth." Experts from the academic world led the discussions, which generally were well attended by lawmakers. But the heart of the weekend was less formal and more personal. Many of the lawmakers were accompanied by their families—children were everywhere, nearly two hundred of them. And because of them, there was almost no room to swim in the indoor pool. The bowling alleys were bustling with kids day and night as well; friendly lobbyists paid for the games.

Lobbyists also underwrote adult activities. One of the most popular was trap and skeet shooting. Hotel limousines regularly drove clusters of green-garbed lawmakers up the road to the resort's shooting range. One of the lobbyist-sponsors was James Free, a former aide to President Jimmy Carter and now a lobbyist-for-hire for corporations at Charls E. Walker Associates in Washington. His firm's clients included a smattering of major paper-products, insurance, and financial companies.

Dinners were communal, and a great opportunity for conversation. On Friday evening, Thevenot's date was a fellow lobbyist named Laura Ison. She managed to get a seat next to the crusty but colorful Representative Jack Brooks, chairman of the House Judiciary Committee, and his wife, Charlotte. The two couples were not strangers. Brooks and Ison had met before on the duck-hunting circuit of which Thevenot was a part. Thevenot sat next to Charlotte Brooks while Ison had the chairman's ear, and the two couples had a jolly time over drinks and their multicourse meal.

Thevenot regaled everyone with stories from his days as a staffer on Capitol Hill. The favorite story that evening was Thevenot's rendition of his second day in Washington in 1963. Fresh from the backwoods of Louisiana, and under the wing of the state's legendary Senator Russell Long, Thevenot was thankful to get one of the Capitol's few patronage jobs: operating one of the "members only" elevators in the Senate. He had hoped to start there, and slowly learn the ropes in Washington, literally from the bottom up. But he hit the big time with his very first passenger, Vice President Lyndon Johnson. Accompanied by two burly Secret Service agents, Johnson stepped brusquely into Thevenot's elevator and ordered the young man to take him down to the first floor. Flustered, Thevenot pushed the wrong button, and took the Vice President to the third floor instead. "I was white as a sheet," Thevenot recalled amid laughter from the others at the table. "I had just arrived yesterday and was already being chewed out by the Vice President. I thought my career was a shambles."

The cigar-chomping Brooks told some stories of his own about Johnson, who as a fellow Texan was one of his political cronies. Everyone at the table listened attentively. Questions were asked deferentially. Brooks answered in full voice and with broad gestures. When in the company of lobbyists, lawmakers always held center stage. That was the order of things. Sometimes, though, lobbyists went too far. After an extended Brooks monologue, A. J. Harris, a lobbyist for CIGNA Corporation who was also sitting at the table, said without any hint of embarrassment, "We're just basking in the glow of your emanations, Mr. Chairman." To which an obviously revolted Thevenot responded, "What does that mean?"

Thevenot could ingratiate himself with the best of them, and often did. He once declared at a lobbyists' Christmas party that he wished one day to be the "kissee rather than the kisser." But he was not cloying in his demeanor. He could be full of country charm and bawdy wit, with a hail-fellow manner to match. Yet he carried himself with the broad-shouldered confidence of the weight lifter he once was. He drove big cars and worked for big money. But more than that, he was a big man in Washington, a member in good standing of the political fraternity there. He might have been just a lobbyist, but in some circles he was a near equal of the lawmakers whose votes he worked to influence. He had been around for so long, he said, that to many lawmakers he was "as familiar as an old shoe." And he liked it that way.

At age fifty-four, Thevenot was sometimes bored by the repetitiveness of the legislative process. Other times he was frustrated by his inability to get things done. And having come of age in the Washington of the 1960s and early 1970s, he was forever bemoaning the "bullshitters and hurrah merchants" who were calling themselves politicians in the 1980s. But he still had not lost his touch or enthusiasm. He said he was "barnacle-encrusted," and deep down, still found fun—and, more important, profit—in playing the insider's game.

Thevenot was an access man. He survived on his ability to be accepted and trusted by the people with clout in Congress; his reputation rose and fell on having his telephone calls returned. He was not a technician. When he lobbied for changes in the tax code, for instance, he usually was versed only in the basic facts of the matter. For answers to deeper questions, he brought along an expert. But almost no one considered his need for backup a deficiency. Thevenot's job was more about strategy than details. He had to know whom to ask, when to ask, and how to ask for help, none of which was a simple question in the Byzantine world of Washington.

The secret of Thevenot's entrée was buried deep in the bayous and cotton fields of rural Louisiana. The third-oldest of eight children, Thevenot was the son of a failed farmer. "We built a house, started a farm, and proceeded to get poor," Thevenot recalled. "We also were the only ones who spoke clear English" in a region where Cajun patois was more the norm. His skill with language and his interest in government had brought him to where he was.

In the early 1960s, Thevenot worked as a television reporter for the NBC affiliate in Baton Rouge, and was part of the gang that covered the antics of the colorful governor, Earl Long. In 1963, Thevenot went over to the other side and became campaign manager for Gillis Long, a cousin of Russell's, who was waging an uphill fight for the U.S. House of Representatives against a two-term incumbent. Thevenot did a tremendous volume of work: everything from hiring hillbilly bands to trying to keep the candidate's driver out of jail. And when Gillis Long won, Thevenot's ticket to Washington had been punched.

The only problem was that the headstrong Thevenot was not interested in working for the even more headstrong Gillis Long. Thevenot told Long that he would be his friend forever, but never again his employee. So Gillis Long telephoned Russell Long, then a U.S. senator, and asked him to find Thevenot a job. The one he found turned out to be as an elevator operator, but, in the hands of the resourceful Thevenot, it became a job with possibilities.

Between trips, Thevenot wrote speeches for his Senate patron. Soon, he moved out of the elevator and into more responsible positions on the staffs of committees that were run by Russell Long. These included panels with jurisdiction over small-business and post-office legislation. No matter what his title was officially, Thevenot always functioned as a top aide to Russell Long, who went on to become one of the most powerful men in Washington as chairman of the Senate Finance Committee.

When Russell Long had been drinking and was bruising for a brawl, Thevenot was there to spirit him away. He was also confidant to the mighty and friend to those who would become that way. He knew "Johnny" Breaux when he was a fellow staffer on Capitol Hill; Breaux went on to become a U.S. senator—in the seat vacated by Russell Long. Thevenot knew "Tommy" Boggs when he was the chubby teenage son of House Majority Leader Hale Boggs of Louisiana; in 1989 Boggs was running one of the biggest lobbying law firms in Washington. In short, Thevenot belonged to Washington's tight-knit Louisiana mafia, which like the Tabasco sauce from back home, wielded a fiery punch even in small quantities. "Thevenot's a piece of work," Senator Breaux explained. "He adds color to an otherwise bland city."

When Thevenot first left the Hill in 1975, he worked briefly for an investment-banking firm. But he soon realized that his life was too closely tied to Congress to abandon the Hill completely. Besides, he thought, becoming a lobbyist would get him faster to what was then his goal: making lots of money. "I decided that there was a point of diminished returns to being a staffer. I got to a point where I just sort of ran out of good ideas," he said. "I also had a family and financial obligations. I was making thirty-five thousand dollars a year, with four kids who had to go to college eventually. It was just not enough. So after nearly thirteen years it was just time to get out and cash in.

"I gave up the idea of changing the world. I set about to get rich."

With two friends, Thevenot set up the lobbying firm of Thevenot, Murray and Scheer. They represented a variety of business interests, but Thevenot was most drawn to real estate. After a few years, he left the partnership to become president and chief lobbyist for the National Realty Committee, one of the burgeoning new trade associations that represented specialized industry factions. The business world had grown too complex and too fragmented for huge umbrella organizations, such as the U.S. Chamber of Commerce and the National Association of Manufacturers, to represent adequately. So in 1969 the biggest real estate developers banded together to form an elite group. In the early 1980s, Thevenot became its most successful and best-known mouthpiece, and helped lead it to many victories on Capitol Hill.

The National Realty Committee's most sweeping win came in 1981, when real estate was lavished with new tax breaks at the prodding of President Reagan. That caused a spurt in development around the country, which redefined the skylines of the nation's cities and filled the pockets of Thevenot's clients with gold. Projects were planned not so much for the rent that they would bring in as for the tax benefits. The boom, however, was so excessive that it was not long before the tax goodies were taken away. "See-through skyscrapers" with no occupants to speak of were becoming a national embarrassment, and there was nothing that Thevenot could do about it. The Tax Reform Act of 1986 made real estate one of its biggest victims. Not only were the 1981 benefits excised, but some tax breaks of older vintage were trimmed away as well. It was a bloodbath for the industry. But, in typical form, Thevenot expressed his chagrin with a smile. "At least our people have nice big buildings of their own to jump from," he said.

Thevenot was not blamed for the disaster. Lobbyists rarely are when the industries they represent lose a legislative fight. He could have stayed with the National Realty Committee forever; indeed, he was on retainer to the group though 1989, at $7,500 a month plus expenses, and continued to function as its top lobbyist. But he wanted a change, and a chance to make more money. So he decided to leave the full-time employ of the real estate industry and go out on his own. He affiliated with William Boardman, a tax lawyer and lobbyist for the engineering and construction industries, who had rented some fancy new office space (at about $45 a square foot) in the Willard Office Building, which had been renovated with the help of Thevenot's early 1980s tax breaks. The two men called themselves Concord Associates, a reference to Boardman's Boston-area roots; on the elegantly papered walls they hung drawings of Revolutionary War scenes from battles around Concord.

In appearance, Thevenot was an odd mixture that mirrored the competing demands of his vocation—one part soft, another part hard as nails. He had the cherubic face of a Kewpie doll, and only slightly more hair. But he also had the beefy hands and swagger of the roughneck he was during the hardworking summers of his youth in sweltering Morgan City, Louisiana. Thevenot had come a long way since then. When Congress reconvened in January 1989, he had been an invited guest at some of the fanciest gatherings in the nation's capital, and he spent most of his time hopping from one private party to another. Senator Charles Robb of Virginia had held a bash for three thousand people at Union Station to celebrate his election. But thanks to the National Realty Committee checks that Thevenot had delivered to Robb's campaigns in the past, Thevenot had been invited to a far smaller, more intimate party in the new senator's office.

What Thevenot did there was collect information, which for him was no insignificant task. He explained: "We're talking to everybody we can about what the general mood of the Congress is. What issues are they going to deem important? How are the members lining up? How strongly they feel, for example, about new taxes to deal with the deficit problem. That is what we do, it's a network, it's a game. All the people that we know, and we've done favors for, gotten jobs for, sent them business, are part of it. What you know and your ability to interpret it—your ability to understand what's important and what's not—is what it's all about."

Thevenot was always testing for the possibility of a tax increase, an issue always of deep concern to his real estate clients. In particular he was curious about the chances for a value-added tax, which is a kind of national sales tax. "If I thought there was going to be a strong move to put in a value-added tax, I would say to the real estate industry, 'Now is the time to commission a study by someone, to see what the effects of the various formats of a value-added tax would be on real estate,' " he said.

For the time being, though, Thevenot dismissed the notion of a value-added tax. But in anticipation of at least some type of tax bill in 1989, Thevenot planned an assault by the real estate industry on some of the more painful changes enacted in 1986. His goal was to have a set of extremely complicated anti-tax-shelter rules eased in a way that would help his clients. To that end, he stayed in constant contact with the staffs of Republican Representatives William Thomas of California and Richard Schulze of Pennsylvania, who were carrying the industry's water on the issue. "They call and ask for advice," Thevenot said matter-of-factly about the congressmen's staffs, "and also to tell us what they are thinking of doing."

Thevenot, like "King of the Lobby" Sam Ward before him, acknowledged that being a lobbyist was not commendable. "Obviously the vested interests gain at the expense of the great mass of people," he said. But there was a need, he thought, for corporations to get involved in Washington, and that was what kept him in business. "The modern government is huge, pervasive, intrusive into everybody's life," he said. "If you just let things take their course and don't get in the game, you get trampled on. You ignore it at your peril."

Much of Thevenot's work was directed not at taking anything away from the public at large, he asserted, but at refereeing between competing business interests. "What's the public-interest side of a contest between the stock and mutual life-insurance companies?" he asked. "It's a contest between the two, with the third party being the Congress. Who's got the better argument is anybody's guess. That's one I don't feel strongly about one way or the other." But his allegiance was for sale. "I don't have a dog in that fight, and don't have a position," he added. "I will have a position as soon as I get a dog." And in not too long a time, he would.

* * *

The after-dinner entertainment at the Greenbrier that first night, Friday, February 3, was singer-dancer Louise Mandrell, who decided to have some fun with the mostly political audience. At the conclusion of her foot-stomping performance she pretended to call a press conference, and asked if there were any questions for *her*. Only one was shouted out—by lobbyist Robert Juliano. "What are you doing after the show?" he asked, and everyone laughed. *Oh, there goes Bobby again*, they thought.

Like Thevenot, Juliano had been busy trying to weave himself deeper into the social fabric of the U.S. Congress. He was already pretty thick with the group. Later in the weekend, he would play pool and share some beers with a handful of lawmakers at 1 A.M. The next day he would hold court with some of the same people around a coffee urn. Most of his chatter was purely social—but not all of it. At one point he grabbed the arm of Representative Ronnie Flippo of Alabama and said, "I want to come by and talk to you about two little things." Flippo smiled and happily agreed. "Sounds good, Bobby," he replied.

The group that paid Juliano's $6,000 entrance fee to the weekend was the Hotel Employees and Restaurant Employees International Union, an AFL–CIO affiliate. But his client list was broader than that. He was also retained as a lobbyist by major corporate clients such as American Express and the National Motor Sports Committee, which oversaw the NASCAR and Indianapolis 500 races, among others. Like Thevenot, Juliano said he was proud to play a part in bringing lawmakers together for serious talk about significant issues. But he also conceded that "the good part" of the Greenbrier retreat was getting a chance to meet freshmen members of the House. "It's tough to keep on top of that because of all the changes," he said. The event also presented a much more efficient way to talk to lawmakers. "Here there aren't the bells ringing with them running off to vote," he said. "There's more of an opportunity to do it in a concise way."

Juliano was a congressional regular, and no one minded his sniffing around for facts and gossip, even during a conference at which there was supposed to be no lobbying. Like Thevenot, he repeatedly asked lawmakers, "Is there any chance of enacting a value-added tax?" The budget deficit was so huge that his clients were forever being picked on to defray it. A revenue source as gigantic as a national sales tax might provide enough money to get Congress off their backs, he thought. This was a peculiar stance for a lobbyist who represented a union, because the burden of a national sales tax would fall disproportionately on low-income working people. But Juliano represented corporations as well.

Juliano's interest in the budget deficit was well informed. The previous month, his union had lured a handful of Washington's most prominent politicians to its board meeting in Palm Springs, California, by paying them speaking honoraria plus expenses. Each politician had given a speech about the legislative outlook, and almost every one of them had emphasized the need to stanch the government's red ink. The early warning had been a great advantage to Juliano, but not to many others. Minutes of the meeting were not publicly disclosed until March, and only to the limited readership of the union's in-house magazine, *Catering Industry Employee*. But Juliano knew firsthand and from the start that something big was on the horizon.

At the January meeting, Dan Rostenkowski of Illinois, the chief tax-writer in the House, had confided that the deficit "worries me more than anything else." "How are we going to service that debt?" Rostenkowski had asked. He had predicted that Congress and President Bush would begin to answer that question, and perhaps in a major way, but not before late summer at the earliest. According to others who had spoken at the meeting, such as Representative Marty Russo, also of Chicago, "sin" taxes on alcoholic beverages and tobacco were likely to be eventual targets for increase.

Juliano was unapologetic about the advantage he had had. He was even boastful about his role in making Palm Springs a mecca for paid speeches by politicians. Juliano was a lobbyist, and loved it. For every member of Congress who passed by, he had an inside joke. For every eligible woman, he had a proposition. And for every major piece of legislation, he had a pretty good sense of where it was likely to go, thanks to his friends, paid and otherwise, in high places.

Like other big-name lobbyists, Juliano did more than beg favors of the people in power. By careful design, he managed to be a presence on behalf of those people who paid his fees. Sometimes loud, ever flashy, he was part host, part spy. His job was to know and to be known, and to always, always be there. Unlike most lobbyists, who represented either business or labor interests, he was in the unusual position of representing both. That gave him access to as wide a range of decision-makers as anyone in town. And access was Juliano's stock-in-trade, as it was Thevenot's. To members of both Congress and the Bush administration, his face was familiar, if somewhat well-fed. But that was completely appropriate. He was the lobbyist for restaurant dining, the lobbyist for having a good time, the lobbyist for tourism and travel.

He worked for—and managed to personify—the garish, brazen world of business meals and entertainment. The combination made the forty-eight-year-old Juliano a one-stop shop for anyone who wanted to know what was up in the world of going out. He also was often in the center of some of the most heated political catfights in Washington, including the perennial squabble over the tax deduction for the "three-martini lunch."

In the mid-1970s, the Internal Revenue Service tried to force waiters and waitresses to withhold taxes on tips on the basis of the amount shown on credit-card receipts. With the help of American Express, Juliano lobbied successfully in Congress, first to delay the regulation and then, in 1982, to enact a compromise that avoided such mandatory withholding. In 1985 and 1986, when President Reagan and Congress wanted to severely limit the tax deduction for business dining and entertaining, Juliano headed a broad business-labor coalition that did not win, but did blunt, the effort; in the end 80 percent of those expenses were made deductible, down from 100 percent. In 1989, he was among the many lobbyists battling to prevent any further cutback.

In all of his endeavors, Juliano strove to work closely with both business and labor. His model, he said, was his experience with the collective-bargaining method of negotiating labor contracts. Tremendous things could be accomplished, he noted, when business and labor officials worked together and dealt in good faith with one another. Surely the same principle could apply to legislation, he reasoned, and his career for the most part had proved him right. "When I walk up and say I represent the hotel and restaurant workers union, American Express, and NASCAR," Juliano said, "it makes people stop and think."

He was, in essence, a walking coalition, maintaining two offices just a couple of blocks apart—one for labor, the other for corporate clients. The first was located on the ornate first floor of the three-story hotel and restaurant workers building at 28th and M streets. The second was on the third floor of a nondescript office building at 26th and M streets. But the twain often met, and that was the secret of Juliano's success. "Many times business and labor are perceived to have disparate interests, while in fact they often have identical ones," he said.

The Juliano prototype was being followed all over Capitol Hill—though usually by more than one lobbyist at a time. "The [lobbying] business is more complex than it used to be," said George Gould, a lobbyist for the postal workers' union. "There is no way that any single union, or any single business, can survive without going into coalitions. That's just the way it is going to be."

Indeed, to hear lobbyists talk, there was no such thing as a special interest anymore. Sure, there were still plenty of trade associations and lobbying factions; the 723-page *Washington Representatives* directory attested to that. Lobbyists continued to represent everything from soup (Campbell Soup Company) to nuts (the Peanut Butter and Nut Processors Association), and from head (the American Academy of Otolaryngology–Head and Neck Surgery) to toe (the American Academy of Podiatric Sports Medicine). But increasingly, lawmakers saw fewer of these individual pressure groups. Instead what they saw was a coalition of interests that claimed to care about the public good, often led by organizations that, politically speaking, were less offensive to an elected official than were the self-interested corporations that tended, in reality, to bankroll such efforts. Lobbyists even had a term for this type of special-interest manipulation. It was called creating coalitions of nontraditional allies.

The idea behind these odd couplings was to "raise the comfort level" of lawmakers when they were being hit up for some taxpayer-paid benefit, according to lobbyist Anne Wexler, a master of coalition lobbying. Most voters were working people, not corporate chieftains, the theory went. So the front man for each coalition had to be close to the people and not even remotely associated with the executive suite. Indeed, effective coalitions had to possess a public profile far prettier to the average legislator than the relatively ugly countenance of the corporate interests that lurked not far in the background.

Juliano was perhaps the best illustration of a business-labor alliance. To some insiders, though, Juliano's dual representation was a blatant conflict of interest that ultimately shortchanged the labor side. Partly out of jealousy for his big paychecks, and partly out of a belief that he was, at times, a traitor to the labor movement, some fellow union lobbyists belittled him. "Bobby is a good lobbyist. He is very effective. He knows the players," one union lobbyist said. "But there's always a concern, 'Who is he working for now?' " Some labor lobbyists also disliked the fact that Juliano was not as much a team player as were the lobbyists for other AFL–CIO unions. "He doesn't take on a lot of the agenda for the rest of the union movement," the lobbyist added.

In response, Juliano was equally uncharitable about organized labor. Though he was careful to maintain close ties to a small cluster of union-lobbyist buddies, he saw the bulk of the others as shortsighted bureaucrats who had failed to change with the times. The result, he believed, was an added threat to the already crumbling future of the labor movement. Of some high-ranking AFL–CIO leaders, he said, "I don't give those guys the time of day."

Corporate interests outside of the tourism and entertainment fields were intrigued by Juliano's ability to bridge the divide, and hired him regularly. With largely Democratic lawmakers, he had the access and credibility of a union lobbyist, but he also was willing to argue on behalf of corporations. "He works in mysterious ways," said William Harman of the law firm Davis & Harman, who had worked closely with Juliano on life-insurance taxation issues. People skills were Juliano's chief ability. "He's a very unusual guy: very smart and very, very perceptive," said Harry Freeman, a former executive with American Express.

This reputation for effectiveness had made the one-man Robert E. Juliano Associates one of the best-heeled lobbying shops in town. Juliano made in excess of $250,000 a year thanks to multithousand-dollar monthly retainers from several clients. According to his filings with the Congress, in 1989 Juliano was paid in the range of $34,000 a quarter by the hotel workers' union; $15,000 a quarter by both American Express and the Stock (Life Insurance) Information Group, and $9,000 a quarter by National Speedway Corporation, the race-car outfit. "I work my ass off, there's no question about that," he said. He was, in any case, well paid for his time.

Juliano's dual role as a lobbyist for hire by both labor and business interests began in 1978 at the board meeting of the hotel workers' union in Palm Springs. Rostenkowski and House Speaker

Thomas P. (Tip) O'Neill, Jr., were having a drink with Edward T. Hanley, the union's president. After a while, Hanley was struck by the number of corporate lobbyists who came over to thank him for Juliano's assistance on one issue or another. Afterward, he called Juliano aside and said, "Bobby, you've worked hard all your life, and this is not right." Thus began a negotiation that in 1981 freed Juliano to take on other clients in addition to the union.

Juliano's first new paying client was American Express, which formalized a nonpaid relationship he had had with it on many issues. When Juliano was still with the union full-time "we formed a very strong alliance," recalled Freeman, the former American Express executive. Placing Juliano on retainer was more or less just to "allow him to keep doing what he was doing," Freeman explained. "He brings a perspective that you usually don't get in a corporate environment." National Restaurant Association lobbyists were not pleased with the affiliation, Freeman remembered. "But I said I preferred to win rather than lose, so that was that."

Juliano's roots were in the working class. He grew up on the West Side of Chicago; his father was an immigrant from Pescara, Italy, who sold leather to shoemakers. After just two years of college Juliano quit to go into the hotel business. He started as a personnel clerk at Chicago's Palmer House hotel, but moved up rapidly. Soon he was a full-fledged manager with a blossoming career as a hotel executive.

Early on, though, Juliano had an encounter with organized labor that would influence the rest of his life. In 1962, at the age of twenty-one, Juliano, then a clerk, was helping the Palmer House beat back a threatened city-wide strike by hotel workers. The chief negotiator for the hotel workers was another young man—Ed Hanley. Watching from afar, Juliano was greatly impressed by the labor leader's willingness to negotiate and his ability to accommodate. After the talks ended with the strike averted, Juliano's boss at the time, Fred Guest, introduced him to Hanley in the lobby of the Palmer House. "This guy is going to be president of the international union one day," Guest said. And a decade later, Hanley was.

In the meantime, Juliano and Hanley kept in contact. Hanley moved up in the union hierarchy, and Juliano worked here and there in the hotel and financial-services industries. Then, in 1973,

Juliano received a phone call. Hanley said he was in a hotel room in Miami waiting to be anointed president of the international union. He offered Juliano a job, though he didn't quite yet know what it would be.

"Are you with me?" Hanley asked.

"You got me," Juliano replied.

Sometime later, the two men met in Chicago to talk.

"What do you know about lobbying?" Hanley asked.

"A lot," Juliano responded. "You know how much time I've spent in the lobby of the Palmer House."

Despite his nearly complete inexperience, Juliano became the union's first lobbyist. He arrived at Washington's National Airport on June 4, 1973, and hailed a cab.

"What do you do for a living?" the driver inquired.

"I'm a lobbyist," Juliano replied with newfound pride.

"What does a lobbyist do?" the cabbie asked.

"You really shouldn't ask me those technical questions," Juliano answered.

It was not long before Juliano learned the technicalities. He did so by devoting himself, day and night, to his new career. Night was especially important. Over dinner he would sit and listen to elder statesmen, especially former Democratic Representative Johnny Dent of Pennsylvania, at whose dormitory-style apartment he poured drinks for some of the great men of Congress. He also spoke to so many senators that he was once admonished for talking too much. Back then, lobbyists were supposed to listen, not talk, to members of the upper chamber.

In 1989, Juliano was still out almost nightly, attending cocktail-party fund-raisers, usually with a union check in his hand. Other nights he wined and dined this congressman or that, one night hosting a dinner for Senator John Kerry of Massachusetts, another night picking up the tab for what he called the Redneck Caucus, a group of more than a dozen moderate-to-conservative Democrats, mainly from rural districts.

But Juliano's most influential and important dinner companions by far were part of what had come to be known as the Tuesday Night Group. Juliano's connection to the group was his longtime friend Representative Marty Russo of Chicago. They both had attended the same Catholic high school; when Russo ran for Congress, Juliano and his union were early financial backers of his campaign. And after Russo was elected, he prodded Juliano into taking to dinner an obscure group of young Democrats of which he was a part. They had little in common except that they had left their families back in their districts, and spent three days and two nights in Washington each week that Congress was in session.

This group eventually came to include some of the most influential lawmakers in the House: Budget Committee Chairman Leon Panetta of California; soon-to-be Interior Committee Chairman George Miller, also from California; Banking Committee powerhouse Charles E. Schumer of New York; and Russo, who was Rostenkowski's right-hand man. Representative Barney Frank of Massachusetts referred to them, only half-jokingly, as the Rostenkowski Youth.

The real value of these dinners was information gathering; Juliano's companions were among the best-connected lawmakers in town. It was from these encounters that Juliano got a good sense of how his clients might fare in the increasingly top-down world of legislation. More specific lobbying contacts with those lawmakers would come later, on an as-needed basis, and usually they were quick and businesslike. But they certainly did come. A friend like Bobby was never denied an audience.

"The most effective lobbyists here are the ones you don't think of as lobbyists," Budget Chairman Panetta said, "and I don't think of him as a lobbyist. He's almost a constituent, or a friend." Democratic Representative Barbara Boxer of California, another Tuesday-night diner, agreed: "He's a lovely, wonderful guy. In the whole time I've known him, he's never asked me to vote for anything." At her husband's fiftieth-birthday party at the Army-Navy Club, Boxer joked to her guests that Juliano was not a lobbyist, but a member of the family.

At almost any time of the day, Juliano could be found standing in the ornate Reception Room outside the Senate chamber or near the elevators en route to the House floor. He was obviously a favorite of many of the most senior lawmakers; there was hardly a member who would not stop to shake his hand, acknowledge a recent favor of one kind or another, or ask when they would have spaghetti together again.

One of Juliano's closest pals was the senior senator from the tourist state of Hawaii, Democrat Daniel K. Inouye. Inouye was a minor potentate in Congress: chairman of an appropriations subcommittee but, more important to Juliano, a senior member of a tourism subcommittee. Their bond had been sealed years before in typical Juliano style when the lobbyist had cooked pasta for the senator one lazy afternoon on hot plates in the lawmaker's secluded Capitol hideaway. Their friendship was maintained over more food that Juliano paid for at Giorgio's, a downtown Washington restaurant that boasted a dish called veal Juliano in his honor.

Juliano's tenure as a lobbyist had not been without controversy. Over the years, the hotel workers' union had been investigated for possible ties to organized crime by at least four grand juries, the Labor and Justice departments, and the Internal Revenue Service. No action was ever taken against the union, in court or elsewhere, but a three-year investigation by the Senate Permanent Subcommittee on Investigations concluded in 1984 that the 400,000-member union was under the "substantial influence" of organized-crime interests. Because of all the attention his employer got, Juliano worried for a time that he, too, might become the subject of an investigation, but that never happened.

Still, the lawmaker who served as chairman of the investigative subcommittee warned that caution was advisable when dealing with the union. "I don't know the lobbyist or anything about him. I would not want to characterize him individually," said Republican Senator William Roth of Delaware. "But in view of the background of the union, I would certainly say, 'Buyers beware.' Anyone dealing with that union should be extraordinarily careful. If I was dealing with them I would want to look into the background a little."

Juliano's response to questions about his union's possible links to organized crime was "Ignore them." And almost everyone who dealt with him never asked. "These people have not been charged. They spent a lot of money investigating them," Senator Inouye said. "If spending a lot of money is a test, they've been tested." In fact, Juliano was widely regarded as an "honest" lobbyist—one whose word was good and whose facts were straight. He had earned respect from Republicans as well as Democrats. "He's a great guy, easy to work with, no high-pressure stuff," said Senate Republican Leader Robert Dole of Kansas. "I know he's a Democrat but he's a good guy. People like him, and he levels with you, that's the key. He's willing to compromise, or he'll tell you he can't."

Juliano was more than just a business-labor coalition. He was a business-labor-government coalition as well. Thanks to Inouye's sponsorship, for fourteen years he was a member of the Commerce Department's U.S. Travel and Tourism Advisory Board, a quasi-governmental group on whose behalf he traveled, at the expense of his clients, to such faraway places as Tokyo, Berlin, and Moscow. And wherever he went, Juliano, unlike most lobbyists, was completely bilingual. He spoke the languages of both labor and management fluently.

Lawmakers appreciated this flexibility, and displayed some real affection for the lobbyist, as was evident at the Greenbrier. "Juliano, my man!" Representative Marvin Leath of Texas shouted to him as he passed by during the Greenbrier weekend. "Great guy," he added to anyone who might be listening. Leath scoffed at any suggestion that lobbyists like Juliano should be barred from the Greenbrier event. "I don't think it's unhealthy at all" to have them there, he said. "We keep trying to make the system sterile. It never will be." Besides, he added, "You can *learn* from these people. It's the way the system works."

• • •

On Saturday night at the Greenbrier, the lawmakers and lobbyists pretended that it was the 1950s again, and came dressed in period garb to dance in the main ballroom. They also were treated to a slide show that featured childhood pictures of themselves. Thevenot was among the most flamboyant of the guests. He came dressed as a greaser, complete with slicked-back hair, and a pack of Camels rolled up in his T-shirt. He and his date, Laura Ison, danced the night away, rubbing elbows with their friends, the members of the House.

The next morning, Thevenot was a standout again, though this time in a casual sweater. He played emcee to the first seminar of the day. "This morning's program is a subject near and dear to your hearts," he told the bleary-eyed lawmakers. "How to get elected and stay out of trouble." He then introduced Representative Beryl Anthony of Arkansas, the chairman of the House Democrats' campaign fund-raising committee.

Anthony thanked Thevenot, who, like chairman Jack Brooks, was an old duck-hunting companion. Before he began his talk, Anthony took time to say, "I had more fun last night than I think I've had in a long, long time," and the audience applauded warmly. At the end of Anthony's speech, the program went back to Thevenot, who reminded all present to place their luggage outside their rooms.

The return trip on the Amtrak special was long. Many people napped, and they needed the rest. When the lawmakers returned to work the next day, Monday, February 6, they were forced to face what they had been able to avoid for at least one pleasant weekend in the woods: the pay-raise issue. House Republicans blocked a routine motion to adjourn, and that act forced Speaker Wright to take the floor to announce that the House would vote the next day on a bill that would stop the pay raise entirely. Republicans applauded, and the outcome was preordained. "It's a thing of the past," growled Brooks, lamenting the lost salary increase. "Forget it."

On Tuesday, the House voted 380–48 to kill the hike, and the Senate endorsed that action with a lopsided vote of its own. Acrimony ruled in the House, and Wright would later pay a price. His colleagues would remember his fumbling of the pay-raise issue when the Ethics Committee announced its conclusions about him.

• • •

In the meantime, lawmakers' days continued to brim with meetings. From morning until night, they scurried from place to place on Capitol Hill, guided by a secretary's typed reminders on a stack of index cards. Many of the meetings lasted only fifteen minutes, but most had one thing in common. They were held with lobbyists of one kind or another. The encounters seemed breezy and casual, but they rarely were.

In a corner office on Pennsylvania Avenue, a half-block from the White House, a group of lobbyists conferred over a catered sandwich lunch about how to approach their latest attempt to twist the fiscal debate away from benefits to the public at large and toward America's corporations. This was not the lobbyists' first discussion of the issue; it had been on their minds for months. But this day in early February they spent nearly two hours discussing how to approach a single meeting on the subject, which was scheduled for that afternoon.

"I think Gradison is genuinely interested," pronounced Charls Walker, the longtime lobbyist for big business in whose office the luncheon was held. He referred to the respected Representative Willis D. Gradison, Jr., Republican of Ohio, whom Walker and his colleagues had chosen to be the champion of their latest legislative initiative: the fiscal equivalent of an environmental-impact statement. What Walker wanted was to require every new tax bill to be accompanied by an analysis—called the capital-costs impact statement—that would detail how the measure would affect corporations' ability to raise money. Presumably, if lawmakers knew that their proposals would increase costs to corporations by a significant amount, they would think twice before pressing ahead.

Lobbyists come at the federal government from many angles, and Walker's angle was from the top down. His group's proposal was just one in a long list of ideas they had dreamed up to, as they liked to say, "change the terms of debate." Lobbyists like Walker did not just try to shoehorn small, self-interested provisions into legislation, as many lobbyists did. Such lobbyists promoted entirely new ways of thinking into which such smaller changes might naturally fit. In the 1970s, Walker was in the vanguard of heavy-industry lobbyists who pushed one such big notion, "capital formation," which preached the need for government to create incentives for "savings and investment." The rhetoric had all the political sanctity of motherhood, and cleverly masked the lobbyists' deeper intention: to channel more government aid to corporations. Capital formation had its heyday in 1981, when tax write-offs for plant and equipment purchases were made more generous, and corporate taxes were dramatically reduced.

But in the ensuing years, the huge cost of that change came home to roost. Budget deficits surged, and Congress was forced to raise taxes on Walker's corporations. The 1986 tax bill was the biggest corporate-tax increase of all: $120 billion over five years. It was a bad year for Charly Walker. It may in fact have been his last year as a full-fledged, full-time corporate lobbyist.

In that year he sold a 30 percent stake in Walker Associates to the public-relations firm Ogilvy & Mather. Soon thereafter two of Walker's most prized young associates, Stewart Van Scoyoc and Lindsay Hooper, left the firm to create a new lobbying shop with John Winburn, a lobbyist who was an expert on politics in the House. In short, Walker was battered by the ebb and flow of Washington, and was slowly withdrawing from it. To his friends, he seemed to be more interested in his teaching at the Lyndon Baines Johnson School of Public Policy at the University of Texas in Austin. Even in his lobbying, he took on more of the persona of a professor. He spent less and less time in the office.

In early 1989, Walker was still involved in the lobbying game. But he was clearly a figure in eclipse. At this meeting in his office, his recollections of tax bills past consumed much of his conversation. The meat of the meeting was led by a much younger man who sat across the table from him: Mark Bloomfield. Bloomfield was president of the American Council for Capital Formation, and by all accounts was the new Charly Walker.

The council was a lobbying group that endeavored to dress up its efforts to lower corporate taxes in the garb of economic theory and "scholarship." It was able to do this in high style thanks to a million-dollar budget provided by some of the biggest companies in the country, including such capital-intensive concerns as the Aluminum Company of America, the Chrysler Corporation, the Scott Paper Company, and the Weyerhaeuser Company, and financial-services companies such as Merrill Lynch.

While Walker asked a few probing questions at the meeting, it was the thirty-nine-year-old Bloomfield who answered them. He shaped how, and to whom, the latest Walker ploy would be pitched. "What's going to be the chairman's reaction?" Walker asked about Representative Dan Rostenkowski of the tax-writing Ways and Means Committee. Bloomfield was sure that Rostenkowski would not like the idea, but suggested that the lobbyists find out anyway. "We should go through Rob," he said, referring to Robert Leonard, the chairman's top committee aide.

"And what about the Senate?" Bloomfield asked, anticipating Walker's next query. He then answered his own question: "You start out by saying, 'Who's the equivalent of a Bill Gradison on the Finance Committee?' The obvious thing is to go see the chairman."

Walker grimaced at the mention of Chairman Lloyd Bentsen of the Senate's tax-writing panel. "Tell him what you're doing and sit back and listen," he said, as he pictured the meeting in his own mind. "You might not hear anything, but you can sit back and listen."

Bloomfield tried to be reassuring. " 'Savings' is an all-American word," he asserted. "I've tried it on a number of members. It's a good buzzword."

The table itself was a snapshot of modern lobbying. Increasingly, more than one person, and more than one skill, was needed to wield significant influence in Washington. Walker was a former deputy treasury secretary under President Richard M. Nixon; his long experience in town gave him access to some of its most senior Republican officials. Also at the table was an economist, Margo Thorning, whose expertise was needed to devise the impact-statement amendment. Then there was Bloomfield, who held both a master's degree in business administration and a law degree from the University of Pennsylvania. He was the archetype of the hybrid that the modern lobbyist was fast becoming: half political strategist, half technocrat.

"My bias has always been to find a good Democrat to start this dialogue," Bloomfield said. "I would prefer him to be on the [Ways and Means] committee."

"I could think of some good nominees off the committee, like a Charlie Stenholm," Walker offered, referring to the conservative Texas Democrat.

"On the other hand I could come up with an Ed Jenkins," Bloomfield persisted, suggesting the Democrat from Georgia, who was a respected member of the Ways and Means Committee. "He would do it," he added.

Bloomfield then combed through the personalities again. A talk with the ranking GOP members of both tax-writing committees in Congress would be appropriate, he said; they would surely "fall in line" with the idea. Then he returned to the Democrats. "The question is whether you do a [Robert] Matsui or maybe a Jim Moody, he's an economist, right?" he said, mentioning the Democrats from California and Wisconsin, who both sit on Ways and Means. In the end, the issue of a Democratic sponsor was left open.

Thorning, the economist, then began a detailed discussion about how the impact statement should be structured. What was needed, she said, were serious academic studies of the issue. And she tossed around names, mostly of Democratic economists, who might be paid by the American Council to produce such studies: Alan Auerbach of the University of Pennsylvania, or maybe Lawrence Summers of Harvard University, who had been the chief economic adviser to the Democrats' 1988 presidential nominee, Michael Dukakis. Thorning said that Gradison had already covered the government angle of the enterprise. At the lobbyists' request, he had asked the Congressional Research Service to conduct its own study of the amendment.

Such scrupulous attention to detail was absolutely necessary, Bloomfield asserted. Gradison would demand it. Bloomfield recalled that he once brought a study about capital-gains taxes to the congressman without first reading it thoroughly. Gradison told Bloomfield that the study was fine, except for footnote number 9. Bloomfield was completely at a loss, but was saved from attempting an explanation: The voting buzzer sounded and Gradison had to rush off to the House floor. "I said to myself, 'This is a lesson,' " Bloomfield said. "I will never again show up at a meeting with Mr. Gradison unless I have read all the footnotes." So, having discussed every possible angle, the group piled into Walker's black limousine for the short drive to Capitol Hill.

In his office, Gradison was full of pleasantries and good wishes. The first few minutes of the meeting were spent discussing football and season tickets. Then Walker decided it was time to get down to business. "The first question is, 'What about the merit of the idea of starting a movement up here to get, for lack of a better word, a legislative mandate to consider a capital-costs impact statement whenever you are considering any tax legislation?' " Walker said, stopping midsentence to clear his throat.

"I have no question of our goal," Gradison began ominously. "But if we do it, we ought not just look at the tax code." In measuring competitiveness, he said, the federal tax burden "is an important element, but it's not the biggest element."

Walker's jaw dropped. He was simply flabbergasted at Gradison's misgivings, but he struggled to recoup. A tax change, he noted, "is the one most amenable to public policy."

Gradison was unconvinced. He made clear he was not interested in measuring the effect just on corporations. A broader measure of the economic impact on society was what he most wanted
to see. "I think the objective is related to productivity and the long-
term standard of living," Gradison insisted. "The question isn't
just capital-recovery costs. There are some industries that are affected more than others."

All of this was bad news for Walker, but he pretended not to
hear it. He and Gradison went on to discuss the political funda-
mentals of enacting a law, including which Democratic lawmaker
to choose as cosponsor of the bill. Gradison was not shy about
giving advice. First, he said, "it ought to be somebody who's on
the committee. It's so much better when someone is pushing it
from Ways and Means." But it probably should not be Matsui.
"Matsui is running for Senate," he said. "Furthermore, Bob Matsui
has stretched himself so thin on this committee some people are
questioning his effectiveness."

On the other hand, Gradison advised, "Ed Jenkins would be
very good on this. Ed's a very clever fellow, not in the crafty sense.
He plans ahead and he knows how to count votes." Gradison
cautioned that he was not sure whether Jenkins would be "comfortable" with the provision. That would depend, he suggested, on
whether the textile industry, with which Jenkins worked closely,
would object.

Again, Walker was not listening. Instead of Jenkins, Walker
proposed Beryl Anthony, the chairman of the House Democrats'
campaign committee. "He's very sensitive to business views on
the outside, he's out raising money for his cause there," Gradison
said, in a backhanded compliment. "I don't think there's any comparison between him [Jenkins] and Beryl, in terms of their standing
around here," he continued. But he concluded, "Beryl's okay. Tell
him you talked to me."

Before the lobbyists left, Gradison made a pitch to them for
one of his own special interests: the American Enterprise Institute,
a Washington think tank. Instead of going to the University of
Pennsylvania or Harvard for an outside study on the impact statement, Gradison suggested, maybe someone at AEI could be hired.
"They have some very good people," Gradison said. "It would be
a very good organization to sponsor work on the outside." And

then he disclosed, "I am chairman of their fiscal-policy advisory committee."

Walker also had a last word about his own pet interest: imposing a value-added tax. To Walker, VAT was the perfect way to find the billions of dollars it would take to pay for the massive reduction in corporate income taxes he sought. A VAT, in essence, is a national sales tax, which would be imposed at each level in the chain of a product's distribution. At the end of the chain, the consumer—not the corporation—ultimately pays the tax. Walker dreamed that someday such a tax on consumption would replace the tax on corporate profits. The impact statement, he confessed, could well lay the groundwork for making such a change.

After the meeting, the lobbyists tried to keep a brave face. But they knew their initiative was in trouble. Walker was mostly silent. But typically, Bloomfield chattered on—not about capital costs, but about an allied topic, capital gains. For years, he and the American Council for Capital Formation had been deeply involved in efforts to reduce the tax on capital gains. The issue was quietly advocated by Bush in his election campaign, and Bloomfield was hopeful that the new President would follow through now that he was in office. His hopes were not idle; he had been working for weeks with Bush officials to devise a capital-gains plan.

In recent days, the newspapers had carried stories claiming that Bush was backing away from a capital-gains proposal. "That is not the case," Bloomfield said as he left Gradison's office. "They're looking at six options," he said, and listed them all. He said he would not place odds that the capital-gains tax would be cut in 1989, but, he suggested, there was good reason it might be. The Democrats, who controlled Congress, wanted to raise taxes to reduce the deficit; President Bush had based his entire campaign on a refusal to raise taxes. "When the Democrats come to September, they might say, 'Why don't we give the President something to help him sign this tax bill?' The most obvious tradeoff," Bloomfield continued, "is capital gains [in exchange] for higher ordinary rates" on upper-income individuals.

Bloomfield was obviously excited at the prospect. Walker was less enthusiastic. When he was asked about the prospect for a capital-gains tax cut, he shrugged and pointed to his young protégé.

A mainstay of the Washington establishment for more than

twenty years, Walker had never been a workaholic. President Lyndon Johnson once called him "an SOB with elbows." But he was, in fact, much more laid-back than that. He loved his golf, rarely ventured out to working dinners at night, and coveted his time at home in leafy Potomac, Maryland. To his fellow lobbyists, Walker had always been known as a Tuesday-to-Thursday kind of guy. It was good fortune that he had acquired a disciple so devoted that barely an evening or a weekend did not find Bloomfield in the office. "I don't want to overstay my welcome," Walker said. "We've been putting Mark out front more. It's good for him and it's good for the council."

Officially, Bloomfield was president of the American Council, Walker's main platform for promoting pro-business economic policies. But in fact, he was increasingly taking the lead on the bigger-picture corporate issues that once were almost exclusively Walker's domain, including fighting for tax write-offs for the purchase of factory equipment and reducing the tax burden on businesses generally. With bonus, Bloomfield's pay came to more than $200,000 a year.

In many ways Bloomfield was an echo of Walker, and in other ways a foil. The two talked alike, they thought alike, and they were on the phone with each other almost constantly. But Bloomfield was a lawyer, Walker an economist, and, true to their vocations, Bloomfield served at times to moderate Walker's strident economic beliefs. On another, more practical level, Walker served as chairman and Bloomfield as the day-to-day manager of the American Council, which combined economic research with direct lobbying of Congress and the executive branch. "Charly loves to get involved in the political and media strategy," said Richard Rahn, chief economist of the U.S. Chamber of Commerce and a longtime ally of the council. "Mark has done a good job managing the council; it's in good financial shape."

The ever-cautious Bloomfield played down his emergence as Walker's heir-designate. He noted, for instance, that he walked only half of Walker's beat—the more public half. Bloomfield said modestly: "I don't think he's grooming me, or that he thinks he's grooming me. But as time has gone along, our relationship has grown and changed. Now I'm taking more of a public role and we both feel comfortable with that."

Bloomfield had charge of Walker's most expansive issues, like capital gains, which fell under the aegis of the nonprofit American Council. Walker also had his separate, for-profit lobbying firm, Walker Associates, which represented individual corporations on narrower issues and had its own set of next-in-lines, such as Phil Potter and Jim Free, the popular former Carter administration official who sponsored skeet shooting at the Greenbrier. Though the two organizations were officially separate, one clearly helped the other. Walker was better able to drum up clients for one or both of his entities thanks to the contacts he made through the other. For many years Walker Associates advised the Business Roundtable, which was a group of top corporate chieftains, many of whom were also members of the American Council.

To casual observers, Bloomfield appeared to be little more than Charly Walker's shadow. But Bloomfield was much more than that. Over more than a decade of apprenticeship, he had developed into one of the most well-rounded lobbyists in Washington. He was an expert in the details of his issues, an adept political strategist, and, with certain lawmakers, a first-rate person-to-person advocate. To many members of Congress, especially the younger ones whom Walker didn't know as well, Bloomfield *was* the American Council. "Mark is highly reputable and knowledgeable; he's an extremely able person," said Representative Ed Jenkins, who was one of the House's chief Democratic advocates of a capital-gains tax cut. "I've relied on him for a lot of technical information on capital gains through the years."

Even Bloomfield's adversaries liked him, and respected his methods if not his views. "Mark and I went to law school together and one of us turned out bad. We debate which one," said Robert McIntyre, head of the labor-backed Citizens for Tax Justice and Bloomfield's nemesis on capital gains. "He goes out of his way to be nice to everybody so that nobody gets personally upset with him." Speaking of the American Council, McIntyre allowed: "They do a good job of lining up academic support for their position. Their position is wrong, but it's probably a good strategy." He also noticed that "Mark is getting more prominent. Five years ago you would have said that Mark just works for Charly; now you would say, 'Mark runs the council.' "

Bloomfield was part absentminded professor, part dandy, and

part hard-charging salesman. In his early years in Washington, he once purchased a suit, only to somehow lose the pants as he was walking back to his office. He was distraught at the loss and roamed the streets for a long time before he conceded they were gone. He also could be unrelenting, some would say pushy, on behalf of his pet project, cutting the capital-gains tax.

Without question, he did talk too much, a problem he shared with the often preachy Walker. When Bloomfield introduced someone, he started the details from birth. And when he discussed capital gains, there was no stopping him at all. At a Christmas party, he once subjected two reporters to his usual capital-gains harangue until fellow lobbyist Nicholas Calio interrupted him. "If you say one more word about capital gains," Calio warned, "those people are going to douse themselves with lighter fluid."

Characteristically, though, Bloomfield took the criticism to heart. He fretted about it for weeks, and thereafter tried to hold himself back. Most people detected this sensitivity in him, and though they got exasperated with him at times, they rarely stayed angry for long. They liked him—and indeed, Bloomfield worked at being likable, sometimes to the point of being unctuous. But then again, some would say, That's just Mark, what can you do?

Unlike Walker, who came from Texas, Bloomfield was sometimes stiff and formal. He always looked as if he'd just walked out of Brooks Brothers. In fact, on many afternoons, he probably just had. He was all pinstripes and horn rims, suspenders and bow ties. At leisure he was pure L. L. Bean. When he recounted the events of a day, he invariably started with a description of what he had been wearing.

If his manner seemed almost European, that was because it *was* European. Bloomfield was born in Vienna and was raised overseas, mostly in Eastern Europe, by his diplomat parents. He did not learn about America firsthand until he was in high school, when he lived with his older sister in California. Even in 1989, after more than twenty years in an English-speaking country, he was still hazy about exactly who the Beatles were and how they differed from the Rolling Stones.

Bloomfield's parents were born in Poland; they immigrated to the United States when Bloomfield was still young. His father had fought in three armies—the Polish, the French, and the American—during World War II and was educated at the Sorbonne in Paris in the 1930s, where his best subject was legislative law. "That's essentially what I do now," Bloomfield said, stretching the facts a little.

In the United States, his parents joined the Foreign Service and then traveled the world. As a result, Bloomfield lived in Berlin, Munich, Madrid, and Sofia, Bulgaria, as he was growing up. His first language, he said, was "British," but he could still speak snippets of German and French. He took correspondence courses and had private tutors. He lived from 1962 to 1964 in Bulgaria, where his English teacher was a disillusioned Communist and his math teacher was a leader of the Young Communists. Ultimately, he chose anticommunism for himself, which helped explain his fealty to the Republican party.

Bloomfield attended Swarthmore College, outside Philadelphia, and got his law degree and master's in business administration degree from the nearby University of Pennsylvania. But from his earliest days, he was mostly a political junkie and a devoted Republican hanger-on. During the 1972 Republican National Convention, he served as a member of a committee chaired by Representative Bill Steiger, Republican of Wisconsin, who was one of the fathers of capital-gains tax cuts. He later worked as a staff assistant to Representative Herman Schneebeli, Republican of Pennsylvania, who was a member of Ways and Means and a friend of Charly Walker's. Bloomfield also struck up a correspondence with Walker after Walker once visited Penn. Walker did not recall that connection. But for whatever reason, Bloomfield joined Walker's capital-formation team in 1976.

The American Council had its roots in an organization known as the American Council for Capital Gains and Estate Taxation. In the early 1970s, it was a shell of a group whose biggest boosters were Robert Keith Gray and the public-relations–lobbying firm he headed in Washington, Hill & Knowlton. In 1973, Walker had just finished his stint as deputy treasury secretary under President Nixon and was asked by Gray if he would try to do something with the floundering group.

At first, Walker said no. The group's base was too narrow, he said; capital-gains and estate taxes were not enough of a draw to get significant backing from corporations. Instead, Walker suggested a bigger idea: capital formation. The phrase, which was all the vogue among corporate economists such as himself, encompassed a whole raft of business tax breaks. These included investment tax credits for the purchase of equipment and the speeding up of write-offs for the equipment once it was purchased. Surely those kinds of proposals would be attractive to the heavy-hitter executives whom Walker wanted as clients in his own lobbying business as well.

And so the new think tank was born. Walker became chairman of the group, and hired Richard Rahn, a young economist with an eye patch, as its executive director. After a time, Rahn decided he needed an assistant, and with the concurrence of Walker picked the twenty-seven-year-old Bloomfield.

By the end of the 1970s, the energetic Rahn was ready to move on, and was hired by the Chamber of Commerce. But who would replace him at the American Council? One candidate was a lobbyist named Kenneth Duberstein, who refused the offer and stayed with the Committee for Economic Development. "At least he got a good raise out of it," Walker joked. Duberstein went on to become White House chief of staff under President Reagan, and later a top lobbyist with his own company.

"We finally determined that Mark could do the job," Walker said. But he conceded: "I wasn't sure. I hadn't worked that closely with him. He was very young." Rahn insisted that Bloomfield would be fine. "I thought Mark would grow into it," Rahn recalled. "I knew he had the smarts and the talent. He would put the time and energy into it."

The hunch worked out. As a team, Walker and Bloomfield went on to triumph on several fronts. They were major players in cutting the capital-gains tax in 1978 and in reducing corporate taxes generally in 1981. They also developed the American Council into a model of modern lobbying. They would never focus on giving campaign contributions, though Walker did do some of that through Walker Associates. Instead, the group's goal was to put the patina of academic respectability on its issues, which, at the bottom line, were invariably designed to nudge Washington policymakers toward funneling more aid to corporate America. With a combination of academic seminars, lectures, books, and studies, the American Council worked relentlessly to indoctrinate politicians in its view that consumers should be taxed more and corporations and wealthy individuals less. Its board came to include the biggest names in the business and economic worlds, both Republican and Democratic. Its methods were copied around town by other, smaller business groups also professing to have high-minded goals, which happened to coincide with the self-interest of the corporations that paid their bills.

Despite the council's Herculean efforts—or, in fact, because of its surprising success in 1981—the political winds changed in the mid-1980s. With Walker receding as a force, and Bloomfield moving forward to take his place, Walker intentionally put Bloomfield out front on the capital-gains issue. Walker began to rest the elbows made famous by President Johnson, and to give more elbow room to his apprentice.

"It's sort of a natural evolution, a coming-of-age," Rahn said of Bloomfield's new repute. And though Walker would later become active in the reignited capital-gains debate, it was Bloomfield who stood out as "Mr. Capital Gains."

· · ·

During that damp February of 1989, Congress was not the place for a gentle debate about the merits of capital formation. With the House in disarray over the pay-raise issue, the Senate became embroiled in its own nasty spat: a bitter fight over whether to confirm the President's nomination of John Tower as secretary of defense.

At first, no one expected Tower to have a problem. The diminutive Texan had been a senator for twenty-four years, until his retirement in 1985. From 1981 to 1984, he chaired the chamber's powerful Armed Services Committee. President Bush thought that surely the Senate would easily approve one of its own. But the arrogant Tower faced rising opposition.

The most spectacular complaints about him involved his alleged drinking problem and his womanizing. One by one, senators entered a special office in the Capitol to read a confidential FBI report about Tower. And one by one they emerged dazed and concerned. Although the report was never made public, Washington was abuzz with talk about the outrageous exploits it allegedly detailed. There were unsubstantiated rumors about drinking bouts during sensitive arms-control talks, and about an affair with a Russian ballerina who might have had ties to the KGB. Conservative leader Paul Weyrich testified before the Armed Services Committee that "the smoke surrounding the nominee's personal life seems rather intense. I have made enough personal observations of this man, here in Washington, to have serious reservations about his moral character." In response, the twice-divorced Tower acknowledged that he once was a drinker, but said all of that was behind him. "I am a man of discipline," he said.

But personal indiscretions were only part of the rap against the sixty-three-year-old Tower. He was also dogged by a lobbying problem—his own lobbying, that is. After he retired from government, he had become a highly paid consultant to a half-dozen defense contractors—a lobbyist, in other words. The extent of his work for these companies, and the gargantuan sums he was paid by them, compounded his difficulties with confirmation in the Senate. From 1986 to 1988, he had hauled in an astounding $1,028,777 from companies that had extensive dealings with the federal agency he had been nominated to head. By his own accounting he had received $246,860 from LTV Aerospace & Defense Company; $166,750 from Rockwell International Corporation; $116,000 from Martin Marietta Information Systems; $154,167 from Hicks & Associates; $70,000 from Textron Incorporated; and $10,000 from Jeford-McManus International Incorporated. He also received fees of $265,000 from British Aerospace Incorporated, a unit of British Aerospace PLC.

The complaint about Tower's close ties with contractors was voiced by no less a personage than his successor as chairman of the Armed Services Committee, Senator Sam Nunn, Democrat of Georgia. "Frankly, the difficulty here is not that you have worked for a contractor as a consultant, but the number of them," Nunn said. "Five or six or seven of the major corporations. If you were to recuse yourself on all of them, you couldn't be secretary of defense."

Tower tried to deflect the criticism by promising not to participate in any case involving any of the companies he had worked for. He also said he would step away entirely from any involvement in a small airplane program, called C-FIN, for which he claimed to have actively lobbied. His consulting work, he testified, was "within the bounds of law and ethics." He added: "I intend to be very, very objective."

Tower was far from alone in turning to lobbying after years of service as a member of Congress. At the time, approximately two hundred former lawmakers continued to reside in Washington, and most of those, whether they admitted it or not, lobbied for a living. What that word meant to Tower was unclear. Much of what he did was simply give advice about how to approach government; he rarely did the approaching himself. But that advice, and the prestige associated with who was giving it, obviously was worth a considerable sum. Donald A. Hicks, a former under secretary of defense who became a private consultant with his own firm, told *The Washington Post* that he had hired Tower in mid-1987 because some of his clients "wanted some capability to interpret what was going on in Congress. Not lobbying—they have their own office for that." Hicks paid Tower more than $100,000, because he said it "added to the prestige of the firm."

Such an intangible commodity as prestige was what drove much of lobbying. Corporations figured that if Tower backed their causes, they would have an easier time making their cases to the government officials who once worked with him. His name could also help them get in the door. One Washington lobbyist candidly told the *Post* that Tower was a prized commodity because corporations believed that they needed a former insider in order to make their case inside government. "The corporate guys say, 'Who can get us in?' They never ask, 'What will they say?' " the lobbyist explained.

If appearances were what made Tower rich, appearances were also what led to his fall. The combination of personal and professional foibles proved to be too much for his former colleagues to stomach. Despite the unwavering support of President Bush, Tower was unable to gain the backing of the respected Chairman Nunn, and he lost the support of some of his fellow Republicans as well. A crushing blow came when the influential GOP Senator Nancy Landon Kassebaum of Kansas declared her intention to oppose him. She said she did not believe he would show adequate concern for women in the armed services; this was a thinly veiled reference to the womanizing charges. But she also said that Tower's lobbying demonstrated "an enormous insensitivity" to concerns about possible conflicts of interest in the Pentagon procurement system.

On Thursday, February 23, the Armed Services Committee voted 11–9, along party lines, against the nomination. On Thursday, March 9, the Senate killed the nomination by a vote of 53–47. In one of the most backhanded defenses of Tower, Republican Senator John McCain of Arizona said, "At least John Tower did some work for those companies. . . . The rest of us take political-action committee money" and are expected to have no bias toward the donors.

Congress sank deeper and deeper into an ethical quagmire. But lobbying went on and on.

• • •

On Thursday, March 30, Charly Walker was conducting business as usual. After disembarking from a private plane, the sixty-five-year-old lobbyist was chauffeured in a big black Olds '88 to a luncheon speech in Columbus, Ohio. The topic, for a group of bank executives there, was to be his favorite: the state of things in Washington as seen by himself.

But fate intervened. With an ear-shattering explosion, one of the car's tires blew out just as a huge tractor-trailer truck was bearing down behind it. The eighteen-wheel monster rammed into the car and knocked it thirty feet into the median strip. Walker, who was sitting in the front passenger seat, had only enough time to think, "My God, I'm still alive!" Then he watched helplessly as the truck jackknifed and bashed the car one more time.

Walker was alive, but badly injured. His seat belt saved him, but it also caused a severe contusion to his left chest, among other aches and pains. The car was so mangled that the driver had to be cut out of it. The speech, of course, was canceled, and Walker's life was changed for good. Maybe it was time, he thought, to accelerate his efforts to make room for someone else—even faster than he had been doing already.

"Once I was confronted with my mortality as drastically as I was in that car wreck, you look at things a little differently. You get more interested in your teaching and writing and working with young people," he said. Then he added: "I plan to stay in an active role, but I see active roles for others. After all, I'm getting older." The person he made the most room for was Mark Bloomfield.

. . .

In a private back room of the dark and expensive Pisces Club in tony Georgetown, some of the biggest-name lobbyists in town were having dinner. Wayne Thevenot, the real estate lobbyist, was among them. It was Tuesday, April 4, and the event was not a casual affair. Around the table with him sat his old Louisiana friend Tommy Boggs, Tom Korologos of Timmons & Company, J. D. Williams of Williams & Jensen, Robert Barrie of the General Electric Company, and Horace Godfrey, the city's ever-dapper sugar daddy, who was the author and chief defender of the multi-million-dollar federal subsidy to the U.S. sugar industry. They called themselves the Washington Discussion Group, and that night they were hosting Senator Daniel Patrick Moynihan, who was one of the capital's most erudite conversationalists.

The senator talked of taxes and of tribunals, of politics and of probabilities—the usual Washington fare. But Thevenot wanted him to talk about something different. He wanted to hear about trains. Very fast trains. Maglev trains—which, Thevenot knew, Moynihan cared about deeply. Now that he was on his own as a lobbyist, Thevenot was always searching for new clients. And in Moynihan he saw the potential for a bonanza. The lawmaker had a vision of transportation's future that Thevenot saw as an important part of his own future in the lobbying business. Where Moynihan saw trains, Thevenot saw dollar signs.

"Maglev" is short for "magnetically levitated transportation." By means of this technology, powerful electromagnets lift a train inches above a metal guideway and propel it forward at up to three hundred miles an hour. Almost alone among major policymakers, Moynihan hailed Maglev as a clean, quiet, and safe way to help reduce congestion on highways and at airports. Indeed, he saw the technology as the inevitable next generation of transportation, and almost single-handedly had been trying to force the federal bureaucracy and his colleagues in Congress to pay attention to it.

Moynihan's first task, he knew, was to provide some modicum of federal support. "No major transportation revolution has ever progressed in the U.S. without substantial federal involvement," he wrote in an essay for *Scientific American* magazine. "Maglev will be no exception." Thevenot had read that essay and had agreed. Surely he could find a way to profit by lobbying for such a good cause.

Maglev was an American idea that had been taken over by foreign competition. It was developed at the Brookhaven National Laboratory on Long Island and at the Massachusetts Institute of Technology in the 1960s and early 1970s, and was backed and tested by the U.S. government. But when the federal deficit first began to loom, Maglev was one of its first victims. U.S. development of the technology died when its federal funding did, in 1975. In the meantime, Japan and West Germany each poured about $1 billion into developing the technology; now they boasted working models of the train and were preparing to sell the system abroad.

The notion of rejuvenating a U.S.-built Maglev was probably a long shot. But Moynihan was leading the charge to bring Maglev home to the United States again. The Maglev field in general was filled with some high-powered hyperbole. To hear some zealots tell it, Maglev trains would be speeding passengers to work almost any day. In fact, there was not a single commercial Maglev system anywhere, and there was some doubt whether there would be one any time soon. "The Maglev business brings out a lot of oddballs," said Robert Kiernan, coordinator of Maglev 2000, a trade group. There also was some serious opposition to Maglev. Advocates of expanding urban mass transit, for instance, worried that pie-in-the-sky hopes for Maglev might take funds away from their less flashy but more utilitarian systems. In addition, they asserted that Maglev was completely incompatible with existing transit systems and was ill-suited for most mass-transit uses, which entail making frequent stops. "There's nothing inherently wonderful about it," groused Frank Cihak, chief engineer of the American Public Transit Association.

Still, Moynihan was a believer, and Thevenot wanted to be one too. During a cocktail break at the dinner party, Thevenot saw his chance and sidled up to Moynihan. "I want you to know that we are interested in Maglev," he said, and described the group of U.S. manufacturers that he had begun to recruit as a lobbying coalition. Moynihan's blue eyes brightened and fixed on Thevenot, whom he had known before mostly as a real estate lobbyist. During a similar gathering of lobbyists with Moynihan some years before, Thevenot had distinguished himself by saying that his real estate association was actually a constituent of the senator's. "I represent Leona Helmsley," he said, to loud laughter around the table.

During the dinner part of the evening at the Pisces Club, Thevenot again asked Moynihan to talk about Maglev, which the senator did with great enthusiasm and at great length. He mentioned that a group of experts he had assembled, including people from Grumman Corporation in his home state, were studying the issue. Thevenot again mentioned that he, too, was beginning to put together a group of companies to lobby the U.S. government for aid. Moynihan said he thought that was an excellent idea.

"Well, he really *is* interested," commented Barrie of GE in an aside to Thevenot.

"Obviously, he is," Thevenot whispered back with satisfaction.

After the dinner, Thevenot was grabbed by Andrew J. Samet, one of Moynihan's top aides, and they arranged to meet in Moynihan's office to discuss their plan of attack.

3

Spreading
the Word

At 8 A.M. on the windy Wednesday of April 12, the American Trucking Associations invited Representative Ed Jenkins to a meeting to speak about anything he wanted. He was happy to attend. The event, known as an honorarium breakfast because of the payment that was usually dispensed to the speaker, was conducted informally, around a huge conference table in the spacious third floor of the associations' fortresslike town house on Capitol Hill. Fittingly, images of trucks were almost everywhere—from paintings of trucks on the walls to toy trucks on many desks.

The truckers and affiliated groups regularly paid members of Congress as much as $2,000 for the minor inconvenience of driving—or even walking—the short distance from the Capitol to deliver an even shorter address. It was easy money, and many lobbying groups gave out similar fees. House members could keep $2,000 from each such appearance, up to $26,850 a year, which was equivalent to 30 percent of their congressional salary. Senators likewise were limited to $2,000 per speech but could keep 40 percent of their salary, or $35,800 in total. Lawmakers did not have to do much for this money. This was the case with the truckers' breakfasts. They were held two short blocks from the House office buildings and lasted just forty-five minutes.

Jenkins did not take any cash for his speech that day. Thanks to wise real estate investments back home in the fast-growing region of northern Georgia, he was a wealthy man and did not need extra income. Instead, he, like many lawmakers, wanted something from the lobbyists in the audience that transcended the few extra dollars he could have put in his pocket. He wanted their help to pass legislation. So what transpired at the truckers' office that morning was a bout of mutual lobbying: The lobbyists pressed their causes with Jenkins, and Jenkins tried to enlist them for his own. "I was doing a little missionary work," Jenkins said.

Other missionaries to the truckers' domain in 1989 had already included some of the biggest names in Congress, including Representative Richard Gephardt of Missouri; Senator Bob Packwood of Oregon; and the new Senate Budget Committee chairman, James Sasser of Tennessee. The topics of their speeches were wide-ranging. The questions, however, were often quite pointed. The two dozen or so lobbyists who attended the truckers' breakfasts—and paid the speakers—got the privilege of asking some of Washington's most important people about the fate of issues that were important to them. And with Jenkins that morning it was not long before the dialogue, over eggs and coffee, turned to the truckers' favorite topic: whether excise taxes, especially the motor-fuels tax so critical to their industry, would be raised.

Jenkins made clear that he personally opposed a gas-tax increase. A typical commute in his rural district, he said, was eighty to a hundred miles a day. That precluded him from favoring any gas-tax increase—at least for the time being.

All of this pleased the audience, especially Kenneth Simonson, the truckers' economist. But the tenor of Jenkins's answer also worried Simonson a little. So he asked Jenkins to expand on his response. "It seems like there is less opposition to other sorts of excise taxes," Simonson suggested. "Would there be other excises that could pass?"

"Yes," Jenkins replied forthrightly. "Other excise taxes, especially tobacco, are more likely." Then he added, with a laugh: "I didn't mean to scare you, but it will help pay your salary for today."

The congressman went on to mention his own pet project and, tacitly, to seek the lobbyists' help in pushing it. He revealed that he was putting together his own tax package. In it, he said, was a tax cut that, miraculously, would actually raise revenue: a cut in the tax on capital gains—anathema to most of his own Democratic party but of keen interest to the business world the lobbyists represented. He told the group that he wanted to cut capital-gains taxes and also raise the top tax rate on individuals to 33 percent from the existing 28 percent top rate.

The capital-gains/top-rate plan, Jenkins said, would raise $9 billion in new revenue a year—a bounty that piqued the interest of many lobbyists around the table. But in fairness, Jenkins disclosed, part of that money was already spoken for. He was the chief backer in the House for tax credit for research-and-development expenditures, he said, and extending that tax break surely would be part of his plan.

The breakfast ended before nine o'clock. Few of the lobbyists who attended understood how prescient Jenkins's underspoken disclosure would prove to be. They had just been given the road map that would guide legislation—and almost all of their efforts— for the next two years. And unlike most of the rest of the world, they and their clients had had the chance to see it in advance.

Jenkins was an unassuming source for such weighty intelligence. He was a compact man with wiry salt-and-pepper hair, always smoking and never, seemingly, in a hurry to do anything. The son of a barber, he had worked for years as a country lawyer in the rolling hills of North Georgia. But his eye had always been on coming to Washington. Before being elected to the House, he had served as a top aide to his predecessor, Representative Phil Landrum, who also was a member of the Ways and Means Committee. One of his best boyhood friends was Zell Miller, who went on to become governor of the state.

With his thick glasses and even thicker Georgia twang, Jenkins struck some more as hayseed than high-flyer. But, as George (Boots) Ramsay, a Toccoa, Georgia, attorney, said: "He's a lot smarter than you think he is." As a legislator, Jenkins was cunning and disarming, a quiet power whose forte was informally testing the attitudes of his colleagues and finding ground for compromise. "He's one of the real leaders, respected by all of us," said Representative Charles Stenholm of Texas. "He helps find that middle ground, a little bit to the right of center." In public forums, Jenkins could be a persuasive speaker, with a trial lawyer's gift for debate and a storyteller's wit and timing. He also commanded respect from Republicans. "He has the ability to pick the right issues and he knows how to deal," said Representative Raymond McGrath, Republican of New York. "He brings a lot of people with him on this side."

For many years, Jenkins had contented himself with small victories. Thanks to him, farmers got a special federal program that provided money to prevent soil erosion. And a tax-free bond issued by rural communities was known as the Jenkins Bond. But lately, he had tried to broaden his interests. In 1987, he had served on the Iran-Contra committee. In 1988, he had championed the drive to give special protection to the U.S. textile industry—legislation for which he became infamous in the Far East. The *South China Morning Post* once declared him "the man Hong Kong loves to hate." His only weakness, friends said, was that he lacked the killer instinct, and was reticent to press the many political advantages he had accumulated. He was a lawmaker with considerable, but largely untapped, potential. And the floodgates were about to open.

· · ·

The next day, Thursday, April 13, many of the lobbyists who had listened to Jenkins's pitch assembled again, but this time at a press conference in Room EF-100 of the Capitol itself. It was a small, cold-looking room with stark stone walls and a shiny gold emblem of an eagle above the door. It was located near a concession stand and a small post office in the center of the building. Tourists often hovered there, and even at 9 A.M. plenty of them were around, poking their noses inside to see what was happening.

Most of what lobbyists do is kept closely under wraps. But sometimes they do their lobbying by getting their message to the widest audience—the voters in general—and not just to the lawmakers the voters elect. The lobbyists going public this day were part of a group called the Coalition Against Regressive Taxation, or CART. The press event was typical of the second stage of Washington lobbying: spreading the word. Sometimes lobbyists went door-to-door. Sometimes they used the back door, by appealing to lawmakers through their constituents. And other times they tried to advance their issues through the press. That was the mission of CART and the truckers this day in 1989.

Their subject, though prosaic, was fundamental to the forthcoming budget fight. CART unveiled an economic study to prove that raising excise taxes was a bad idea. Excise-tax increases disproportionately hurt poor people, and CART had paid an accounting firm to prove it was so. In point of fact, though, not a single poor person was a member of CART. Quite the contrary: CART was a coalition of very large and very profitable businesses. But through CART these corporate interests used—some might say exploited—the populist argument against regressive taxation to keep taxes on their products low.

The little conference room was lined with lobbyists who represented members of the coalition: Philip Morris Incorporated, the diversified tobacco company; Anheuser-Busch Companies, the beer maker; and the Distilled Spirits Council of the United States, Incorporated, which represented makers of hard liquor, to name just a few. Lobbyists outnumbered the mere handful of reporters who attended, but CART was not disappointed. If the issue of raising excise taxes ever got hot, the study surely would come in handy for a reporter in a pinch for facts. In the meantime, CART sent the study to lawmakers as soon as the press conference was over.

A few minutes after nine o'clock, a white-haired man wearing a crisply pressed blue suit moved toward the microphone at the front of the room. "My name is Tom Donohue; I am president and chief executive officer of the American Trucking Associations and president of CART," he said. Then he introduced what any lobbyist like himself would have considered the most important people in the room: two lawmakers who supported his cause, Republican Representative Don Sundquist, of the tobacco state of Tennessee, and Democratic Representative Louis Stokes, from Ohio. "Thank you very much, gentlemen," he said, ignoring the lobbyists and reporters in attendance. "We know you're pressed this morning. We very much appreciate your coming by."

Now to the issue at hand: excise taxes. Donohue's angle that day was that such taxes not only hurt poor people more than rich people, but that any attempt to offset that inequity was unlikely to succeed. CART had long made the argument that excise taxes were regressive. The reason: Poor people spend a larger portion of their income on consumer products that are hit by excise taxes than rich people do.

But CART and Donohue were trying to think ahead. Regressivity was already a well-accepted drawback of raising excise taxes. So proponents of raising them had been busily looking for ways to correct the problem. One way growing in popularity was to increase a tax subsidy called the earned-income tax credit, which went directly to the low-income people who would be most burdened by an excise-tax increase. In this press conference, CART tried to show that even that maneuver would not help.

The person who devised the argument was the bookish Simonson, who was seated near the front. The economist was not a lobbyist in the traditional sense. He was Donohue's detail man, and his importance to the CART effort could not be underestimated. He hung on to his boss's every word. He had written most of them.

"The budget deficit is everyone's responsibility," Donohue said. "But excise-tax hikes are a quick and dirty fix that won't work." Behind Donohue were charts and graphs prepared by the Policy Economics Group, a research unit of the giant accounting firm KPMG Peat Marwick. At the urging of Simonson, CART paid Policy Economics $25,000 to prepare the study, and Donohue noted that one of its top economists, Harvey Galper, recently of the Brookings Institution, was in the audience "to answer the technical questions that I choose to duck."

It was the job of CART, Simonson, and Donohue to prevent any increase in excise taxes. And in his prepared remarks, Donohue spoke for the coalition about all sorts of excise taxes: on tobacco, alcoholic beverages, and gasoline. But in answering reporters' questions, he concentrated on his own bête noire: the excise tax on motor fuels.

The chance that excise taxes would rise increased as Congress's appetite for new revenue rose, Donohue said. Excise taxes brought in big money, and were likely to be tapped only when lots of new revenue was called for. That day's study assumed that Congress wanted to raise a whopping $20 billion in taxes, all from increases in the levies on gasoline, cigarettes, beer, wine, and whiskey. According to the study, the share of federal income, payroll, and excise taxes paid by low-income and middle-income families had already risen 12 percent since 1979. The $20 billion package would increase the burden on low-income families by 18 percent over 1979, while leaving upper-income families with a 5 percent smaller share of total federal taxes.

That really was not news. What was surprising about the study was that excise taxes were shown to have an uneven impact within each income group. In the low-income group, for instance, one-third would pay a steep 20 percent more in taxes, while another third would pay only about 5 percent to 10 percent more. That meant that increasing the tax subsidy to low-income people through the broad-gauge earned-income credit would not help everyone in need. "Increasing this credit by enough to counter the unfair excise-tax hikes would cost the U.S. Treasury more than five billion dollars of the twenty billion to be raised," Donohue said, "and the system still would be inequitable."

More precisely, he added, "such a tax package would give a substantial cut to nearly two million lower-income families, but would leave another three million with a high-percentage tax increase." He then ad-libbed a little: "You can't take the tax credit and balance this out. All it would do is add more confusion."

Donohue got few questions from the audience, so he filled the time by talking about trucking issues. He volunteered, for example, that fuel taxes were dedicated to the highway trust fund and should not be used for deficit reduction. Finally, he got a cynical question: What was CART really? His answer was straightforward: "We are clearly an interest group, a self-interest group. We are saying in a combined voice for our mutual self-interest that these taxes are unfair. Together we might have a little more influence than we might have alone."

He then was asked whether a recent proposal by Ways and Means Chairman Dan Rostenkowski to increase the gas tax by fifteen cents a gallon would succeed. "It is clear this is an ongoing matter. We hope that we will prevail. What he puts on the table at first isn't always there in the end," Donohue responded. Then, in a saccharine tone, he added: "I would not dare to speak for the chairman of so distinguished a committee." At the conclusion of the press conference, Donohue left the microphone to extend a warm handshake to Democratic Representative Mervyn M. Dymally of California, who had arrived late. "Thank you for coming," he said with a broad smile on his face, stepping past the other people standing in the aisle.

· · ·

At that moment, almost no one in Washington believed that excise taxes would be increased. True, Rostenkowski had floated the idea of raising the gasoline tax, but he seemed to do that almost every year, and so far nothing had happened. What was more, it appeared that Congress was not going to do much deficit cutting in general, despite the obvious problem. The Gramm-Rudman deficit-reduction law demanded only minor budget cuts in 1989, probably a mere $15 billion total, only part or none of which would have to come from higher taxes. Compared with the trillion-dollar federal budget, that was not much. And President Bush, of course, was dead set against tax increases.

To cement the President's resolve, Donohue and his confederates had conspired to get his intentions in writing. In the closing days of the 1988 presidential campaign, they had written asking Bush's view about gas taxes, and had gotten it in a strongly worded letter. Prior to the press conference, CART members distributed copies of Bush's letter as a reminder and a warning to the new chief executive. Written on October 19, 1988, to J. Kay Aldous, vice president for public and government policy of the American Automobile Association, it read:

Dear Mr. Aldous:

Thank you for your letter of October 5, 1988, and your question regarding the possible imposition of a federal gasoline tax increase to fund deficit reduction. It gives me the chance to say what I've said so many times before: No New Taxes!

The problem with the deficit isn't that we tax too little, it's that we spend too much. A gas tax increase to balance the budget would particularly hurt lower wage earners, families with both spouses working and farmers and residents of Western states who have to drive long distances. I think it's ironic that at a time when there is genuine concern for the working poor, liberal policy makers would consider so regressive a measure.

Let me say it one more time: As President, I will oppose any attempt to raise taxes to balance the budget. That means gas taxes, too. I hope you and your members will join me in fighting for a more productive economy, with more jobs—and for a budget balanced not on the backs of the taxpayers, but through budgeting and prudent management.

Sincerely,
George Bush

. . .

Thomas J. Donohue was a fifty-one-year-old former college administrator turned ardent Washington Republican. A native of Brooklyn, New York, Donohue came to Washington in the early 1960s to work for the U.S. Postal Service. He ended up as a regional postmaster general, and then moved on to the U.S. Chamber of Commerce as a group vice president. But the loud-spoken Donohue always wanted to be top man. And in 1984 he won his chance: He was named chief executive of the American Trucking Associations. His base salary in 1989 was listed as $331,000.

A lot of Donohue's time on the job appeared to be spent flying from speech to speech, promoting trucking in Florida one day, and talking to truckers in Minneapolis the next. The gossip at the truckers' headquarters was that he wanted to lease a bigger plane so he could catch at least some sleep in between engagements. In Washington, he kept offices in Alexandria, Virginia, and on Capitol Hill, and was chauffeured between them in a limousine.

Donohue was boastful and blustery. "I am an advocate," he liked to exclaim, as if to justify the sometimes ridiculous positions he took. His alliance with tobacco companies against excise-tax increases was a good example. "Quite frankly, I can't stand cigarettes," he said, leaning forward for effect. "You know, I hate the goddamn things. But the right of those companies to object to a tax that requires them to pay for everybody else's deficits is correct. And if we can legitimately work together to get up enough votes to head off any excise tax, we're a lot better off than pissing all over each other's legs."

Donohue loved to hear himself talk. He loved to see people's reactions when he cursed, which he did quite often. He also had a habit of talking before he thought things out fully, a dangerous trait for someone in so visible a job. "I'm a guy who sometimes figures out what he thinks after he hears what he has to say," Donohue said candidly.

This tendency sometimes led to incredible missteps, such as the time he compared White House Budget Director Richard Darman to Machiavelli, or the occasion that he belittled the abilities of the House Democratic leadership during a cocktail-party conversation with Barry Toiv, a senior aide to House Budget Committee Chairman Leon Panetta, one of the most important Democrats in the House. "I'm outspoken," Donohue confessed to the *National Journal*. "I can be tough. If some guys get into a meeting and pile up the bullshit, I'm liable to cut them off at the knees. . . . Some people would say I'm a little too brusque or overstated."

Many said just that, but not Simonson. The economist was one of Donohue's early hires at the association, and he had never let his boss down. Simonson was Donohue's greatest defender, and one of his most important staffers. As a press junkie, Simonson also helped get his boss the media coverage he craved, wrote many of his speeches, and helped formulate almost everything Donohue said about taxes and the economy. Despite their obvious differences in style, both were deeply conservative in their views. They strongly opposed tax increases and honestly believed that deficits could be solved by cutting social-spending programs.

. . .

The details of the Peat Marwick study were not a minor matter to the ever-precise Ken Simonson. In 1987, he had worked with the accounting firm to put together a basic analysis of the regressivity of excise taxes. By 1989, he wanted a new twist, but not just any gimmick. Something fly-by-night would just not have done. And something too broad also would have had no meaning. "We spent a lot of time deciding what sort of study might be most helpful,"

Simonson explained. "We felt the '87 study had really given us a handle and that we needed something new. We continued to cite it, and others have cited it. But by 1989, it was getting a little threadbare. Just to repeat the same study would not be that useful, so we wanted a new hook. And so we discussed the various possibilities, for instance, showing macroeconomic effects of an excise-tax increase. Frankly, I argued against that kind of study. I just didn't think that those have the credibility that maybe they once had."

The final study was anything but shoddy. Its summary alone was thirteen pages long, and it was accompanied by a "technical appendix" nearly twice that length. Most of it was a blur of charts and statistics, but its basic conclusions were not disputed by anyone. After the press conference, at least one wire service carried a story about it.

That was all in a day's work for Simonson, who did not like to think of himself as a lobbyist. But, in fact, he and people like him in Washington were an increasingly important part of the lobbying industry. He rarely talked to members of Congress, and his bosses liked it that way. He was not the least bit outgoing or vivacious. Still, he personified a major part of what lobbying had become— a highly technical, green-eyeshade sort of business that ran as much on facts and analyses as it did on wit and charm.

Simonson was well suited to his task. He was a certified Washington drone. Born in the District of Columbia, the son of a civil servant, Simonson had worked there as a tax and budget economist his entire career. He bumped from an economic-consulting firm to the Federal Home Loan Bank Board to the U.S. Chamber of Commerce. He joined the American Trucking Associations in 1984, after a stint on the staff of a presidential commission on industrial competitiveness.

For entertainment, Simonson read the text of tax bills and technical journals, searching for misspellings and typographical errors. He then took odd pleasure in writing to the authors to point out their mistakes. During his summer vacations on the Eastern Shore of Delaware, he had been seen more than once reading the latest issue of a trade publication while pushing one of his two young children in a stroller.

But Simonson was not a cold fish. Nor was he colorless. Behind his scratchy monotone voice was a good-humored, good-hearted forty-one-year-old who was known as the proud owner of a 1978 Toyota Corolla called the Green Bomber. Once, when he drove his van to work, his entire office was buzzing with the rumor that the Bomber had finally been retired. Not so, he told his friends; the Bomber was still alive! And everyone was pleased. Simonson would probably drive the car until it died—or until its sun-cracked dashboard, which was held together with duct tape, broke completely in two.

Over the years Simonson had managed to insinuate himself into Washington's economic establishment. Six years earlier, he had founded a breakfast group he called the Tax Economists Forum, which had started small, but by 1989 had sixty-five economists on its mailing list, including staffers of virtually every major fiscal agency in government from the Treasury Department to the Congressional Joint Taxation Committee. It met every other Wednesday for an hour and a quarter, and its topics ranged from the tax-withholding tables to tax reform in New Zealand. Simonson's participation in this and other forums, he believed, helped keep the truckers' interests on the agenda. "I can't stop somebody from saying, 'We really ought to tax trucks more,' but I can counter the impression they leave that their ideas are unchallengeable," he said. As the trucking associations' chief economist, he was paid $110,000 a year.

Most of what Simonson cared about was mind-numbing to laymen. He worried about such tax-law esoterica as whether truckers employed by trucking companies were "independent contractors" or "leased employees." The distinction made a difference in the tax treatment of the pension and health-insurance plans the companies provided for their full-time workers, and the Treasury Department was not necessarily going to side with the companies. So the trucking association put Simonson on the case. On the same issue, it also retained no less a lobbyist than Randolph Thrower, a former commissioner of the Internal Revenue Service.

The "independent contractor" fight was ongoing. But another battle that Simonson had already won even better explained what he did. In 1987, Congress passed a 12 percent excise tax on sales of new trucks, trailers, and tractors. Retailers of these types of vehicles complained that their sales would suffer unless a special

surcharge were levied on truck-leasing companies, which the retailers saw as competition. The leasing companies could, in effect,
offer discounts that would also entail lower excise taxes. So Congress decided that bulk sales of trucks should be assessed more to
make up for the disparity.

The size of the surcharge was left to the Treasury Department,
and that was where Simonson went to work. The dealers were
insisting that the leasing companies pay an extra 7 percent to
10 percent. Simonson, whose association members often bought
trucks in bulk, held out for a markup of 1 percent or less. The final
compromise was 4 percent—a victory of sorts for the truckers. On
each $50,000 rig, the tax saving amounted to hundreds of dollars,
which translated into millions of dollars in savings to the trucking
industry each year. "That's not a big deal," Simonson said modestly, adding, "It's not necessarily good to get your victories in
print."

・　・　・

The American Trucking Associations was a $27 million, four-thou-
sand-member trade association with its main offices in an exceed-
ingly unattractive section of Alexandria, Virginia. Outside almost
every window in the angular glass-and-steel structure, truck traffic
could be seen whizzing by at any time of the day or night. That
was because the building overlooked the far southern end of the
Beltway, the famous highway that encircles Washington. Appropriately enough, the headquarters was located inside the Beltway.

It maintained the annoyingly self-conscious name of the American Trucking Associations because the organization was a confed-
eration of fifty-one affiliated trucking associations, one in each
state plus one in the District of Columbia. Together they represented more than thirty thousand trucking companies. The mission of the American Trucking Associations encompassed much
more than lobbying. Its 280 employees spent a lot of their time
trying to help trucking executives navigate the maze of regulations,
both state and federal, that were forever bedeviling the industry.

The associations had their own in-house law firm, research
foundation, information clearinghouse, and customer-service center. It published a newspaper with a circulation of 31,000 and
directed a small political-action committee that contributed to the

campaigns of office seekers. It had divisions that worried about such disparate issues as driver's licenses and hazardous wastes. And in the way that it dispensed all of these services, it was typical of any one of hundreds of trade-association and lobbying organizations that had come to thrive in the nation's capital.

One of the trucking associations' greatest assets, though, was located far away from suburban Virginia. It was the associations' four-story town house on Capitol Hill, which was used for the honoraria breakfasts. So convenient was it that a caterer was kept on staff full-time to service not only trucking functions but many other receptions as well. "A lot of members of Congress have fund-raisers there," Simonson said proudly.

And the truckers needed all the capital help they could get. Since deregulation in the 1970s, the industry's profit margins had shrunk and it was going through a wrenching consolidation. And in Washington, railroads, always the truckers' enemy, had been able to bat the truckers around like a cat with a ball of string.

Yet trucking remained a major economic force, and a player of some consequence in federal policymaking. At last count, the trucking industry earned about $240 billion, which at the end of the 1980s represented 77 percent of the nation's freight bill and 5 percent of the gross national product. Trucks carried 2.45 billion tons of freight, which represented more than 40 percent of the total intercity tonnage carried by all modes of transportation. The industry employed 7.5 million people and operated 5.5 million vehicles. Truckers also paid a lot of taxes: $5.6 billion of the $12.8 billion contributed each year to the Federal Highway Trust Fund.

At its Capitol Hill office, the associations maintained a separate staff of four full-time lobbyists, each of whom had responsibility for individual congressional committees in which truckers had an interest. Robert S. Reese, the truckers' Ways and Means Committee lobbyist, was especially well plugged in. "I'm sure that Bob has spoken a lot to Rob Leonard and to other staff members," Simonson said. "He plays golf with those guys and hangs out around there a lot and so forth, and basically has a very social relationship with a lot of those people."

Still, the Rostenkowski gas-tax proposal was a fact of life. So the truckers tried to turn it to their advantage. In an effort to persuade trucking executives to pay their dues to the associations,

Simonson briefed telephone salespeople about the gas-tax-increase threat and about the vigilant—and always underfunded—efforts of the trucking associations to stop it.

. . .

On the morning that CART and the truckers lobbied through the press to kill an excise-tax increase, *The Washington Post* published a story that would send Congress into a tailspin. On April 13, Charles R. Babcock reported on the *Post's* front page that the number three Democrat in the House, Representative Tony Coelho of California, had made a highly questionable investment with the help of powerful businessmen friends. In effect, the story accused Coelho of becoming too greedy and using the power of his office to enrich himself.

The hyperactive Coelho was surely in a position to be tempted. From 1981 to 1986, he headed the Democratic Congressional Campaign Committee, where he raised millions of dollars for the election campaigns of his colleagues in the House. Much of that money came from the wealthiest business interests in the country and from the lobbyists who represented them in Washington. His tireless fund-raising was credited with saving his party from losing control of the House in 1982. But, in the process, he may also have sold its soul to the special interests—the same ones the Democrats had once prided themselves in opposing.

Certainly, Coelho had sold out his own political career. It was special-interest money that raised him up, and money from the same private interests that would bring him down.

Coelho had built his reputation by finding ways to entice business executives and their lobbyists to shower Democratic candidates with campaign cash. When he first took over the House Democrats' reelection committee, business political-action committees—or PACs—contributed little to his party's candidates. But he successfully turned that around by aggressively marketing the traditionally pro-labor Democrats as increasingly pro-business, often during candidate forums for corporate PAC managers. The forums were nicknamed meat markets or cattle calls.

There was little that Coelho would not do in his pursuit of campaign dollars. He went so far as to sell access to the Democratic leadership of the House. He set up the Speaker's Club, which granted lobbyists and their clients the ability to meet socially with the Speaker of the House and other top Democrats for $5,000 a year for individuals and $15,000 for a PAC. A brochure about the club stated: "Members of the Speaker's Club serve as trusted, informal advisers to the Democratic Members of Congress." It also quoted then-Speaker Thomas (Tip) O'Neill, Jr., as saying, "I have learned to listen. Tell us what you think—at a time and place where we can really hear what you have to say."

Coelho even arranged, in effect, for lobbyists to put money into the personal bank accounts of Democratic politicians. He acted as a broker, putting together politicians who needed extra funds for their families and lobbyists who had ample honoraria to dispense. In *Honest Graft*, Brooks Jackson's book about him, Coelho is quoted as saying: "People came to me with real serious financial trouble. What I've done is, I've gone to people and said, 'I want to have these people speak to you, or include them on a program, or do whatever you can to help them out.' "

One of the companies from which Coelho personally took honoraria was Drexel Burnham Lambert, the high-flying investment-banking firm. And the *Post* article suggested that he eventually took more from the company than the law allowed. Babcock reported that in his last year as chairman of the campaign committee, Coelho made an unusual $100,000 investment in the high-yield junk bonds for which Drexel was famous. The lucrative though risky investment was generally available only to institutional investors and regular customers of Drexel. Still, Drexel listed Coelho's campaign committee as the purchaser of the bonds; this suggested a possible violation of election rules. Lawmakers were forbidden to use their campaign funds for personal gain.

Coelho was quick to say the listing was in error. But the issue did not die there. At first Coelho told the *Post* that the investment had been recommended to him by "a friend from southern California." Later, the friend turned out to be Thomas Spiegel, a Beverly Hills executive for a savings-and-loan institution with close ties to Drexel. What's more, it was Spiegel who actually "bought the bonds for him in early May [1986] and held them for a month until Coelho obtained $100,000 in three loans—including $50,000 from

Spiegel's savings bank—to pay him," the *Post* reported. In just four and a half short months, Coelho earned $13,230 on the investment, netting $6,882 after he paid interest on the loans. And in another possible violation of election rules, the $50,000 loan from Spiegel's Columbia Savings and Loan Association was never disclosed.

The *Post* traced a long list of unsavory connections between Coelho and the bond deal. During the period when Coelho had held the bonds, Drexel and its employees were among the largest contributors to his Democratic campaign committee: About $110,000 was received from Drexel's political-action committee and from some of Drexel's employees, including the disgraced junk-bond dealer Michael R. Milken. The Drexel PAC also gave $8,000 to Coelho's personal PAC, the Valley Education Fund, during 1986 and 1987. Coelho also accepted $4,000 in honoraria from Drexel for two speaking appearances those same years. Coelho denied any wrongdoing, but he knew that the public's perception of all this was devastating.

Disclosure tumbled upon disclosure. The *Los Angeles Times* reported that Coelho had recently joined other members of the California congressional delegation in urging the Securities and Exchange Commission not to force Drexel to close Milken's Beverly Hills headquarters as part of an expected settlement of a civil fraud investigation. Another *L.A. Times* article reported that Coelho had arranged a meeting in early 1988 between a member of the House Banking Committee and a lobbyist for his own banker, Thomas Spiegel. Coelho began to fear that the drip, drip, drip of charges and revelations about his ties to special interests would sink not only himself but the Democratic party. As if to underscore this possibility, the campaign committee for House Republicans distributed a package of press clippings about Coelho's financial misdeeds entitled "Democrats in the News."

When he was first elected to the House in 1978, Coelho's investments were small and cautious. A month after his election he bought his house in Alexandria for $170,000, with a conventional mortgage, putting 20 percent down. But under the influence of rich friends and lobbyists, he stepped up his life-style considerably. Over the years, he made extensive renovations and began to refer to "the house honoraria built." He refinanced three times, ultimately raising his mortgage to $430,000. He used some of the extra money to pay off debts, and to send $60,000, presumably for investment, to the trustee of his growing blind trust.

"I think that the process buys you out," he confessed to author Brooks Jackson. Coelho backed away from that statement later in the book, but admitted that money from business interests did influence lawmakers. Just how much it did was not fully clear until the results struck Coelho himself.

• • •

On Monday, April 17, four days after the *Post*'s Coelho bombshell, the twelve-member House Ethics Committee sat solemnly together in front of a packed news conference to accuse Speaker Jim Wright. The day had been long in coming. But few could have guessed how harsh a judgment was about to be placed on the top Democrat in the House. Ironically, the event was held in the Rayburn House Office Building, which was named for Sam Rayburn, Wright's role model as Speaker. Wright foolishly emulated Rayburn's long-outmoded, tyrannical style of managing the House, and was about to suffer the consequences.

The panel announced that it had found "reason to believe" that Wright had broken the rules of his own House in sixty-nine instances. The alleged violations stemmed from his extensive financial dealings with George A. Mallick, a Fort Worth businessman and lobbyist on his own behalf. They also involved an outright shakedown by Wright, mostly of business lobbyists, to put more cash into his own pocket. Ethics Committee Chairman Julian C. Dixon, Democrat of California, slowly read the charges. He described the shakedown as a "scheme" to avoid the limits placed on honoraria by selling in bulk to special interests Wright's privately published book, *Reflections of a Public Man*. Dixon also said that Wright improperly accepted gifts worth $145,000 from his longtime friend Mallick, a man who had extensive interest in the outcome of Wright's legislative work.

Although panel members had disagreed over individual violations among the sixty-nine counts, it voted unanimously to make Wright the first Speaker ever to be formally cited for possible violation of House rules. He had "failed in his duty to exercise reasonable care to avoid even the appearance of impropriety," Dixon said.

The panel's "statement of alleged violations" against Wright was the legislative equivalent of an indictment. And under such pressure, he clearly would not last long as Speaker, the top elected Democrat in the nation. Pressure for his resignation had been building for the ten months during which the Ethics Committee had investigated his finances. His mishandling of the congressional pay raise and other acts of political ineptitude certainly did not help his cause.

According to the panel, Wright had received—and failed to disclose—gifts from Mallick, who was his partner in a closely held company called Mallightco, a combination of their two names. The alleged gifts, given to him from 1979 to 1988, included the use of an apartment in Wright's home district of Fort Worth and a 1979 Cadillac Seville owned by Mallightco. In addition, the panel agreed that there was reason to believe that the partnership had paid Wright's wife, Betty, $72,000 in salary over four years, although she did little or no work.

Mallick was not just some Joe off the street. The committee said there was reason to believe that Mallick might have been making these payments to influence the Speaker to help his legislative causes. Lawmakers are prohibited from accepting more than $100 per year in gifts from anyone with a direct stake in legislation. Mallick had far exceeded that limit.

Mallick was deemed to be a player in public policy as a result of his large real estate and oil and gas investments. He also actively sought financing for a revitalization project in Fort Worth's historic Stockyards area, and was considered to be an interested party in savings-and-loan legislation as a result of his financial exposure on a $2.2 million loan from a thrift institution that he had guaranteed for his son.

The Ethics Committee also saw Wright's sale of his book as just another way to funnel income to himself from lobbying groups in potential violation of House rules. It found reason to believe that seven bulk sales of the book in 1984 and 1985 constituted disguised and unreported honorarium payments. Royalty payments from book sales, it turned out, were exempt from the

House's limits on honoraria. So when Wright's honorarium income exceeded the House limit, his staff directed the people to whom he spoke to purchase the books instead.

The purchasers included Mid-Continent Oil & Gas Association, which paid $1,000 "in lieu of an honorarium" and asked for only three copies of the book; Ocean Spray Massachusetts Growers, an agricultural cooperative, which paid $2,000 in connection with a speech by Wright in 1985, but agreed to let him distribute the books on its behalf; and Southwest Texas State University, which agreed to accept books only after sending $3,000 as an honorarium for a speech by Wright, who endorsed the check over to the Fort Worth printing company that published the book. Another example involved an appearance by Wright before the Fertilizer Institute, which had wanted to give him a memento "such as a plaque or small gift" for his speech, but which instead bought $2,023 worth of books at the suggestion of Wright's office. The National Association of Realtors, the law firm of Hamel & Park, and Van Liew Capital clients each also bought $2,000 worth of books.

After these damaging charges were brought, Wright sought advice about what he should do. And, of course, many of the advice givers were lobbyists. Some of the Speaker's oldest and closest friends were hired guns of Washington. In the past he had gotten crucial financial help from lobbyist J. D. Williams. And in the end, one of Wright's chief advisers was Clark Clifford. The Speaker had audiences with a parade of other lobbyists as well, including Robert McCandless, a lobbyist for the insurance company Transamerica Incorporated and former aide to Senator Bob Kerr of Oklahoma. After he saw the Speaker, McCandless walked glumly down the front stairs of the House and reported that Wright was in good spirits and was clearly being victimized. "There's just something about people from our part of the country," the lobbyist said. "They think we have oil oozing out of our skins. We wear big hats and big boots, we're different."

In downtown Washington, a large group of lobbyists was called together in the vast conference room of the offices near Georgetown of Tommy Boggs's lobbying law firm, Patton, Boggs & Blow. More than a dozen lobbyists with long-standing ties to the Democratic party were in attendance, including Wayne Thevenot.

Others there were Howard Paster of Timmons & Company, and Pat Griffin, a former aide to Senator Robert Byrd and a principal in his own lobbying firm. The late-afternoon meeting lasted slightly more than a half hour.

By all accounts, it was an odd event, designed for the Wright forces to lobby the lobbyists. Charles T. Manatt, a former chairman of the Democratic National Committee and currently a lobbyist, introduced the Speaker's lawyer, William C. Oldaker. In turn, Oldaker asserted at length that his client had a better case than those in attendance probably were being led to believe. He laid it out; the audience sat, mostly, in silence. The idea of the meeting, apparently, was to persuade this important component of the Washington establishment—the lobbying community—that Wright's political life should not be allowed to end. "They want more conversation that's positive about Jim Wright around town," Thevenot concluded.

Judging by Thevenot's reaction, though, the Wright forces did not get what they wanted. Oldaker's arguments were clearly beside the point. Jim Wright was politically dead, and the old hands in the conference room knew it. For the sake of their party, he had to go. "Their arguments were strictly legalistic," Thevenot said. "That's not his problem, though. The problem has more to do with perceptions."

• • •

"The timing of this day could not be better," exulted lobbyist Kenneth Kay, just nine days after Speaker Wright was charged. "It's just perfect," he said, ever ready to go to work.

The youthful-looking Kay was executive director of the Council on Research and Technology, or Coretech, the coalition that lobbied for the research-and-development tax credit. He was not referring to Wright's travails, and was not much concerned about such passing matters. Kay was a lobbyist with the right connections, and he was sitting where only lawmakers were usually allowed: behind a microphone in a congressional hearing room on the first floor of the Dirksen Senate Office Building. The room was loaned to him and the sixty engineers and technicians he was addressing by Democratic Senator Max Baucus of Montana, Kay's former boss and a chief backer of the tax legislation Coretech was pushing that morning. The wood-paneled room smelled of coffee and old leather. It served as the staging area from which Coretech would launch a lobbying barrage that would touch more than a hundred members of Congress in the next eight hours.

It was Wednesday, April 26, the day that Kay and his followers dubbed Lobby Day. It was an annual exercise in pressure from the "grass roots." Although some Washington-based lobbyists were sprinkled through Kay's sleepy-eyed audience, most of these people were scientists from as far away as California and Oregon. For the moment, their job was to be lobbyists for a day and guarantee that their local representatives and senators would open their doors to Coretech's plea for research aid.

Coretech was more than just a lobbying coalition; it was an archetype of corporate manipulation. In structure, it was a coalition of interests that had agreed to work in tandem to pressure lawmakers to pass four pieces of special-interest legislation. But its design was meant to disguise those special interests in the costume of the general good. Coretech lobbied for more "research and development," which almost everyone agreed were good things to have. And most of the dues-paying members of Coretech were universities, which civic-minded lawmakers considered to be "good guys" in the spectrum of interest groups. Half of Coretech's legislative agenda for more research and development catered to them.

But behind these "good guys" and good goals loomed profit-hungry corporations, whose image was not as pristine as the universities'. In fact, corporations quietly financed most of Coretech's activities, and through it lobbied for federal handouts that were even more expensive than the legislation sought by their university allies. The largest beneficiaries of Coretech's legislative agenda were not scientists or even science, but the shareholders of a few dozen big-name corporations.

Such unholy alliances between business and nonbusiness interests were the latest rage in Washington lobbying. "Black hat" corporations spent a lot of effort—and money—seeking to associate themselves with "white hat" organizations of various political stripes, ranging from labor unions to consumer groups. Though most of the financing for these groups came from corporations, their front men were inevitably the white-hat groups that the corporations recruited. Such artifice was becoming as important as, if not more important than, campaign contributions in the world of influence buying in Washington.

"Lobbying is no longer somebody coming with a bag full of money and laying it on a member's desk or relying on personal contacts to have that member do you a favor—if it ever was," explained Coretech lobbyist Stuart Eizenstat. "The difficulty of passing legislation has increased exponentially. To make common cause with people who would not be your traditional allies is important." In the case of Coretech, the cash-starved universities acquired a lobbying machine to press their small-time issues and the corporations got a single organization that they could pay to be responsible for protecting a particular set of tax breaks. They also got some very persuasive white hats to cover up their black ones.

Coretech comprised seventy-two universities and forty-six companies. On behalf of the universities, it lobbied to double the budget of the National Science Foundation to $3 billion, and also to authorize an increase of millions of dollars in U.S. spending on research facilities. But Coretech's largest issues were clearly corporate: It wanted a permanent extension of the soon-to-expire tax credit for research-and-development expenditures, a more than $1-billion-a-year proposal, and the reinstatement of a related, approximately $800-million-a-year R&D tax break that dictated how multinational corporations could divide their research expenses between U.S. and foreign operations.

In some years, Coretech was a million-dollar operation. Usually, though, it cost somewhat less to run—around $700,000 a year. Universities became members for $2,000 each; corporate dues ranged from $5,000 to $30,000, depending on the extent of the companies' research expenditures. For the companies, the dues had been a worthwhile investment: tax savings from the R&D credit for some of Coretech's biggest corporate members, such as Hewlett-Packard Company, Digital Equipment Corporation, Merck & Company, and International Business Machines Corporation, reached into the tens of millions of dollars a year. The average Coretech member saved at least a few million dollars a year from the R&D credit.

But as a matter of public policy, the tax legislation Coretech advocated was of debatable merit. Critics said that the credit, which was given to companies that increased their R&D spending each year, was basically a waste—a cash reward to major corporations for doing what they had to do anyway. "It's used frankly more for tax avoidance than to spur research and development," contended Democratic Representative Brian Donnelly of Massachusetts, a member of the Ways and Means Committee. "In a market-driven economy, these people are forced to invest [in research] by their desires to make profits."

A congressional investigation bolstered Donnelly's point. In a ninety-one-page study, the nonpartisan General Accounting Office concluded that taxpayers were not getting much bang for their R&D bucks. The GAO estimated that from 1981 to 1985 the credit stimulated between $1 billion and $2.5 billion of new research spending; but the credit itself cost U.S. taxpayers $7 billion in forgone revenue over the same period. That meant the federal government spent $1 to get, at the very most, 36 cents' worth of extra R&D, and probably much less.

This conclusion was made even more credible by one of the nation's largest research companies, General Electric, which permitted one of its Washington lobbyists to criticize the credit publicly as, essentially, a triumph of symbol over substance. "It's really a distortion," said GE lobbyist Anne Canfield. "It helps the companies' cash flow, I guess. But does it create more R and D? No!"

Even advocates of the credit conceded that it had not been as effective as it could be. But that, they said, was because it had been allowed to lapse periodically since being established in 1981. "I can't think of one discussion I've had internally or externally that said, 'What about the R and D credit?' because we don't know if it's going to be there," said Robert Gilbertson, chief executive of Data Switch Corporation of Connecticut. "It's better than nothing, but you might as well forget it because it's not doing any good. It's just throwing money down a rat hole."

And who benefited most from the R&D credit? Almost exclusively the largest U.S. corporations. The GAO found that corporations with assets over $250 million, of which there were only about 3,500, accounted for 80 percent of the credit's use. And an even more elite group was helped by the R&D credit's sister legislation, which allocated R&D expenses between the United States and abroad. One Treasury Department study early in the decade suggested that most of the hundreds of millions of dollars of benefits that flowed from that legislation went to just a few dozen of the nation's largest corporations.

Coretech's job was to sidestep these problems, and play up other issues. In this task, it was a master.

*   *   *

Before they set off on their rounds for Lobby Day, the researchers-turned-lobbyists convened in the Senate hearing room at 8 A.M. Led by Kay and Eizenstat, the meeting was part pep rally and part seminar. It was meant to ensure that everyone was singing from the same song sheet.

"Thank you for coming," Eizenstat said, speaking into the mike set up at the head table. "It makes a big difference to members [of Congress] to see that people from their home states really are interested."

"We've had a very, very good start," Kay agreed, pointing out that a majority of both congressional tax-writing committees had sponsored Coretech's bills. "The goal is to get a majority of both chambers. The basic job today is to ask for cosponsors," he said. If the lawmakers have already agreed to cosponsor the bills, which were authored by Coretech partisans, Kay said, then butter them up anyway. "Tell them thank you," he advised.

But the ever-vigilant Eizenstat was interested in more than getting in the door and being complimentary. He tried to prepare his lobbyists-on-loan for some of the questions that they might face, and he tried to arm them with arguments, carefully dictating what their answers should be.

"Doesn't the marketplace do this on its own?" he asked, pretending to be a lawmaker.

"Of course companies will do it anyway, but there are great risks," he suggested as a reply. Society as a whole gets two to three times as much benefit from research as the research company itself derives. So, Eizenstat said, "there is a gap between research for self-interest and what society should have done." Therefore, he concluded, it is up to the government to stimulate the extra research that society needs.

"Why not use grants instead of tax breaks?" he asked himself.

A grant would "hamstring the private sector" with "an army

of bureaucrats," he replied, emphasizing the catchy phrases. Also, he pointed out, the credit was reasonable in price. It had even been cut back over the years. When first instituted in 1981, he recounted, the credit was 25 percent of increases in research spending. In 1986, it was reduced to 20 percent. In 1988, its value was trimmed again, this time by one-sixth. By the end of 1989, Eizenstat said, the credit was scheduled to expire again, and Coretech was dedicated to preventing that from happening.

What's more, Eizenstat went on, there was "demonstrable evidence" that the credit worked. To prove his point, he pulled out the big gun: the venerable Brookings Institution. Years ago, Coretech had hired Martin Baily and Robert Lawrence, two scholars affiliated with that eminent Washington think tank, to study the credit's effect on corporate research. Their conclusion was that despite the credit's flaws, from 1981 to 1985 it inspired 7 percent more research-and-development spending than there would have been without the credit. That 7 percent worked out to about $4 billion. "The credit has worked," Eizenstat said triumphantly.

The credit was also a big winner politically, he went on. "President Bush specifically mentioned making the R and D credit permanent before a joint session of Congress," he boasted. The President also "placed a great emphasis on the R and D credit" in his written budget proposal. "There was a page and a half on making the R and D credit permanent," Eizenstat said. "It wasn't just a line item."

Eizenstat asked the researchers to use their common sense, and to draw upon what they knew from their own vocations. Surely they knew in their hearts that the R&D credit was right. "You know these things from your own experience," he said. "We have to compete by being at the cutting edge of change. At the bottom of innovation has to be research and development." Eizenstat appealed to his audience's own corporate self-interest as well. "If we have the R and D credit, it gives you that extra argument with your CEO for more research money," he said. "We're trying to increase on the margin. That is the purpose and the beauty of the R and D credit."

On the stickier question of the U.S.–foreign allocation tax break, Eizenstat gave a quick primer. "What is it?" he asked. "It treats some R and D as if it were done abroad." But he quickly added, "I don't think many of the members understand it." Internal Revenue Service Regulation 1.861-8, he explained, was issued in early 1977 by then–Treasury Secretary William E. Simon. It dealt with the question of where R&D expenses should be accounted for on the balance sheet of a company that conducts business in several countries. Since research benefits a company in more places than just the country in which that research is done, the Treasury Department said that some of the expenses had to be allocated around the world: half in the United States and half elsewhere.

Companies protested, however, saying the arrangement unfairly deprived them of needed tax deductions in the United States. They also argued that the rule was an incentive for them to do research outside the United States, since they would get no benefit from keeping their plants at home. After much angry lobbying on Capitol Hill, Congress heeded these complaints and postponed the implementation of what became known in shorthand as 861. Over the years, other moratoriums were also imposed. What Coretech wanted, Eizenstat said, was a permanent moratorium on the original regulation, and the enactment of a rewrite, which he called the 67 percent solution. Under the new proposal, a company could claim as much as 67 percent of its research spending on its U.S. income-tax returns.

"Our problem," Eizenstat confessed, to his audience of lobbyists-for-a-day, "is money. There's not a lot of money around" to pay for the 861 fix that Coretech desired. Of the original regulation, he said, "No one likes the rule; everyone admits it's wrong." But in Washington, where deficits were king, even good ideas were left wanting for lack of financing.

Besides, Eizenstat said candidly, the 67 percent solution "is criticized as a giveaway program to the multinationals." And at this complaint, he became visibly agitated. "Of course it goes to the multinationals," he said, "So what?" But he offered no rebuttal.

"One more charge you may hear is that we are greedy when we ask for it to be retroactive," he said about 861. The answer to that, he said in effect, was to duck the question. "We would like a permanent solution to pick up from the last moratorium. We think it's a matter of principle and intellectual honesty." The theme for the day, he said, should be "the permanent solution."

Eizenstat finished and turned the program back to Kay, who reminded the researchers about the noncorporate part of Coretech's agenda. "The beauty of Coretech is that the corporate and academic areas work together," Kay concluded. "That's our strength." But his explanation of the noncorporate issues did not take long at all.

. . .

At 11 A.M., a Coretech team crowded into the office of Representative Michael A. Andrews, a Democrat from Houston and a member of the Ways and Means Committee. Eizenstat made sure to attend this meeting, because the ambitious young Andrews was a major supporter of Coretech's legislation. "Hi, Mike, I just came from seeing Sandy Levin," he told Andrews, referring to Representative Sander M. Levin, the Michigan Democrat. After he sat down, Eizenstat dropped the casualness and went right to business. "This is our Scientists' Lobby Day," he said. "We do this once a year, using scientists and engineers who are doing the actual research. We want, first, to thank you."

The rest of the thanking was done by Houston-based scientists. Alvin Hildebrandt, a physics professor at the University of Houston, led the chorus. He reminded Andrews that "we really need some of the tax credits and incentives." But the usually genial Andrews decided to be disagreeable, for the moment. "One of the criticisms is, 'Wouldn't they do it anyway?' " he said. And Eizenstat almost leaped out of his chair with his well-rehearsed answer. "It's the right question to ask," he said, and cited the Brookings study. Then, sticking to the script, he added: "If you do it with a tax credit, you let the system work."

"That's a real good point," Andrews said with his more typical enthusiasm. "It could allow a University of Houston to compete with MIT [Massachusetts Institute of Technology]." With that happy thought, Andrews dropped all pretense of playing devil's advocate. "I'd be glad to help," he said. "Research is becoming a big part of the future of the city. We're desperately trying to diversify." For good measure, Hildebrandt mentioned the need to double the National Science Foundation budget—a change that would help the university greatly—and Andrews nodded his assent.

Before the meeting was concluded, Eizenstat quizzed Andrews about the outlook for fiscal legislation. Andrews said he did not know what would happen, but might have a better idea after the weekend, when the Ways and Means Committee went on retreat. He promised to bring up the issue of extending the R&D tax credit. Then Andrews gave some lobbying advice to Eizenstat. He mentioned that Representative Thomas Downey of New York, another committee member, would be coming to Houston soon to attend a congressional field hearing. "It would be a good time to meet with Tom and others on the subcommittee," Andrews suggested. As he was leaving, Eizenstat handed Andrews a study on the credit, and said with a laugh that the report could be used "if you have trouble sleeping one night."

• • •

Eizenstat was excited about the day, even though he had spent a good part of it in a wheelchair. The forty-six-year-old suffered from a bad back, and just the night before Eizenstat had taken an acupuncture treatment to soothe it. The acupuncture worked well enough for him to walk into most office visits. But, in between meetings, he was rolled around the hallways by a young employee of his law firm.

"When they hear from the people who are doing the research it makes a difference," he asserted as he was being chauffeured in his brown Grand Marquis from the Cannon House Office Building back to the Dirksen Senate Office Building. "They see us enough. We're there just to provide continuity, not to be doing the major talking."

The political background was not where Eizenstat was usually found. During the late 1970s, as President Carter's assistant for domestic policy and a member of the President's inner circle of advisers, he had been one of Washington's most prominent citizens. He held this high-powered job as a remarkably young man, still in his thirties. Educated at Harvard University and serious to a fault, Stuart Eizenstat, with his long, gaunt face, became a respected fixture of the Washington scene.

When his boss lost a bid for reelection, Eizenstat was torn

about what to do next. His roots were in Atlanta, and his whispery voice still had enough of a trace of the South to fit there nicely. But much of his adult life had been spent in the Northeast. At age twenty-four, he was on President Johnson's research and speech-writing staff. Later, in 1968, he was research director for Hubert Humphrey, whom he called "my hero." Public policy, he once told *The Washington Post*, was "what has really animated my life since college."

His father, Leo, finally gave Eizenstat the advice that made the difference. He told his son, "I'd rather have you happy five hundred miles away than less than happy next door." So Eizenstat stayed to become a very young elder of the Washington establishment. In a community populated by once-close-to's like himself, he was absorbed easily as a big-name Democrat, a pro-Israel activist, and a lobbyist for the corporate cause. His going rate as a lawyer-lobbyist was $350 an hour, colleagues said.

In the car on the way to the Dirksen Senate Office Building, he telephoned an ABC News producer who was trying to arrange an interview with him. The network was preparing a story about Bush's first hundred days in office, and the quotable Eizenstat was a natural choice. In fact, for days he had been fielding calls from a variety of news outlets on the same topic, and he had his patter down. Bush was doing a fine job, he told each of them. But all the President was doing, he added, was "reacting to the next problem." "Where is his positive agenda?" Eizenstat inquired, obviously proud of the line.

Like prominent lobbyists before him, Eizenstat was a man of parts. He was a professor at Harvard's John F. Kennedy School of Government, where he taught a course each summer on presidential decision-making. He was a passionate writer and lecturer on Israel and a leader of the Jewish community: president of the Washington-area Jewish Community Center, which was one of the nation's largest, and a former chairman of the advisory committee of the Institute for American Jewish–Israeli Relations of the American Jewish Committee. He also served as an informal adviser to the hottest politicians in his party, reviewing speeches for such Democrats as Governor Mario M. Cuomo of New York, Senator Charles Robb of Virginia, and Senator Joseph R. Biden, Jr., of Delaware.

Along the way he also managed to build one of Washington's more successful law-lobbying firms. After leaving the White House, he rejoined the fledgling Washington office of the Atlanta-based Powell, Goldstein, Frazer & Murphy, and built it steadily from there. By 1989 the firm's clients included IBM, Westinghouse, and the International Paper Company. Eizenstat's office overlooking Pennsylvania Avenue was always stacked high with documents, many of which Eizenstat had written. He was always writing, always thinking, often getting by on just five hours of sleep a night. "He is one of those magical people who doesn't need to sleep," said an admirer, Carolyn Seely, who worked at Eizenstat's law firm before she joined the staff of Senate Minority Leader Robert Dole of Kansas as his top tax aide.

Eizenstat's reputation as a policy expert was one of his greatest strengths as a lobbyist, and one of the main reasons he was retained by Coretech. Kay said Eizenstat had a "policy gloss." What he meant was that Eizenstat, unlike other lobbyists, could actually deal with the substance of issues. Most lobbyists were known for whom they knew and not what they knew. But in the complicated world of Washington, that was changing. "You've got to have both an outstanding public-policy position and the ability to do effective lobbying on a day-to-day basis," said Bruce Holbein, manager of government relations for Digital Equipment Corporation. "There are very few lobbyists in Washington who bring both of those skills together." Eizenstat, he said, was one of them. David Rubinstein, who was Eizenstat's deputy at the White House, called him "incredibly diligent," and few would disagree.

One R&D lobbyist was bowled over by the effusive compliments heaped on Eizenstat by Democratic Senator John D. (Jay) Rockefeller of West Virginia during a routine meeting in the senator's office. The lawmaker thanked Eizenstat for advising him to work quietly in the background during his first years in Congress. Now, Rockefeller said, other senators relied on him to shepherd issues that he really cared about, such as health care. Similar accolades for Eizenstat also came from some Republicans as well. Treasury Secretary Nicholas Brady once told one of his aides that if "Eizenstat wanted a meeting, I'll have a meeting"—such was his reputation for businesslike honesty.

Where Eizenstat fell down as a lobbyist was in his rough manner and partisan leanings. Notable lobbyists of the past had possessed a charm and a grace of which Eizenstat had little. Friends claimed his wit was dry; detractors suggested that, if that was true, the Mojave Desert was a swamp. One top congressional aide likened him to a bulldog who would not let go of a pant leg. Republican aides added, with some distaste, that he was a purely Democratic bulldog. Early on, the R&D lobby had retained both Eizenstat and a former Republican member of the House in order to convey the impression that research was a bipartisan issue. But the Republican was dropped when Eizenstat persuaded everyone that he had plenty of contacts with the GOP as well. In perception-conscious Washington, that ultimately proved to be a bad decision.

Still, the need for government subsidy of R&D *was* widely accepted in Congress. But "support is a mile wide and an inch deep," Coretech's Kay said. At a time of budget deficits, federal aid to private corporations "tends to be one of those things that gets pulled off the table." With regret in his voice, he said he realized that some people considered stimulating research of this kind "a luxury."

Kay was a veteran of research wars. He had lobbied for R&D issues since he "left the Hill" in 1984. Before that, he had worked as an aide to Representative Edward I. Koch of New York (who went on to become mayor of New York City) and to Senator Baucus of Montana, who was known as one of the best-looking but not one of the most intellectually rigorous of senators. Kay served as Baucus's brain on the Senate Judiciary Committee and elsewhere. Now that Kay was in the private sector, he continued to serve his old boss, especially on research issues.

When asked about Kay, Baucus had only good things to say. He said the lobbyist did things for "the right reasons" and was careful never to steer him wrong. Baucus delighted in recounting how well-liked Kay was by both Democrats and Republicans on the Judiciary Committee. He had been a particular favorite of GOP Senator Alan K. Simpson of Wyoming, who referred to him as Bright Eyes. Kay was still thick-haired, handsome, and engaging. He was forever describing things as "upbeat." But his most impressive features were his huge, almond-shaped eyes and long eyelashes, which gave the impression that his exuberance was indeed wide-eyed.

An avowed baseball fan and dedicated parent, Kay was none-theless a nearly nonstop worker. One of his favorite expressions was "of course, we all work hard and try our best," as if everyone really did. The son of Eastern European immigrants, he was raised on Long Island. In his mother's fiftieth year in America, he hosted a family party in her honor, and presented her with an American flag that had flown over the Capitol—at the direction of Baucus's office.

These days, Kay was a partner in the Washington office of the Seattle-based law firm Preston, Thorgrimson, Ellis & Holman, which later changed its name to Preston, Gates, Ellis & Rouvelous, Meeds. At age thirty-seven, Kay served as Coretech's coordinator. That meant his firm was paid more than $100,000 a year to keep the coalition together, coordinate its lobbying efforts, and serve as a clearinghouse for information about the fate of its issues. Much of his time was spent in telephone conversations with one or more of his coalition members, collecting and dispensing the latest intelligence about the R&D tax credit.

Kay's faith in the tax credit at times bordered on the extreme. News articles that gave even the slightest hint that the credit might not be good public policy set him to sputtering. And so sure was he of his legislative strategies that some of his colleagues considered him arrogant. Still, by Washington standards, Kay was a young lobbyist, and he professed still to be learning his trade. The next two years would prove to be a true learning experience.

Coretech, too, was relatively new. Born in December 1986 at the Hyatt Regency Hotel in Washington, it was the offspring of CAIT, the Council for the Advancement of Industrial Technology. CAIT was a coalition that lobbied for the R&D tax credit, but had a relatively limited amount of university representation. (Coretech, on the other hand, had big backers of all sorts right from the start.) The featured speaker at the kickoff meeting was Richard Darman, who was then the deputy treasury secretary and by 1989 was the White House budget director.

"We spent several months developing an agenda for Core-tech," Eizenstat recalled. The 861 issue previously had been lob-bied by a separate group of companies with an uninspiring name: the 861 Companies. Coretech included 861 in its agenda to bring them—and their substantial financial wherewithal—into the fold. Two nontax issues were also included, to appeal to the universities: a new bill to provide matching grants for the modernization of research facilities on university campuses, and the proposal to double the budget of the National Science Foundation in five years.

The combination worked. Soon after the initiation of the new coalition, Coretech was able to win enactment of the grant program. And in 1987, it participated in an extraordinary negotiation with administration and congressional officials that produced the 67 percent solution. Representatives of Coretech, the Treasury Department, and several congressional staffs holed up in a Capitol Hill meeting room to devise the compromise, which was included word for word in bills passed separately by the tax-writing committees of the House and the Senate. But, through no fault of Coretech's, the compromise died in a House-Senate conference. In October 1987, the stock market crashed, and all fiscal legislation was thrown into chaos. One of the victims was the widely accepted, but expensive, 67 percent solution.

In 1989, the R&D credit and the 67 percent solution were still awaiting a long-term place in the law. And the Republican administration remained a loyal backer. In January, Coretech had brought a delegation to visit Treasury Secretary Brady that included the chief executives of two major drug companies, Roy Vagelos of Merck and James Burke of Johnson & Johnson. Brady had told the group that the executives would be "pleased" with President Reagan's last budget proposal, but that no decisions had yet been made about Bush's first budget. He left the clear impression, though, that Coretech's causes would not be forgotten.

In effect, the secretary went on to ask the group to help the incoming Bush administration lobby the Congress. President Bush was interested in proposals that would promote long-term investment, and Brady said he wanted an "ally" in that fight. "He said you've got a big coalition. We hope you'll help us lobbying Congress because this is something we believe in," Eizenstat recalled. The delegation did not say no. And President Bush did his part by backing Coretech's issues thoroughly when his own budget plan was later unveiled.

. . .

After lunch on Lobby Day, the researchers had one more round of congressional visits. Not all of the encounters were pleasant. But none was more contentious than Eizenstat's meeting with Democratic Representative Fortney H. (Pete) Stark of California, an archenemy of most tax credits, but especially R&D. Stark came loaded for bear. He brought to the meeting held in his office both his own tax aide, Anne Zeppenfeld, and the Ways and Means Committee's top tax counsel, the able Janice Mays. Eizenstat brought along a couple of lobbyists from California companies and a physicist from Stanford University.

"Stuart, I thought you were bringing two people!" Stark complained the minute he saw the Coretech contingent. Gesturing at the limited space in his office, Stark added, "I guess they can stand or sit on the floor."

Undaunted, Eizenstat began his pitch as soon as he and the others had squeezed into the office and found seats. "The two tax issues are 861 and R and D," he said.

"Those would come under the umbrella of 'tax shelters,' " Stark immediately challenged.

Eizenstat chose to ignore the attack. He mentioned the Brookings study and said that a reformulation of the credit Coretech wanted would serve an even broader range of companies.

"I don't believe you, but that's an interesting theory," Stark said. He then turned to Eizenstat's companions and said he doubted the credit helped spur any research at all. But then again, he added sarcastically, "you've probably never run a company."

Here he was wrong, and the Stanford physicist, Robert Byer, was happy to set him straight. "I have had several start-ups," he said with a thin grin on his face.

"Pay any taxes?" Stark asked. When Byer nodded in reply, Stark pressed on anyway. "It didn't stop you, did it? You guys are all here for your handout." He then added, "Half of research dollars are in defense. Why not take it out of the defense budget, not out of taxpayer dollars?"

By now Eizenstat had had enough. He did not raise his voice. In fact, his pent-up fury made his voice even more hushed than usual. He decided to remind Stark that he had helped keep the R&D credit alive during the tax bill of 1986. "You were really one of our chief champions in 1986," Eizenstat said coldly. But Stark was on a roll.

"Let the government choose what research ought to be done," the congressman suggested. Stark then mentioned that pharmaceutical companies were among the biggest beneficiaries of the credit.

"You've allied yourself with some squirrelly characters," Stark said. "You've got bad companies, that's all."

"We shouldn't be blinded by your problems with the pharmaceuticals," Eizenstat said, asserting a new air of authority. "I have worked here on and off for twenty years. We have to compete on innovation, being a step ahead. R and D can do that," he said, gaining momentum. "Any person sitting on Mount Olympus would want this done. The credit is an efficient way to do it. Otherwise we would be encouraging companies to go abroad with their research."

Stark pulled back after Eizenstat's rebuttal, and they began to talk like two old political pros. "You're not looking for a long-term extension this year, are you?" Stark asked.

"Unless the tax situation changes, I don't see how," Eizenstat confessed, giving the lie to the rhetoric of the "permanent solution."

"Let's talk politics," Stark continued. "The practical politics are that if you don't do all of the extenders, like [the credits for] low-income housing and targeted jobs, you don't do any of them." Stark was referring to the dozen tax breaks that were set to expire at year's end along with Coretech's. All of these so-called extenders usually passed together, because as a group they commanded so much support from a wide range of lawmakers.

"So," Stark continued, "you guys should be praying for a big tax bill. That's when you have a chance."

"That's what we are praying for," Eizenstat conceded and then added with a smile, "Let me just thank you for your previous championing of this."

Only Mays allowed herself a laugh.

· · ·

The next meeting was far more congenial. Eizenstat and a crew of fellow Georgians met with Ed Jenkins, whom Eizenstat had recruited in 1989 as a new lead sponsor in the House for the R&D credit. Both Eizenstat and Jenkins had come to Washington in 1976, and Eizenstat was eager to enlist the congressman as R&D's champion when the previous sponsor, Representative Jake Pickle of Texas, decided he had gone as far with the issue as he could. Coretech had considered others, especially the ever-popular Robert Matsui of California. But Jenkins was a more natural fit. "We felt Jenkins was an excellent person. He was very effective, had good credibility with the committee, and knew the chairman well," Eizenstat explained. "He also doesn't take a lot of issues up," meaning he would focus on the R&D matter to the exclusion of other issues.

Getting Jenkins as a sponsor had been easy. First, Eizenstat had talked to him by telephone and had sent him a memorandum explaining the history of the tax credit and its status. Eizenstat also had told Jenkins whom he would represent, naming everyone in the coalition. Later, Eizenstat, Kay, and a lobbyist from IBM, John Boyd, met with the congressman in his office to seal their deal.

The Lobby Day visit, then, was mostly pro forma. But it was also designed to gather information. "We wanted to come mostly to thank you," Eizenstat said, and Jenkins sat back in his big leather chair to explain why he cared about R&D. His district was largely rural, he said, but "I do have a parochial interest; it is becoming very high tech." His constituents included some computer companies in the Gwinnett County suburbs of Atlanta, he said, as well as an amazingly automated carpet industry in Dalton, Georgia. Dalton was famous for such natives as NBC's Deborah Norville and Donald Trump's girlfriend, Marla Maples. But to Jenkins, Dalton meant carpets spun by computer. "If you can draw it," he said, "you can make a carpet." He pointed to the carpet on his own office floor as an example.

For the moment, though, Eizenstat was interested in finding out Jenkins's assessment of the chances for the R&D tax credit. "Will there be a tax bill, or will we have to wait for a bigger tax bill next year?" Eizenstat asked him.

"I envision doing whatever extenders we do with this year's bill," Jenkins answered. "We're going to have a tough fight."

At the end of the short meeting, Eizenstat handed Jenkins a letter inviting him to a reception in his honor back in Gwinnett County. "I'll take a look-see at my schedule and get back to you," Jenkins said.

. . .

In seeking to keep the tax credit alive, Coretech faced one big problem. "There is no constituency for research," Eizenstat said. "Our job is to create one." So Coretech developed an elaborate network of home-state contacts, from both the corporate and college communities, whose job it was to keep congressmen happy. Both the reception for Jenkins and, in its own way, Lobby Day were parts of that effort, which Coretech called the Adopt-a-Member program. Coretech even devised instructional materials to teach researchers how to cozy up to lawmakers back home in just the right way.

The instructions were quite explicit. For one thing, they said, only certain kinds of lawmakers should be targeted: the ones who belonged to the fiscal committees in Congress, such as Ways and Means, Finance, and Appropriations. And it was quite clear how important these people really were. The word "member" was never mentioned in the multipage instructions without being capitalized. For example: "An informative meeting with a Member of Congress and the at-home congressional staff can be extremely helpful, especially when you give local examples to illustrate your policy arguments," it stated. "Invite Members of Congress and their staff to tour your plant or lab facilities," it went on. "Give them an opportunity to talk with your researchers and technicians."

The message of the document was simply this: Members of Congress needed a reason to back Coretech's causes, and Adopt-a-Member lobbyists needed to find—and to foster—those reasons. This should be done, the instructions said, with a variety of kindnesses, especially the favor of publicity:

> Members of Congress want to be strong supporters of American research and development. Recognize their support through presentation of a plaque, or similar item, that commends the Member of Congress. Couple this award with a lunch

or reception of some sort. Feature the presentation of the award in your internal newsletter or magazine and see that the Member of Congress receives a copy of the story. In addition, perhaps, invite local media. If it's appropriate, ask other members of the industrial and academic R & D community to also attend receptions, award ceremonies, and so on, that you hold for Members of Congress. Invite your Member of Congress to attend and participate in ceremonies when your company or institution is recognized for its excellence or when your company or institution awards gifts to others. For example, ask your Member of Congress to participate when your company awards a corporate gift to a university.

Lawmakers need attention the way other humans need to breathe, and the Adopt-a-Member program was designed to meet that need. The home-state researchers were encouraged to generate news stories, editorials, and letters to the editor about their lawmakers, and to grant radio and television interviews in praise of them. But they were warned to "be aware of deadlines," and to meet them assiduously.

Coretech lobbyists tried to practice what they preached when it came to recruiting folks back home. And Ed Hatcher, a former aide to Representative Matsui and now a lobbyist for the American Electronics Association, went by the book when he had his opportunity with Representative Jenkins. Hatcher was a balding man in his early thirties who seemed anxious even when he was at ease. He rarely left anything to chance. So when a group of electronics executives fêted Jenkins in Washington one day, Hatcher showed up with camera in hand. He snapped a picture of Jenkins being presented an award for his "outstanding contributions" to the high-tech industry. Hatcher sent the photo and a press release to local newspapers in Georgia—with eight copies to Jenkins. Soon thereafter, a huge photograph of the smiling lawmaker holding a plaque appeared on page nine of the *Dawson County* (Georgia) *Advertiser*. The brief story that accompanied the photo quoted an electronics-association official saying that Jenkins was "on the verge of making history by making America more competitive."

Mission accomplished, Hatcher said later, and it was all "perfectly sincere."

. . .

In May, the Coelho and Wright affairs came to a sudden end. After the *Post* story, Coelho consulted closely with his staff and, appropriately enough, with a lobbyist—Martin Franks of CBS Incorporated, the broadcasting company. For years, Franks had been Coelho's top aide, and he still functioned as the congressman's senior adviser even though he was now employed by a private company. On Friday, May 26, Coelho decided to resign. And five days later, on a gray afternoon, the full House was convened to listen to the final official words of Speaker Wright.

Under the bright television lights that helped bring the hour-long address to millions of Americans through a live broadcast, Wright delivered an emotional resignation speech. He stood in the well of the chamber, facing hundreds of his grim-faced colleagues. At times he gestured broadly, sometimes he shouted, and at other times he mumbled his defense. Sitting through it all in the visitors' gallery overhead were the Speaker's wife and one of his daughters, Virginia, who, appropriately enough, worked as a Washington lobbyist.

"Let me give you back this job you gave me, as a propitiation for all this season of bad will," he said, "Let that be a total payment." He acknowledged that he had made mistakes and errors in judgment, but said he preferred to see the battle in terms of politics. "Have I been too partisan, too insensitive, too determined to have my way?" he asked. "If I have offended anybody in the other party, I am sorry." He concluded: "All of us in both parties must resolve to bring this period of mindless cannibalism to an end. There's been enough of it."

After the speech, Wright was embraced by many of his colleagues, as was Coelho. Surely some of them must have been thinking, "There, but for the grace of God, go I." No one in that chamber was immune to the many temptations of private wealth, conveyed by lobbyists, to which Wright and Coelho had succumbed.

4

The
Bumpy
Slide

Huge fiscal problems—particularly the budget deficit—continued to cry out for solutions. And lobbyists were banging down the doors of lawmakers for assistance of one kind or another. But, in the spring of 1989, the House was paralyzed by the Wright and Coelho episodes. Democrats were in a state of shock, and the Congress they controlled was simply unable to get down to the serious business of legislation.

In this frozen, fearful atmosphere, Eben Tisdale, a lobbyist for Hewlett-Packard, visited the office of Representative Robert Matsui. The lobbyist was as laid-back as the congressman was high-strung. But Tisdale and Matsui got along well. As an active member of Coretech, the R&D lobby, Tisdale was responsible for checking in on the Sacramento lawmaker, and Matsui was always glad to see him. The lobbyist's company was based in California, which always made him, and the R&D issue, welcome.

During this visit, Tisdale noticed something new on Matsui's wall: a collection of baseball cards mounted in a frame. The lobbyist knew that the odd wall-hanging was important. Not much about

Matsui's world was random or casual. Matsui was slight of build and soft of speech, but he was also ambitious and fiercely organized. At the moment he was mustering all his energies and resources for a run for the Senate, which explained in part why he helped so many lobbyists. The other focus of his life was his only son, Brian, on whom he and his wife, Doris, doted. The seventeen-year-old boy, it turned out, was the reason for the addition to Matsui's wall.

After admiring the framed cards, Tisdale told Matsui that he had recently found some of his own cards in a box at home, and wondered if he would like to have a few. Sure, the congressman replied eagerly. Brian was a baseball-card fanatic, he said, and would love to have more. So Tisdale sent Matsui six cards, including a Roy Campanella, a Duke Snider, and a Gil Hodges, and other stars of the 1950s Brooklyn Dodgers. "I sent them to Bob and I didn't think anything more about them," Tisdale recalled. "I didn't think these things had any real value."

Matsui excitedly took the cards home. But he didn't get the reaction he had expected. "Dad, are you crazy?" Brian said the moment he saw them. "Do you want to go to jail?" The young man quickly consulted his reference books and discovered that the vintage cards were probably worth more than $100—the limit on gifts from lobbyists. So his red-faced father telephoned the surprised lobbyist to tell him to take them back.

At first, Tisdale tried to laugh off Matsui's suggestion. "This is just fun," Tisdale said.

"It's not fun," Matsui replied with the seriousness of a man seeking higher office. "I would have never thought about it in the past, but there's paranoia going on."

Matsui's dilemma illustrated the new obsession with ethics that was sweeping Capitol Hill. The problems that plagued Wright were giving other lawmakers fits. Early in the year, several House members were caught when their wives received one-ounce samples of a new perfume called Red from Giorgio of Beverly Hills. The samples were valued at $175 at the retail level. Under the Wright and Coelho pall, some lawmakers decided belatedly to return the perfume even though a bottle's wholesale value was less than the $100 limit. Representative Wayne Owens decided to give up something even more valuable—his stake in a ranch. An aide to the Utah Democrat took a hard look at the House rules and discovered that Owens's part-ownership was improper because the property included grazing land leased from the federal government. "I've been brooding about it; I love the ranch," the congressman said. But, he added, "I also love my job."

Lawmakers were always receiving small presents from lobbyists, particularly at Christmastime. Representative Richard Durbin, Democrat of Illinois, had gotten asparagus, aluminum foil, and organic toothpaste and, like many of his colleagues, usually allowed his staff to divide the booty. But during those stressful days in 1989, he decided he had to be more careful. He sent back some books that were given to him by a hometown businessman whom he had once helped with a routine import problem. "You're going to find this hard to understand," he recalled telling his friend, "but I want to save us both a headache."

• • •

In early June, Chairman Dan Rostenkowski of the Ways and Means Committee stole away from the Capitol in his chauffeured Lincoln Continental for a secret meeting at the White House. He and the President had been privately commiserating for weeks about a common problem: how to achieve deficit-reduction goals without violating the President's no-tax-increase pledge. At this meeting, Rostenkowski and Bush tacitly agreed upon a solution that only a politician could fully appreciate: They decided to try to reduce a tax in order to raise revenue. They turned to capital gains. "I'll try to put together a bill that won't attract a veto," Rostenkowski promised his friend the President.

None of this would have seemed possible at the beginning of the year. Back then, there had been no greater opponent of a cut in the capital-gains tax than Dan Rostenkowski. "It's a tax break for the wealthy that will significantly increase the deficit," he had said in response to Bush's budget proposal in February. "I can't imagine any member of Congress willing to take such a step." During a speech in Chicago in March, Rostenkowski reiterated his point. "We are talking about helping the rich here. . . . We're talking about a benefit for the richest five percent of taxpayers that will allegedly somehow help the other ninety-five percent. On its face, it's an argument that defies logic. It's as if someone had suggested that the law of gravity be repealed."

Rostenkowski, a Democrat, had ample reason to oppose a cut in capital-gains taxes: The break would be a boon to millionaires and billionaires, and to almost no one else. According to Congress's Joint Taxation Committee, fully 80 percent of the benefit of the tax cut would go to the approximately 5 percent of all families that had incomes of more than $100,000 a year. More than 60 percent of the benefit would go to the even smaller fraction of families that earned more than $200,000. Advocates of the tax cut contended the break would spur business investment. But they produced little evidence to prove their point. It was mostly a matter of faith to back such a clear giveaway to the wealthy. And Democrats generally did not attend that particular church.

But Rostenkowski was torn. Although he did not want to give a tax break to the rich or to undercut his Tax Reform Act of 1986, which eliminated the capital-gains tax preference, he had become increasingly worried about fulfilling the deficit-reduction requirements of the Gramm-Rudman law. Under it he had to find $5.3 billion in new revenues in the next fiscal year. Most of Washington believed that such a relatively small amount could easily be found somewhere. A new term even arose to describe the situation: "slide-by." This was going to be a slide-by year, everyone agreed.

Everyone, that is, but Rostenkowski. He fretted. He suffered. At times, staffers said, he appeared to be almost desperate to find the right tax increases to meet his revenue obligations without also falling foul of the President's no-new-taxes pledge. Ironically, one increasingly obvious way to raise the money was to cut the capital-gains tax—at least temporarily. Official congressional estimators said that any quick change in the capital-gains rate would produce a fire sale of the stock and property investments that would qualify for the special tax treatment. That, in turn, would bring into the U.S. Treasury billions of dollars in additional revenue. It also would make George Bush happy, something Rostenkowski dearly would have liked to do. Rostenkowski counted himself proudly as one of the President's best friends.

Rostenkowski was a politician in love with the presidency; one of his favorite stories about his youth concerned the trip he made with his father to see Franklin D. Roosevelt's inauguration. But Rostenkowski loved George Bush more than any other President in his lifetime. In the 1960s, Rostenkowski and Bush had served together on the Ways and Means Committee, and they had kept in contact ever since. The first floor of Rostenkowski's sprawling Chicago home was filled with photographs of himself and Bush— including one of Bush driving Rostenkowski in a golf cart. In 1989, Rostenkowski never tired of bragging about how close he was to the President. For his part, Bush seemed to know this about Rostenkowski, and constantly played on it. In effect, the President did some clever lobbying of his own. Before he delivered his inaugural address, Bush conspicuously greeted selected members of Congress from the podium; the greetings included saying "Hi, Danny" loudly enough to be audible to the entire nation. That put Rostenkowski in heaven.

The flattery worked. "I love George Bush," Rostenkowski confided to the *National Journal.* "I think he's one of the greatest guys I've ever met in my life. I talk to him very frankly. And I think— as I never thought he was a wimp, I think he can be a great President because I honestly believe that George Bush will, when the time comes, make the right decision."

In the end, the allure of quick and easy revenue from capital gains and the added advantage of pleasing the President were too much for Rostenkowski to resist. The result was a pact between Rostenkowski and Bush agreed to at that secret White House meeting. It changed the political landscape of Washington. Rostenkowski agreed to cut the capital-gains tax for a single year, thus creating the revenue spurt he needed without *raising* any taxes. In exchange, the President agreed to back some things Rostenkowski and his Democrats wanted: an increase in the earned-income tax credit, which went to low-income working families, and a boost in Medicare payments to inner-city hospitals, a change that would help Rostenkowski's hometown of Chicago.

The importance of the pact could not be overstated. The capital-gains tax cut had no future without the support of the chief Democratic tax-writer in the House. But with his support, capital gains bloomed with new life. Rostenkowski's quiet agreement with Bush let the capital-gains genie out of the bottle, and it was almost impossible to get it back inside.

Soon after he went public with his newfound interest in capital gains later that month, Rostenkowski closeted himself in a cramped room on the second floor of the Capitol to hear what the Democratic members of his committee had to say. And from every corner, he was berated by people who were usually his allies. They complained that the capital-gains tax cut was a break for the rich, which Democrats should have no part in promoting. "Democrats should not be undoing tax reform," one member protested. Some, like the feisty Representative Charles Rangel of New York, even suggested that the chairman was playing footsy with the President to his own party's detriment—which, of course, he was.

In the midst of the protestations, however, the lone voice of Ed Jenkins rose in favor of the capital-gains cut. "I don't want anyone to be under the misapprehension that capital gains won't be offered for a vote," he said. Then he began working behind the scenes to make it so.

He did so with the unspoken backing of Rostenkowski. Over dinner one night that spring at Morton's of Chicago Steak House, a favorite redoubt of both men, Jenkins had tested Rostenkowski on the question of cutting capital gains. The chairman had mouthed the party line of opposition to the cut, but Jenkins saw beyond his words to his meaning. "I can see your lips moving, but I have trouble reading your eyebrows and shoulders," Jenkins had said, and from then on knew he had the chairman's sanction to move forward.

In effect, Rostenkowski had deputized Jenkins to carry out the terms of his pact with the President. When members of the committee wanted extra revenue to pay for their pet projects, Rostenkowski's staff directed them to talk to Jenkins. When Jenkins needed cost estimates for the temporary capital-gains tax cut he contemplated proposing, the chairman permitted him to get them promptly from the Joint Tax Committee. And, more important, when Jenkins maneuvered to get enough votes for his tax package, Rostenkowski did not stand in his way, as he surely could have done.

• • •

One of Jenkins's first Democratic recruits for the capital-gains tax cut was Representative Beryl Anthony of Arkansas, and no one was surprised. Anthony had acquired a reputation on the Ways and Means Committee of being extremely close to lobbyists. Whenever a business lobbyist wanted a favor, he often thought of Beryl first. And Anthony rarely said no.

Lobbyists were an important part of Anthony's life-style. On many weekends he could be found crouching in a duck blind with some of Washington's biggest-name lobbyists. He had even cofounded a duck-hunting club with one of the city's biggest tax lobbyists: J. D. Williams. The Blackwater Hunt Club was a marshy eight-hundred-acre farm in Maryland, only three hours or so by car from the capital. Surely not by coincidence, Blackwater was formed in 1981, the same year that Anthony became a member of the powerful Ways and Means Committee.

Later, when Anthony needed some financial help, his lobbyist buddies were eager to lend a hand. In 1988, Anthony wanted to unload his $34,000 investment in Blackwater. So he turned to Williams and another lobbyist, Tommy Boggs, who was also a club member. By brokering the sale of Anthony's share to a third lobbyist named Colin Matthews, who financed his purchase with a $25,000 loan from the pension fund of Williams's law firm, they made sure Anthony got back the full amount of his initial investment.

Anthony, for his part, always seemed willing to assist the lobbyists. The Jenkins capital-gains plan was a perfect opportunity. Williams's lobbying firm represented both Century 21 Real Estate Corporation and the business interests of Fort Worth multimillionaire Robert Bass, both of which stood to profit mightily from a lower tax rate on gains from real estate sales. Tommy Boggs's firm lobbied for the American Stock Exchange and for PaineWebber Incorporated, which would see stock commissions soar if stock sales could be stimulated by a capital-gains tax cut. A third Blackwater member was Jim Free of Walker Associates, which lobbied for the National Association of Small Business Investment Companies, a trade group of venture capitalists who were pushing strongly for a capital-gains preference. Colin Matthews's law firm, Vinson & Elkins, represented the investment firms Merrill Lynch, Salomon Brothers, and Goldman, Sachs & Company, all of which would obviously benefit from a lower capital-gains tax.

There was also a connection between Anthony's capital-gains

position and a prominent tax lobbyist named R. Duffy Wall. In 1988, the same year he sold his stake in the hunt club, Anthony persuaded the Washington-based Wall to invest with him in a small manufacturing company in his southern Arkansas district. With investments of $190,000 each on the same day, they each became one-third owners of Porterco Incorporated, a Magnolia, Arkansas, maker of soft-sided ice chests.

Wall was one of the most active lobbyists around the congressional tax-writing committees. And like other lobbyists, he did more than just make personal contributions; he organized entire fund-raising events. Lobbyists all over town were forever getting invitations to fund-raisers held in Wall's well-appointed offices near the Willard Hotel. He had so many clients that he was not just a lobbyist, but the head of an entire stable of lobbyists. His lobbying firm, R. Duffy Wall & Associates, employed lobbyists with ties to both Democrats and Republicans throughout the government, so that corporate clients could gain access to important people anywhere.

Wall and his lobbying firm's PAC contributed to Anthony's campaigns and to the House Democrats' campaign committee, which Anthony chaired. What's more, Wall and Anthony were on the same side of important issues before the Ways and Means Committee, including capital gains. One of Wall's longtime tax clients was the Securities Industry Association, which made campaign contributions to Anthony and also paid him a $2,000 honorarium to give a speech. Few issues were more important to the securities association than capital gains.

Anthony was also a champion for a second longtime client of Wall's, the Pharmaceutical Manufacturers Association. Much to the pleasure of Coretech, the R&D tax-credit lobby, Anthony was the chief House sponsor of 861 legislation—the tax break that allowed multinational corporations, especially pharmaceutical companies, to allocate more of their research spending in the United States. For this, Anthony was richly rewarded in both honoraria and campaign contributions from the drug industry. In early 1989, an invitation was mailed around Washington to "a dinner honoring Beryl Anthony," to be held at an upper-crust eatery called the City Club, in downtown Washington. "We hope you will join us at dinner," the letter stated simply. "A contribution of $1,000 is requested and checks should be made payable to: Anthony for Congress." The letter was signed by lobbyists whose employers were active members of Coretech.

Anthony was also treated to an Adopt-a-Member exercise by Ken Kay. For two days early in 1989, Kay and a professor from the University of Arkansas had traveled around the state to visit newspaper editorial boards and sing the praises of Beryl Anthony. Kay had made similar trips for other major Coretech backers. "It's a high-road way of expressing appreciation," Kay asserted. "Politicians are truly appreciative when you get on a plane and spend a couple days in their district talking to opinion leaders about what a good job they've done."

Anthony returned these favors by remaining one of Coretech's most ardent backers. He even appeared on a videotape produced by Coretech to lobby his fellow legislators. The program, *America's R & D Challenge*, starred other lawmakers whose districts Kay had visited, such as GOP Senator John Danforth of Missouri. "I believe that having a tax on section 861 research and development is very punitive," Anthony explained earnestly in his high-pitched voice. "Basically what it is saying is that you're being taxed as though you've done some of your domestic research in foreign countries, and I think that's a disincentive to domestic research."

Because of Anthony's unfailing support for corporate causes, his own fund-raiser in that spring of 1989 was one of the best-attended lobbying events of the season. It was held on the evening of Tuesday, June 6, a glorious night with weather so temperate that it was hard to tell there was any weather at all. Wayne Thevenot attended, with Laura Ison on his arm and a National Realty Committee check in his hand. The event was held in the newly constructed Washington Harbour complex of expensive shops, palatial condominiums, and overpriced office space, which overlooked the Potomac River in Georgetown, just down from the Kennedy Center.

Thevenot was as chummy with Anthony at his fund-raiser as he had been at the Greenbrier. And that sort of open-armed welcome was important to him and to his lobbying business. "It's nice to be seen," Thevenot said afterward. "It's important in a lot of ways. It's important that you be seen as being a player in the game. You show up, members see you there, and over time the cumulative effect is that you are seen as a participant in the process. You are a player. You're a contributor, a benefactor. And that leads to other things. We get hired usually on the recommendation of other people in town. Other lobbyists. And it is important that you be seen and known as a participant in the process at a fairly high level. They take note of who Beryl slaps on the back and says, 'Hey, buddy, let me talk to you about so-and-so.' All of that stuff creates the impression, hopefully correct, that these are friends of mine. For entrepreneurs like myself who represent several clients, it's important that when someone is looking around for a firm to hire, your name pops up as being someone who moves smoothly and easily with the power brokers. When reputation and image are the currency of your realm, you have to keep that stuff going."

When Representative John Dingell, chairman of the House Energy and Commerce Committee, approached Thevenot with a hearty handshake that night, the subject on his mind was the same as that occupying many others at the cocktail party, including the guest of honor. "When are we going shooting?" the big-fisted legislator playfully asked the lobbyist, and the conversation went on from there.

· · ·

In mid-June, the House Democrats finally got around to choosing their new leadership. Jim Wright's successor was never in doubt; he was the respected Representative Thomas Foley of Washington State, who was already the majority leader. But until Tony Coelho decided to bow out, the race to replace Foley was a contest between Coelho, the number three Democrat, and the wily Jenkins, champion of the R&D tax credit and capital-gains tax cut.

For a brief time, Jenkins had a chance to beat Coelho because of the latter's problems with junk bonds. He also had the backing of Rostenkowski. But when Coelho resigned, the dynamics of the race changed completely. Representative Richard Gephardt of Missouri, who had run unsuccessfully for President in 1988, was drafted for the job and was almost immediately a shoo-in to win. Gephardt's presidential aspirations were supported enthusiastically by many of his House colleagues, and they were quick to pick him as their number two leader when fate gave them the chance.

But Jenkins refused to drop out of the race. His run, he said, was meant to make a statement on behalf of other Southerners and conservative Democrats who for too long had been neglected by the party's liberal majority. On Wednesday, June 14, Jenkins got 76 of the 257 votes cast by the Democratic caucus, a respectable tally but not nearly enough to win the job, which went instead to Gephardt.

Afterward, Congress finally drew a deep breath and tried to regain its bearings. It was also then that the next phase of lobbying began: the reactive phase. Now that their messages had been spread and their supporters had been found, lobbyists set themselves up to respond to the actions and requests of the government officials with whom they had worked all year. The decisions of government were not theirs to make. But they had to move quickly to help their friends and, sometimes, to thwart their enemies once legislation began to move. In this case, the direction things took was especially pleasing to Mr. Capital Gains, Mark Bloomfield, and to Coretech.

· · ·

As understated as Rostenkowski was in his effort on behalf of the capital-gains tax cut, Mark Bloomfield was frenetic. At the first whiff of Rostenkowski's interest, he lunged for the telephone. He talked and he plotted and he made notes to himself in his tiny, precise script. His first calls went out to the Capital Gains Coalition, the loose amalgam of trade groups that lobbied for a cut in the rate. They convened in his K Street office and made plans with a new resolve. Then Bloomfield contacted his friends in the executive branch and tried to coordinate his efforts with them. "In many ways, I'm just a glorified staffer," he said, with the assignment of cutting capital-gains taxes.

The Capital Gains Coalition included lobbyists for the U.S. Chamber of Commerce, the National Venture Capital Association, and the Securities Industry Association, as well as timber and small-business groups. Ed Hatcher's American Electronics Association, a mainstay of Coretech, was also an important player with the capital-gains group. With renewed interest on Capitol Hill, Bloomfield also devoted an increasing share of the American council's efforts to capital gains, including its regular breakfast meetings at the Republican Club on Capitol Hill.

On Thursday, June 22, Bloomfield paid Beryl Anthony to speak at the council's breakfast. To Bloomfield's delight, the Democratic lawmaker made a plea for the capital-gains tax cut and proudly showed off one of the Capital Gains Coalition's propaganda buttons. It read: A DIFFERENTIAL MAKES A DIFFERENCE. Another breakfast guest, at a later date, was Deputy Treasury Secretary John Robson. "A lower tax rate for long-term capital gains is a key element of President Bush's economic program," he said, and ended his address by saying that broad support from the business community was critical to passage of the break.

In the meantime, the Capital Gains Coalition tried to build the case that the tax cut had support from the hinterlands. The electronics association, which had categorized its 3,500 members by congressional district and could call up specialized mailing lists instantly, sent letters to its politically active members in key congressional districts across the country. This time, under the direction of Hatcher, it targeted members of the Ways and Means Committee. One letter, to a constituent of Democratic Representative Jim Moody of Wisconsin, read this way:

Dear Mr. Bucolt:

In the next two weeks, the Ways and Means Committee of the U.S. House of Representatives will begin to consider lowering the tax on capital gains. WE NEED YOUR IMMEDIATE ASSISTANCE IN URGING THEM TO DO SO.

As you know, your company is located in the district of a Ways and Means Committee member. Each of these Members will help determine whether or not a capital gains differential becomes law.

Please call your Congressman (or ask for his legislative assistant on tax issues) IMMEDIATELY and voice your support for a differential. The Capitol Hill switchboard is 202-225-3121. Simply dial this number and ask for the appropriate office. You can also send a Mailgram by calling Western Union at 1-800-325-6000.

If you need assistance in identifying your Congressman or have other questions, please call Ed Hatcher with AEA at 202-682-9110. Also, let Ed know once you have made contact with your congressional office.

Our message is a basic one. A capital gains differential will help lower the cost of capital, which will help create more jobs, spur entrepreneurial activity, and enhance American competitiveness. When talking to your Congressman or staff, provide personal examples whenever possible.

The AEA appreciates your assistance on this vital issue.

Sincerely,
J. Richard Iverson
President

The Capital Gains Coalition also tried to inspire some pressure from the grass roots. It decided to target major campaign contributors of selected Ways and Means members, guessing that they would have both clout with the lawmakers and an interest in cutting taxes on capital gains. So, at Charly Walker's urging, the coalition hired Targeted Communications Corporation, an affiliate of his own lobbying firm, to contact voters quickly. Bloomfield decided that he should be the one to sign the letters, which went out in late June. Here are excerpts from one of them:

June 23

Dear Mrs. Tavoularis,

In a matter of days the House Ways and Means Committee of Congress will vote on whether to cut your capital gains tax rate.

The outcome of this vote could have a very big impact on America's economic competitiveness.

However, while bipartisan congressional support is growing, it will take strong public support to ensure passage of a capital gains tax cut.

That's why I'm writing to you today. Because you are a knowledgeable and politically active leader in your community, I'm certain that Congressman William Coyne will listen carefully to your views on the issue.

But, if you agree with us on the importance of a capital gains tax cut, you must act quickly. Congressman Coyne and the other key members of the House Ways and Means Committee could vote on this issue within the next few days.

And so, I urge you to call or write The Honorable William Coyne at his district office: 1000 Liberty Ave., Suite 2009, Pitts-

burgh, Pa. 15222, (412) 644-2870. Or call him directly in Washington at (202) 225-2301.

We at the American Council for Capital Formation are advocating a capital gains tax cut that makes economic sense . . .
is fair to all sectors of the economy . . . and will raise federal
revenue.

We represent a broad group, from advanced technology
companies to entrepreneurs to individual investors as well. For
more than a decade, our coalition has been in the forefront of
all capital gains tax cut initiatives.

I've enclosed a more detailed Briefing Paper for your review,
but here is a summary of reasons why we believe this capital
gains tax cut should be permanent, sizable and broad-based.

And if you have any additional questions, please don't hesi-
tate to contact me here at the Council.

Thank you for your attention to this important matter. Your
opinion could well make the difference on how Congressman
Coyne votes.

I hope that I can count on you.

Sincerely,
Mark Bloomfield
President

In addition to Coyne, the coalition targeted eleven other Democratic members of the committee. According to a memorandum
given to Bloomfield by Targeted Communications, 1,290 voters
were contacted in total, 708 of whom said they would call their
member of Congress. The cost: $34,000, or nearly $50 a call. That
was a big price to pay—but, Bloomfield thought, not too big for
the cause.

* * *

While the capital-gains people worked on the outside, Coretech
worked the inside to extend the R&D tax credit. The Ways and
Means Committee was scheduled to begin drafting its tax bill during the week of July 17, and the R&D lobbyists felt confident.
Thanks to Jenkins's efforts and the success of Lobby Day, twenty-
six of the committee's thirty-six members were cosponsors of the
proposed legislation to make the credit permanent. The only obsta-

cle that remained was budgetary. With the deficit always looming, the lobbyists needed to worry about whether there would be enough revenue to pay for extending the tax break indefinitely.

On the Wednesday before the drafting session, the committee staff handed Jenkins a piece of paper that gave an affirmative answer to that question. The document contained a proposal by Rostenkowski to make the R&D credit permanent—a significant concession that was testament to the credit's popularity on the panel and to the chairman's support of Jenkins. The new proposal served as the starting point of what in the next few days would become intensive negotiations.

Coretech already had done plenty of homework. In response to academic criticism, it had worked closely with the Treasury Department to devise a new structure for the credit. Its intention was not to put more money into the hands of its dues-paying members, but rather to save the credit by answering complaints about how the tax break operated. The result would probably mean less subsidy for some Coretech members, and more to others, but at least there would still be a subsidy there to be gotten.

Coretech's point man on these details was Paul Oosterhuis, a $325-an-hour tax lawyer with Skadden, Arps, Slate, Meagher & Flom, and a former staffer on the respected Congressional Joint Tax Committee. Nearly a decade earlier, Oosterhuis had been one of the few Joint Tax Committee aides to leave government for the more lucrative field of lobbying, a transition that was then considered akin to treason. "The Joint Committee staff is the place where you are naturally suspicious of lobbyists. That's ingrained into you. So when you leave, it's hard to turn around and be one them," he said in an interview in his office, whose coffee table boasted a copy of the 1954 tax code. "We laugh about it now, those of us who have gone out," he added.

The flaxen-haired lobbyist helped lead the ragtag group of electronics-company executives who lobbied successfully for the original R&D tax credit in 1981. His group had won just on the basis of its message's appeal. That had to be the case, since the group had virtually no lobbying organization or political cash. The allure of the message ended in 1984, when Rostenkowski and his staff decided to make the credit just another one of the so-called extenders, the dozen tax breaks that expired annually and for which revenue had to be constantly scrounged in order for them to have any chance of renewal.

This yearly uncertainty was the perennial headache of the research community. But it also had been a steady source of employment for Oosterhuis and Coretech. "We're going to do you the greatest favor," Rostenkowski aide–turned–lobbyist John Salmon used to like to tell Oosterhuis. "There's no way we're going to get this through without a sunset date, and that's going to give you something to do for the rest of your career." Salmon's warning was more than a joke; it reflected Rostenkowski's true misgivings about the public value of the credit.

Oosterhuis also harbored doubts about the tax break. The problem, he said, was that, like all credits, it was an inefficient subsidy. It also was simply too small to do much good; it was a $1-billion-a-year credit in an economy that spent $60 billion a year on research. "I personally feel right now, even with it enacted, that the credit is sufficiently small that it doesn't necessarily accomplish all that much other than something that's symbolic," Oosterhuis said.

Still, it was Oosterhuis's job to write a statute that both his clients and the lawmakers would accept. He did so with great verve and at least some introspection. "I guess where I've changed over the years is that you get cynical about most things government does, and yet you don't want to say government shouldn't do anything," he said. "So you start holding things to a little lower standard."

The standard that Coretech started with in the summer of 1989 was the Rostenkowski proposal it received from Jenkins. Oosterhuis and Kay were thrilled that, for the first time, Rostenkowski appeared to want to make the credit permanent. But the devil was in the details. Oosterhuis and his assistant faxed the proposal—and their interpretation of it—to corporate Coretech members, and waited for their response. First thing in the morning of Thursday, July 13, the reactions rolled in, and they were decidedly negative.

"The tax people didn't understand the numbers," Oosterhuis complained. But that was a reasonable response. The staff proposed to change the credit from a tax break that was calculated solely on the basis of research spending growth to one that was based on a ratio of research spending to corporate sales. The new structure would silence critics who said that corporations were able to tinker with their research spending levels in order to increase their tax benefits. But the change also made projecting the value of the new credit difficult. Millions of dollars of tax breaks hung in the balance.

On Friday, July 14, Kay and Eizenstat met with congressional staffers in their offices to try to better understand what the chairman was suggesting. They asked very basic questions, like the definition of "sales," which were important to the big corporations they represented. Finally, they understood that Rostenkowski was willing to be at least a little flexible so long as his budget for the tax break was not exceeded: about $4.4 billion over five fiscal years, roughly the same size it was at the moment. The lobbyists agreed to talk over the weekend to find a compromise.

Saturday and Sunday were full days of labor for the Coretech team. Since Oosterhuis's law firm specialized in mergers and acquisitions, some Coretech companies were leery of giving their proprietary financial data to him directly. So, according to Oosterhuis, some of the numbers had to be disguised before they were entered into his computer, which was kept behind the high-security locks of Skadden, Arps. The sales numbers were altered in Kay's law firm so that they always totaled an even 100, and everything else was made proportionate. With those numbers in hand, the lobbyists computed and conversed through the weekend—sometimes in four-way telephone calls—to devise alternatives to the Rostenkowski formula. Their goal was to help as many of their clients as they could without busting Rostenkowski's budget.

On Monday morning, the day that the drafting session officially was to begin, Kay and Eizenstat trooped over to the Rayburn House Office Building and reported their findings to Jenkins. He was pleased with their efforts and delegated to them the responsibility for getting the best deal that they could from the staff of the Ways and Means Committee. This was far from a minor assignment. In effect—and in fact—these select corporate lobbyists were not only allowed but *encouraged* to negotiate with committee staffers—emissaries of Rostenkowski—to devise what could well become a new public law.

Late in the afternoon, Kay, Eizenstat, and other lobbyists descended into the basement of the Rayburn building, where the drafting session was to take place in a hearing room. There they met, away from prying eyes, in an anteroom directly adjoining the hearing room. It was white and windowless, and located down the hall from the House's barbershop and a carry-out restaurant. The restaurant came in handy more than once during the extraordinary negotiating session that took place between the lobbyists and the government-paid aides.

The Coretech lobbyists came armed with a checklist of items they would have liked to see changed in the Rostenkowski proposal. One would have helped start-up companies. Another would have benefited small and fast-growing businesses. A third would have assisted a few of the biggest corporations in future years. The negotiations lasted into the evening, and were cordial and businesslike.

In the end, the committee staff, who were mostly Democratic aides, proved generous—to a point. All but one of Coretech's suggestions were accepted. That single provision, the one that would have been most helpful to companies in future years, was deemed to be too expensive. Instead, the lobbyists won the promise of a study on the subject. It was the price they had to pay for getting what they had long wanted: a permanent R&D tax credit.

The next morning, Tuesday, July 18, the lobbyists received telephone calls from the staff. The deal was done, they were told. And, incredibly, it was almost everything the lobbyists had wanted. Rostenkowski had agreed to accept a permanent 20 percent credit that would be applied to the ratio of research spending to sales over a given period. What was more, the provision would be part of the chairman's own starting-point proposal for the drafting session. And that gave it a great advantage.

Oosterhuis telephoned Kay as soon as he got the news. "I'm numb," Oosterhuis said.

"I can understand that," Kay replied, drawing a deep breath.

· · ·

The Ways and Means drafting session was held in a basement because the committee's usual place—a spacious, high-ceilinged room in the Longworth House Office Building—was being refurbished, with the help of lobbyists' dollars. The overhaul was timed for the committee's two-hundredth anniversary that year, an event Rostenkowski took very seriously. The broad-shouldered chairman saw the anniversary almost as if it were his own birthday, and lobbyists all over town were eager to bring him presents.

The celebration was yet another example of how lobbyists reached deeply into the government by pandering to the vanity of decision-makers. This time they opened the doors of power through purely financial means. The event was bankrolled with a staggering three-quarters of a million dollars, almost all of which was raised from wealthy corporations and some labor unions. Sponsors got to send representatives to sit beside the much-sought-after members of the tax-writing committee.

Rostenkowski made sure that every committee member attended. He was especially aggressive about getting one *former* committee member there as well: President George Bush. During one of his visits to the White House, Rostenkowski invited Bush to attend both the lunch and the dinner of the day-long celebration. At first, the President resisted; attending both affairs would have constituted a remarkable commitment for a President. But Rostenkowski continued to insist. "You're going to both of them!" he recalled saying. And in a grand—and calculated—gesture, the President agreed. And during the bicentennial dinner, on Monday, July 24, Rostenkowski repaid Bush with a confession that stunned the audience—and proved how deeply moved by the celebration Rostenkowski actually was. He said he had come just "one step short" of endorsing Bush for President in 1988.

Well before that evening, lobbyists had realized how much of his ego Rostenkowski had invested in the event. And they were quick to exploit this, making a great show of expending energy to raise money for his celebration. Lobbyist Robert Juliano, the one-man business-labor coalition, was an important cog in this fund-raising machine. Weeks before the dinner, Juliano and Ed Hanley, president of the hotel and restaurant workers union, had treated Rostenkowski to cocktails, dinner, and flattery at the union's Georgetown headquarters. About fifteen other union presidents attended as well. "I was a facilitator," Juliano explained modestly. "I helped make sure that people met."

The dinner was meant to smooth Rostenkowski's sometimes

rough relations with the labor-union movement. And in the process more than bread was buttered. During the course of the meal, William Wynn, president of the United Food and Commercial Workers International Union, rose to praise Rostenkowski and to suggest that his bicentennial event was a cause worth contributing to. Wynn's own union chipped in $20,000; Hanley and Juliano's shop gave another $15,000.

Another of Juliano's major clients, American Express, did not need any prodding to contribute to Rostenkowski's bicentennial. The event had gotten its start when Rostenkowski contacted American Express's chairman, James Robinson. At Rostenkowski's behest, Robinson called a few of his friends, notably John Akers, the chairman of IBM, and John Welch, the chief executive of General Electric. Rostenkowski added a few other names, including several from Chicago. "The dollars just came pouring in," said Donald Kennon of the U.S. Capitol Historical Society, the nonprofit group that organized the celebration.

Twenty-two companies gave $25,000 each. Even some that were not asked, such as the Sara Lee Corporation, sent in checks. Real estate developer Donald Trump kicked in $10,000. In all, forty corporations and unions paid for a celebration fund that the historical society said totaled $768,949.67. Companies that gave $25,000 were a *Who's Who* of corporate America, including AT&T, Anheuser-Busch, Arkansas Electric Cooperative, Beneficial Management, the Chicago Mercantile Exchange, General Electric, General Motors, Hewlett-Packard, Johnson & Johnson, Kraft General Foods, Loews, Pfizer, Philip Morris, Price Waterhouse, Pritzker Charitable Fund, Procter & Gamble, RJR Nabisco, Joseph E. Seagram & Sons, and U.S. Fidelity & Guaranty.

Donors were quick to deny they had any sinister motives for their participation. IBM, AT&T, and Philip Morris representatives characterized their companies' contributions as "educational" and "cultural." But W. Minor Carter, a senior vice president of U.S. Fidelity & Guaranty, told *The Wall Street Journal*: "We're not dopes, you know. We know that if you get to do something helpful for a powerful body like Ways and Means, it could turn out good for you later." And American Express spokesman Larry Armour acknowledged: "Everyone wants to be on the good side of the chairman of this particular committee. I would be lying if I didn't admit that."

Congressional critic Ellen Miller of the Center for Responsive Politics went a step further. "It's just another opportunity for the corporate and labor leaders to be benefactors for members of Congress," she said. "And in this day and age, that means access." Every lobbyist who contributed knew that the money went not only to glorify the Ways and Means Committee as an institution, but, more important, to laud its current chairman, who would have a lot of say about the fate of the issues they cared about.

So much money was contributed, in fact, that there was almost no limit to the ways in which the chairman could toast himself. Half a million dollars went for an hour-long documentary on the committee's history. But a full third of the twenty-two-minute preview screened during the bicentennial dinner focused exclusively on Rostenkowski. A 526-page, four-pound history of the committee, which was paid for with at least $100,000 of lobbyists' money, opened with a two-page, full-color picture of the current Ways and Means Committee—with Rostenkowski in the center. Another $100,000 was used to pay for the dinner, which brought together current and former committee members, some of whom were lobbyists. That total included $10,022.65 for gold cuff links and stickpins, and $70,685 for hardcover committee histories, all of which Rostenkowski dispensed as favors.

In the midst of the dinner, a corporate vice president approached the chairman. "I'm surprised your arm isn't in a sling," the executive said.

"Why?" Rostenkowski asked.

"For patting yourself on the back so much."

Rostenkowski barely cracked a smile.

Juliano was not smiling either. Despite his money-raising efforts, he did not go to the dinner. He relinquished his seat at the union's table to a friend of Hanley's who was visiting for the day from Chicago. Juliano gamely asserted that he was not upset, but clearly he chafed a little. One person who might have gotten him in—but did not—was Denise Ferguson, a former Matsui aide who was then a lobbyist for American Express. She was close to many Ways and Means staffers and was known for making her beach house available to tax aides in need of recreation. But, more important, she was Jim Robinson's point person for the bicentennial event. "She snuck people in because she helped with the arrangements," Juliano said.

But she did not make room for Juliano. "This is a very important day," he said with some regret in his voice. But he was not without something to do. For the night he contented himself by dining with a new lady friend.

· · ·

As Rostenkowski celebrated, Jenkins conspired. He worked diligently to knit together a majority of the thirty-six-member committee in favor of a cut in capital gains. And in time he managed to put together a slim, one-vote majority for a proposal. The Jenkins forces consisted of a solid core of six Democrats—known as the Gang of Six—and all thirteen committee Republicans. The Democrats were Jenkins; Anthony of Arkansas; Ronnie Flippo of Alabama; Andy Jacobs of Indiana; and Jake Pickle and Michael Andrews of Texas.

The Jenkins proposal would have reduced the top tax rate on capital gains for two and a half years, to 19.6 percent from the existing nominal rate of 28 percent. After that, the rate would have been set at a maximum of 28 percent, and the gains would have been indexed for inflation. Proponents said the measure would raise revenue in the short run and boost economic growth in the long term.

When word of the Jenkins offensive reached the ears of the House's new Democratic leaders, they tried to counterattack. Speaker Tom Foley got on the telephone and persuaded a few wavering Ways and Means members, such as Representative Frank Guarini of New Jersey, to toe the party line and shun the Jenkins plan. Foley and Majority Leader Richard Gephardt also met privately with the Ways and Means Democrats to emphasize their opposition to the tax cut.

But when Foley appealed to Representative Pickle, one of the Gang of Six, the Texan told him the request was "like waiting outside the delivery room and having your mother say, 'Son, you ought not to have kissed that girl.' " Jenkins had worked too quickly and the still-fledgling leadership had reacted too late to stop him. "I don't see a single one of the six Democrats peeling off," said Representative Andrews, another member of the Gang.

When Jenkins began to design his capital-gains proposal, he turned to his staff for technical advice. In Congress, there were always formats to follow and protocols to protect, and the staff was master of those details. But Jenkins's tax aide, Douglas Ashworth, was as new to the process as the Democratic leaders were to their jobs. So, on the night that Jenkins gave Ashworth the particulars of his evolving proposal, Ashworth bypassed his word processor and headed for the telephone. He called the man who had preceded him in his job: the lobbyist Jim Rock.

Rock had left Jenkins's employ at the end of 1987, after eight years as a staffer on Capitol Hill. His first job on the Hill had been an internship for Senator Lloyd Bentsen of Texas. He then went to work full-time for Texas Representative Kent Hance, who became notorious when, in 1981, he served as the Democratic front man for the Reagan-backed tax-cut bill. Hance left the House soon thereafter, and Rock went to work for Jenkins, a Ways and Means Democrat who was just as conservative. Now, as a lobbyist, Rock was once again part of a team that threatened to beat the leading members of his mentor's political party.

Rock was more than happy to help his old boss. As a lobbyist for Gold and Liebengood, a gun-for-hire lobbying shop, he was always searching for ways to get inside, to learn more about the outlook for legislation, and to become part of the process if he could. His clients included a galaxy of corporate giants, among them Phillips Petroleum, Salomon Brothers, and MCI Communications. "I am the foot soldier, the deliverer of the message," Rock said of his vocation. "It's not much different than the way I worked when I was still with Jenkins—maneuvering and manipulating. Lobbying is the extension of those same skills."

At age thirty-five, the dark-bearded Rock was well trained for his job. He had graduated first in his class from the master's program at the LBJ School of Public Affairs in Austin. And as the tax aide to the pro-business Hance and Jenkins, he had encountered a wide range of lobbyists over the years. "Some people find it distasteful, but I don't," he said. "Why do I lobby? Well, why does somebody who goes to law school want to be a lawyer? I really enjoy this kind of work."

Rock was born in Brownsville, Texas, because his hometown of Port Isabel was too small to have a hospital. Hard by the Gulf of Mexico, Port Isabel was considered one of the most impoverished communities in the nation. Rock's father was a shrimper who barely made $10,000 in the best of years, yet he was considered well off by Port Isabel standards. "My family was poor, but didn't know it," Rock said. He and his father sometimes would spend weeks together on the water, hauling in what catch they could from the sometimes reluctant gulf. His father was Cajun, the son of a trapper and shipbuilder from the bayous of Louisiana. His mother's family had settled nearby in southern Texas after leaving their native Mexico.

In Washington, Rock was determined to leave his working-class roots far behind. As a sideline, he part-owned and rented thirteen houses in northern Virginia; he hoped that this small real estate empire would be his ticket to early retirement someday. One reason he had left Capitol Hill to lobby was to increase his income enough to support his burgeoning business. But he was careful never to stray far from Jenkins, remaining the congressman's friend and adviser.

At first, Rock's arrangement with Jenkins and Ashworth was informal. Before each drafting session during the week, Rock met with Ashworth to update the Jenkins plan. But eventually, Rock cut out the middleman and met directly with Jenkins in his office, which was upstairs from the basement Ways and Means drafting room. The sessions became a daily ritual through much of July.

As a result, Rock became the keeper of the details of Jenkins's plan, an important brief in the information-driven capital. Jenkins dictated the big-picture particulars, and Rock served as his faithful scribe. When Rostenkowski accepted the new R&D credit, Jenkins instructed Rock to place it into the ever-growing Jenkins alternative. Which Rock dutifully did.

On smaller issues, Rock was sometimes able to help his clients. When Jenkins gave Rock leeway to draft the capital-gains cut, for instance, the lobbyist included in the fine print a provision that would benefit real estate developers like his client the American

Resort and Residential Development Association. The provision would have kept in law a limit on the amount of tax benefits that real estate developers were required to refund to the federal government after they sold properties. But in the end, the Joint Tax Committee estimated that such a provision would cost billions of dollars—far too much to keep it in the Jenkins plan. So Jenkins said it had to go. Rock did his bidding with no regrets.

In the hallway outside the closed-door drafting sessions during that muggy July, Rock became known as one of the leading experts on what Jenkins was up to. And, increasingly, it looked as if whatever Jenkins wanted, he would get.

• • •

Another former aide who was busy being an inside player during the drafting session was Kenneth Kies, a former chief tax counsel of the Ways and Means Republican staff. Like Rock, he had left the Hill to become a lobbyist in 1987, but remained close to his mentor, Representative Guy Vander Jagt. The baby-faced Kies had first worked for the Michigan Republican as a summer intern during his college days in 1975, but after law school and four years of private practice in Ohio, he had returned to Washington in 1981 as an assistant minority counsel to the Ways and Means Committee, the panel on which Vander Jagt served. Kies was elevated to the top spot the next year.

The chain-smoking Vander Jagt was a senior, but decidedly distracted, member of the committee. Most of his attention went to his chairmanship of the House Republicans' fund-raising committee. He spent most of his time away from Ways and Means deliberations, speaking on behalf of GOP candidates. It had been Kies's job to keep Vander Jagt informed about taxes when he was on the road.

Even though Kies was no longer on the congressional payroll—indeed, even though his job as a lobbyist was to influence those who were—he continued to serve Vander Jagt in the same way. The lawmaker even admitted, "I am forever calling him and saying, 'Ken, can you explain this to me?' " And Kies added, "What I do now is not all that dissimilar to what I did on the Hill."

The closeness of this relationship came in handy when Kies was hired at $210 an hour by Iron Ore Company of Canada (IOC).

The Ohio-based mining company wanted an exemption from the corporate minimum-tax law that Kies helped draft in 1985, when he was still a staffer. And Kies was poised to make the exemption happen—with Vander Jagt as his champion.

With Vander Jagt's sanction, Kies had met with several Ways and Means members and senior committee staffers over the summer to lay the groundwork for the IOC amendment. Since Vander Jagt was supporting the plan, the only hurdle, the staffers told him, was its cost. In cash-strapped Washington, no problem could be fixed unless the fix was paid for. So Kies was forced to find an ox to gore.

To do this, he sat down with the red-haired James Clarke, the current Republican tax counsel, to come up with a tax increase to balance the tax cut he was seeking. The two lawyers worked well together; Kies, in fact, had helped hire Clarke for his job on the committee. When they were both staffers they had often combed through lists of revenue-raising ideas to find just the right offset for their bosses' proposals. And that summer, they had engaged in precisely the same kind of search, even though one of them was now a lobbyist. They came up with a plan they thought had merit—and little pain for the populace at large. They chose to clobber the nation's nearly ten million cellular-telephone users with a surprise tax increase. In effect, their proposal would have made it harder for cellular-telephone owners to write off their high-tech toys.

Arrangements like those of Kies and Rock were not unusual in Washington, where former staffers formed a close-knit network and support system for the lawmakers and executive-branch officials for whom they once worked. This was especially true if the aides stayed in town to lobby. And increasingly, that was precisely what they did.

In the few short years since the passage of the historic Tax Reform Act of 1986, fully half of the aides who had worked with members of the congressional tax-writing committees had left their Capitol Hill jobs to lobby for many of the same corporate interests that were the bill's biggest victims. The career path did not have any partisan coloration. Democratic aides left to work for business interests with about the same frequency as Republican aides did.

Some critics were aghast at the trend. "It's obscene," contended Representative Pete Stark of California. "They have just sold out for the big bucks to take on special-interest tax deductions on behalf of huge corporations and rich people." Former aides "have a special kind of access," said congressional critic Ellen Miller. "When you work with someone in that staff-member relationship, you develop a closeness that continues off of the Hill. It raises real questions in the public mind about who's in charge here and who's being represented."

But few of the former aides saw anything wrong or even unusual about their transformation. Some even returned to their old haunts to undo some of the tax provisions they had helped put into the 1986 law. "If you spend a substantial amount of time in this area and you want to leave the Hill, there are limited opportunities to utilize all those skills," said Jonathan Keyserling, a former Matsui aide who now worked as a lobbyist with Black, Manafort, Stone & Kelly. Ex-aides often specialized in the same subjects they dealt with while they worked for Congress, and usually stayed on the same side as their old bosses. William Signer left the office of Representative Charles Rangel of New York in 1985, and, as a lobbyist for Keefe Company, still focused on issues important to his former boss: getting funds for inner-city hospitals and retaining a tax credit that encouraged companies to hire economically disadvantaged workers. "I have made an effort to work on those things that I care about, rather than just picking up clients, period," Signer said. "At least, that's what I think I'm doing."

Becoming a lobbyist was increasingly part of the career plans of congressional staffers. Taking a job on Capitol Hill "became more of a means to an end while I was there," said Carolyn Blaydes, a former tax aide to Representative Tom Downey. "People coming up [as staffers] see it as a way to move up: become a lobbyist and probably double their salary." Added David Raboy, a former top tax aide to Senator William Roth, Jr., of Delaware and a lobbyist with Patton, Boggs & Blow: "It's almost like an internship for a doctor. . . . It's a card you have to punch."

It is difficult to pinpoint what effect such job-switching had on legislation. One thing was certain, though: former staffers had a greater chance of getting their message across than many other special pleaders. "They know you, and they return your phone calls," said Mary Beth Riordan, a lobbyist for Verner, Liipfert and a former aide to Representative Raymond McGrath of New York. "It's definitely an advantage."

Tax aides' lives were made comfortable by the lobbyists who pursued them. Their social lives were largely underwritten by corporate lobbyists who understood well what the aides expected: When they were aides themselves, lobbyists had accorded them the same privileges. "When I was on the Hill," recalled Rich Belas, a lobbyist who had been a tax aide to Senator Robert Dole, "all of my social life was paid for." He was not alone. Another former tax aide complained privately that when he moved to another job in government he missed being picked up by chauffeured car at the office. And a senior Ways and Means staffer said he did not recall ever having to take out his wallet to eat at Bullfeathers, a favorite restaurant near his office.

When Jim Rock was still an aide, and in need of recreation, he would sometimes call his lobbyist friends and ask if they could arrange for him to give a speech to a client of theirs in a sunny spot. Over the years, he had made several such trips. Now that he was a lobbyist, he and other former staffers bankrolled an annual skiing trip to Vail, Colorado, on which they took several of their successors.

· · ·

In the midst of the Ways and Means Committee drafting session, on Tuesday, July 25, another ritual of lobbying comradeship—the fund-raiser—took place a block away from the Hart Senate Office Building on the other side of the Capitol grounds. The event was hosted by Senator Lloyd Bentsen for the campaign of Pete Geren, the man who would later take Jim Wright's vacant seat in Congress. The $500-a-head cocktail party was held at a favorite roost of Washington lobbyists, the 116 Club. So, during a break in the action at Ways and Means that evening, Juliano and Thevenot hopped over there.

A bottle of Scope and some Skin Bracer after-shave lotion were always available on the sink of the men's room at the 116 Club. These were two commodities that no self-respecting lobbyist would do without. Appearances are important in their business. And so are disappearances. So it was there, behind what looked like a boarded-up storefront, that lobbyists and lawmakers had long been able to meet and eat in their own world. Only the limousines outside gave a clue to the tenor of what transpired within.

The club was begun in 1959 as the Quorum Club, the old haunt of Bobby Baker, the former secretary to Senate Democrats. The place then was located in the Carroll Arms Hotel, and its reputation declined along with Baker's. The hotel was eventually torn down to make room for a parking lot, and the club moved to 116 Schott's Court, whence it got its new name, in March 1965.

The club moved two more times and by 1989 it was no longer located at 116 anything. (Its address was 234 Third Street N.E.) Its membership was about three-quarters lobbyists and one-quarter government employees. But it was much easier to become a member as a congressional staffer than as a lobbyist. Preference was given to those who were still on the inside, for the benefit of those who no longer were. It was also cheaper for government employees to join: They paid a $100 initiation fee and $15 monthly dues, compared with a $1,500 fee and $40 monthly for nongovernment people. The 116 Club had about three hundred members, and a fifty-person waiting list.

Lunch was served downstairs, where there were about twenty-five tables and a bar. Crab cakes and homemade ice cream were popular fare. Upstairs were private rooms that were as dowdy as the rest of the place. But the 116 Club was certainly convenient and consistently friendly. This was particularly true for the soon-to-be Representative Geren, who hauled in thousands of dollars that night from his patron Bentsen's lobbyist friends.

Thevenot came armed with two $500 checks, one from the National Realty Committee and the other from a private client from Texas with whom he had had lunch that day at the Occidental, another lobbyist eatery next to the Willard. He persuaded the client to write out a check for the evening's good cause right at the luncheon table. "You don't get 'em like that every day," he boasted. Thevenot attended the fund-raising event, not because he liked—or even knew—Geren, but because one of Bentsen's operatives had asked for the lobbyist's help. "Any friend of Bentsen's is a friend of mine," Thevenot allowed. "I'm sure he's a good American."

Juliano showed up with a check from the hotel workers' union, but he had already done plenty of work on Geren's behalf. At Bentsen's request, a couple of weeks earlier he and two dozen or so other lobbyists had gathered together at the Democratic Club on the House side of the Capitol grounds. Over some wine and mineral water, Bentsen asked them for their help, and they had each agreed to contact other lobbyists to raise money for the candidate. They formed a steering committee and served as organizers for the fund-raising effort. Juliano had been a member of Bentsen's steering committees for years, and was pleased to help the powerful lawmaker again.

Juliano spent only a few minutes at the fund-raiser. But over the past weeks he had spent many telephone calls trying to shake some campaign contributions from his colleagues in the labor movement. At the cocktail party, he mostly made sure to thank the few labor people who showed up at his request. Why did he go to this effort? "It just gets you in the door," he said. By doing this good deed, he had won a chit for access to Bentsen that he might one day need to cash.

Thevenot and Laura Ison lingered a little longer than Juliano, basking in the glow of being in the inner circle. Bentsen was there too, of course, and made his gratitude clear to everyone who had assembled. "I can't promise you he'll have a seat on Ways and Means," Bentsen told the assembled 150 people about his young protégé. "But I *can* guarantee you he'll have a seat on the Senate Finance Committee"—referring to the seat he himself occupied. That, of course, was the seat that everyone in the room really cared most about.

The next day, Wednesday, July 26, Thevenot and his partner at Concord Associates, Bill Boardman, were the recipients of more good news. They put all but the final touches on their high-speed-rail lobbying group, which they had decided to call Maglev USA. In Concord Associates' newly remodeled conference room, Thevenot and Boardman met at 11 A.M. with the nucleus of the new group, which included Grumman, CSX, Westinghouse, and General Electric, among others. The cost of joining: $20,000 each, an amount that paid all lobbying expenses, including salaries for Boardman and Thevenot. For the price, the group, according to the tentative wording of its charter, would "foster and expedite the introduction of magnetically levitated transportation (Maglev) technologies to the U.S. surface transportation system" and "stimulate industrial research and development" of a U.S. technology.

Thevenot and Boardman already had done a lot to get their space-age idea off the ground. In April, they had met over lunch at one of Capitol Hill's best French restaurants, La Colline, with a top appropriations committee aide to Senator J. Bennett Johnston of Louisiana. Thevenot had arranged the meeting by drawing on his Louisiana roots. One of his closest friends was lobbyist Charles McBride, who had worked for Senator Russell Long with Thevenot years ago. McBride had made the telephone call that got the lobbyists together with the Johnston aide, Proctor Jones, which in turn helped them get the ball moving in the appropriations committee to fund a Maglev study. Senator Daniel Moynihan had also done his bit by setting his public-works subcommittee to authorize millions of dollars in new funds for the project. He had also whispered to Johnston about the need for appropriated funds. "We're getting close!" Thevenot exclaimed, but there was more work to be done.

• • •

Back at the Ways and Means Committee drafting session on Thursday, July 27, the tax-writers quietly adopted the Vander Jagt amendment that helped Ken Kies and his client, IOC. It cost $2 million in fiscal 1990 and $22 million over five years. The panel then accepted a second Vander Jagt amendment that placed cellular telephones in the same write-off category as cars and home computers, a change that raised $2 million in fiscal 1990 and a staggering $68 million over the five-year period—three times as much as the loss from the IOC amendment. Both amendments, which had been drafted by Kies, were accepted without dissent.

The next week, the Ways and Means Committee moved forward to consider two major tax proposals. One was Rostenkowski's, which, at the Democratic leader's insistence, did not contain a cut in the capital-gains tax; the other was Jenkins's, which did. Both included the permanent R&D credit negotiated by Coretech. Both also contained a slightly reduced version of the 861 legislation that Coretech had wanted. In other words, Coretech would be a big winner no matter what happened, and, as a lobby, it faded into the background for a while.

Indeed, the basic provisions of the rival tax bills, aside from capital gains, were pretty clear by then. For instance, excise-tax increases were not a serious possibility no matter which package passed. Ken Simonson and Tom Donohue of the trucking associations appeared to have done their job and kept any excise-tax increases out of the legislative debate—at least for the time being. Just in case, members of the CART coalition had managed to get hundreds of cosponsors for a resolution opposing gas-tax increases.

Juliano was also having an easy time of it. His three-martini-lunch deduction was too big to fit neatly into 1989's little tax plan. For a brief moment, though, one of his other corporate clients, the coalition of stock life-insurance companies, seemed about to come in for a bonanza. Under prodding by Democratic leaders to find revenue outside of a capital-gains tax cut, Rostenkowski proposed an $800 million tax increase on mutual life-insurance companies—the archrivals of Juliano's stock-company client. The prospect briefly stirred Juliano and others on his side, but the effort was extremely short-lived. The proposed tax increase was so large and so unexpected that it proved impossible to pass in committee. As soon as the proposal was made, mutual-company lobbyists blanketed the Congress with both letters and personal visits. The Treasury Department also lent a hand by expressing its own reservations about the proposal. It went nowhere, but that was hardly the end of the fight between the stock and mutual life-insurance companies.

Thevenot's real estate clients got nicked. Rostenkowski's search for inconspicuous tax increases led him to restrict an obscure but lucrative loophole that allowed real estate owners to escape taxes by swapping one piece of property for another. These so-called like-kind exchanges were big business for the heavyweight developers who paid Thevenot's retainer. But Thevenot had not had his last day. He took his fight on like-kind exchanges to his home turf in the Senate.

During this ebb and flow, Thevenot and Juliano made only token appearances in the hallway outside the Ways and Means Committee room. The hallway was nicknamed Gucci Gulch because whenever lawmakers were at work it was crowded with well-heeled lobbyists. Juliano showed up one day wearing a purple shirt. Another day, he wore a suede jacket. Thevenot wore mostly conservative blue suits. But despite their differences of style, they agreed that loitering there was a fruitless exercise most of the time. "Futile" was how Thevenot described it.

The real lobbying took place prior to such gatherings. The very latest information—which is valuable only to the most hyperactive clients—and pained arches were about all that could ever be gotten by waiting in the halls. All the real work, for both lobbyists and lawmakers, went on behind closed doors, and occasionally in front of the cameras.

Focusing on the capital-gains issues, Gephardt and Democratic Senator Bill Bradley of New Jersey held a press conference to bash the capital-gains forces for attempting a blasphemy against the tax-reform bill that the two men had helped guide to passage just three years earlier. Gephardt and Bradley also flew the flag of populism, asserting that a capital-gains tax cut would benefit only the richest of the rich. According to the Joint Tax Committee, they explained, nearly 80 percent of the tax benefit of President Bush's proposal to reduce the top tax on capital gains would go to those who earned more than $100,000 a year. And 60 percent of the proposed tax reduction would go to individuals who earned $200,000 a year and over. Those who earned $50,000 and less, who made up more than 80 percent of all American families, would get only 8.6 percent of the benefit. Public citizens groups put out their own propaganda along the same lines.

In response, Mark Bloomfield and his coalition put out a publicity barrage of their own. The liberals' numbers were wrong, they said; middle-class people would be the real beneficiaries of a capital-gains tax cut. So would the small but growing companies that create most of the new jobs in the United States. The National Venture Capital Association unveiled a survey showing that 88 percent of the executives who run what *Business Week* magazine dubbed the "100 best small companies" in America believed that the capital-gains tax should be reduced to encourage enterprises like theirs. The survey came complete with quotable comments from the executives themselves.

With both sides of the capital-gains fight still firing furiously at each other, the Ways and Means drafting session ceased on Monday, July 31. Jenkins had the votes to win, so the Democratic leadership demanded extra time to try to turn the tables. The final vote to determine whether the Rostenkowski or Jenkins plan would prevail was postponed until the fall.

. . .

The stifling-hot Augusts of Washington were usually dead periods for lobbying. Congress was out of session, and lawmakers were vacationing, junketing, or both. The August of 1989 was no exception. So the Capital Gains Coalition contented itself mostly with what Bloomfield called makework. As an example, someone even suggested taking out an advertisement in the Kennebunkport, Maine, newspaper urging the town's most famous resident, President Bush, to keep pressing for his favorite tax cut. But the coalition decided against placing the ad. The ad, Bloomfield said, would have served little purpose other than to allow the lobbyists to "indicate they were useful to their clients." He was not interested in doing things just to do that.

At another beach town far to the south—Bethany Beach, Delaware—lobbyist Nick Calio, who had by then switched jobs and was working for the White House as its chief liaison with the House of Representatives, was busy at more serious labors. There were few issues the President cared about more that summer than capital gains. So each morning Calio took time away from the beach and his three children to telephone available members of the House and urge them to vote for the tax cut. He also spoke often to Bloomfield, with whom he was coordinating efforts. "Nick put together a list of prospects and asked if I had any ideas on Democratic votes," Bloomfield said. "I had a few."

Bloomfield's coalition of lobbyists worked closely with their allies in the Bush administration and in Congress to gather the votes they needed to pass the Jenkins capital-gains tax cut. In addition to compiling lists of lawmakers susceptible to their arguments, they also waged a propaganda war. For instance, in response to a two-page letter about capital gains that Gephardt and Representative Don Pease of Ohio had written to their colleagues, imploring, "Don't vote for a budget buster," the Capital Gains Coalition distributed a five-page paragraph-by-paragraph response, which Bloomfield had penned.

The U.S. Chamber of Commerce sent out about fifteen thousand "action calls" to its members encouraging them to ask nearly

150 key lawmakers to vote for a capital-gains tax cut. Chamber of Commerce lobbyists also visited the offices of more than a hundred House members. Indeed, everyone in Bloomfield's group had been busy. "We've made so many contacts I couldn't even begin to count, and we remain very active and very involved," said Allen Neece, a dapper lobbyist for the venture capitalists.

Bloomfield concentrated much of his effort working for Jenkins and the Treasury Department. When Jenkins needed facts and figures to bolster his arguments, he turned to Bloomfield's American Council for Capital Formation. And when the Treasury needed a model for its own propaganda piece to promote the capital-gains tax cut as being beneficial to the middle class, it used a series of vignettes written by Bloomfield and entitled "Ordinary People Get Capital Gains Too." The Treasury's version was called "The Jenkins Capital Gains Proposal Benefits All Americans." But the two series were much the same from that point on.

In reaction to these pro-capital-gains endeavors, anti-capital-gains Democrats tried to recruit a lobbyist force of their own. Representative William Gray of Pennsylvania, the third-ranking Democrat in the House, met with fifteen to twenty corporate lobbyists to urge them not to back a capital-gains tax cut. According to participants, Gray warned that the consequence of passing the cut would be that corporate taxes would later be raised. Rostenkowski also met with about ten lobbyists in his office near the House floor. He asked them either to support his drive to beat the cut or not to lobby on the issue at all.

· · ·

When Congress returned in September after its usual month-long summer break, the Democratic leadership tried at the last minute to derail Jenkins's effort, and floated a plan that was a milder version of the Georgian's tax cut. And, for at least a fleeting moment, at least some members of Jenkins's Gang of Six seemed tempted. But the vote in the Ways and Means Committee remained a foregone conclusion. On Thursday, September 14, the Jenkins plan passed by the long-anticipated vote of 19 to 17.

Now the real fight began: the vote on the House floor. Playing with a weak hand, Speaker Foley hastily proposed his own alternative to Jenkins's. Instead of cutting the capital-gains tax rate, Foley suggested, gains attributable to inflation might be exempted from tax. Rostenkowski was deputized to find a suitable compromise using this so-called indexing proposal. In response, Bloomfield drafted a short primer on why "indexing alone is not enough."

The Capital Gains Coalition tried to win over every lawmaker it could. The American Electronics Association telephoned about two hundred executives in the California district of Democratic Representative Norman Mineta, many of whom, in turn, called the congressman to urge his vote for the tax cut. (He ultimately decided to vote for it, since his district included the high-tech Silicon Valley.)

At the urging of Bloomfield, the capital-gains lobbyists also went after an unlikely target, liberal Representative Ron Wyden of Oregon, who had been a junior high school classmate of Bloomfield's in Palo Alto, California. "I know the man, I think he's bright, I think you ought to talk to him," Bloomfield recalled saying. Wyden was not a predictable choice as a capital-gains backer, but the fierce fight over cutting capital-gains taxes threw the entire political compass into a whirl. The issue was supposed to be a clear contest between conservatives, who wanted to slash taxes, and liberals, who opposed measures helping the rich. But Democrat Wyden ended up backing the capital-gains tax cut anyway, because of Oregon timber interests. "I'm hearing from the people who are basic to the economic future of my state," Wyden said. And at least some of those people were sent to him by the timber lobbyists in Bloomfield's coalition.

Wyden's backing for the tax cut was made easier by arguments developed with the help of the lobbyists. Wyden noted, for example: one, that Oregon had twenty thousand privately owned woodlots covering four million acres; two, that Oregon had one of the nation's largest per-capita concentrations of small businesses; and three, that a cut in the capital-gains tax would, in reality, be a boon to the "middle class." All of these echoed rationales circulated by Bloomfield's colleagues in the lobbying world.

In the meantime, Bloomfield got even closer to Jenkins and his Gang. When the congressman wanted to answer questions about capital gains and economic growth, Bloomfield fired off a memo suggesting which economists he should cite. And though neither Bloomfield nor Jenkins said so outright, Bloomfield actually ghostwrote an op-ed piece that appeared under Jenkins's byline in *USA Today* in September. The duo would concede only that Bloomfield contributed significant amounts of technical advice for the piece. But its theme and tone had a familiar Bloomfield ring: "A cut in the tax rate on capital gains makes good economic sense and is fair for the middle class."

During this same period, Bloomfield was asked by staffers for Jenkins's Gang to draft fact sheets about their plan and its effects. The Bush White House also put on a full-court press. Part of its effort involved enlisting corporate lobbyists for the capital-gains cause. Beginning on Monday, September 18, Bush aides convened a series of meetings of business lobbyists in the regal Roosevelt Room of the White House. On that day, White House Budget Director Richard Darman gave a pep talk and asked the assembled lobbyists for support. A similar group met the next day in the same spot. This time, Treasury Secretary Nicholas Brady was the cheerleader. Yet another meeting was held on Thursday with John Sununu, the White House chief of staff. That evening Bloomfield attended a cocktail party in the Capitol with Maxine Champion, a lobbyist for LTV Corporation. "I just spoke to Sununu," he told Champion. The margin between winning and losing, he reported, "is ten votes either way."

With mounting pressure on the business community to lobby for a capital-gains reduction, Thevenot was brought into the fray as well—though reluctantly. The National Realty Committee board decided to back a capital-gains tax cut, mostly to be sure that real estate sales would benefit along with those of other assets if the tax rate was cut. But Thevenot had misgivings. For one thing, the bill itself contained the offending provision that limited like-kind exchanges of real estate. For another, capital gains was so politically charged an issue that Thevenot feared taking sides could only hurt his client.

Still, he had been given his marching orders and he acted on them. Thevenot telephoned Representative Michael Andrews's office and asked how he might help. Andrews was a friend to real estate and a main cosponsor of some National Realty Committee legislation. So a staffer in Andrews's office was happy to give Thevenot a list of thirty-two names of Democratic lawmakers who the congressman had determined might be persuaded to vote for a capital-gains tax cut. Thevenot telephoned some of them and asked for their votes.

Throughout this period, Bloomfield's capital-gains coalition stayed in constant contact with one another, exchanging intelligence and vote counts via fax machine. On Friday, September 22, Andrews's office faxed to Bloomfield the details of the alternative capital-gains plan being floated by the Democratic leadership. On Monday, September 25, the lobbyists began faxing lists that detailed which lawmakers were leaning toward their position and which were leaning the other way. The September 25 list had thirty Democrats "definitely with us" and seven others "leaning our way." Thirty-nine Democrats were listed as "undecided."

On Wednesday, September 27, the vote-count faxes ceased. "Due to rapid changes and the need for security, we will no longer be transmitting complete lists of our targets," the final fax read. "Please call . . . if you have a report on a direct contact with any member from a previous list or need to know about a particular member."

At this juncture both sides also began to look outside of Congress to give their causes added popular appeal. The Democratic National Committee aired a commercial on Washington television that featured Gephardt saying, "The lines are drawn. George Bush wants to raid the Treasury by reducing capital-gains taxes for the super rich, and he wants you to pay for it." The Democrats also released a letter from prominent economists casting doubt on the GOP's claim that the tax cut would stimulate economic growth.

At the same time, the House Republicans' campaign committee started to show a thirty-second television commercial of its own. It appealed as much to patriotism as to logic. "Why are foreign economies growing faster than the U.S.?" an announcer inquired as the flags of Japan, Taiwan, and Korea appeared on screen. "One big reason is taxes," he continued. "We have one of the world's highest capital-gains taxes." The ad concluded with four American flags moving up the screen and the announcer saying, "Let's get back in the race; let's cut the capital-gains tax."

The day of reckoning finally came on Thursday, September 28. Bloomfield wore a particularly conservative suit. He never wanted to call attention to his clothes when he met with lawmakers. And that was what he did all day. His contacts were bolstered by the delivery of a letter from the American Council to every member of the House.

The Capital Gains Coalition also made a final push through its network of carefully coached constituents. The electronics association sent a delegation of executives to speak to a possible waverer, liberal Republican Representative Constance Morella of Maryland. Right afterward, one of the executives, Wayne Shelton of Emhart PRC, wrote her a note, emphasizing the importance of the tax cut to the local economy. It read in part:

> The capital gains tax issue is an important one for our member firms. Most of them are small, entrepreneurial organizations in need of capital—if not currently, at some time in their development. Some of the larger member companies such as Martin Marietta, Vitro and my own firm need equity capital from time to time to support growth. We [would] sincerely appreciate your vote on the current legislation.

Bloomfield shuttled from lawmaker to lawmaker and then reported what he had learned to Bush officials who were holed up in a small room off the House floor on the Republican side of the chamber. There, Darman and Calio were hunkered down, keeping track of the votes they thought they had. At one point Bloomfield rushed excitedly to tell Darman that he had learned that freshman Democratic Representative Jill Long of Indiana might be a vote for their cause. But Darman scoffed, "We already know," and shooed Bloomfield away.

Undaunted, Bloomfield stood on the long marble steps that led to the House chamber. He had become something of an emblem for capital gains, so when lawmakers saw him, they knew what he wanted. For his part, he knew he was not going to win many votes during his last-minute stand, so he went about his work with levity. When he stopped Democratic Representative Ben Cardin of Maryland on the stairs, for example, he asked him *not* to vote for the Jenkins plan. Bloomfield joked that if Cardin voted for a capital-gains tax cut it could hurt his chances later to push for another pro-business tax he favored—the value-added tax, which also was a priority of the American Council. "I'm here to try to get people to vote for it," Bloomfield said of the capital-gains break. "But as a friend, you probably should not."

All of the work paid off. The tally was never even close. The House voted overwhelmingly, 239–190, in favor of the Jenkins plan, and Bloomfield felt a combination of exhilaration and relief. It was a humiliating defeat for the new Democratic leadership. Sixty-four Democrats—a quarter of their membership—voted with almost all of the Republicans to put the plan over the top. It was a moment Bloomfield had worked to achieve for three long years. Bloomfield burst into the room off the House floor to wish Calio and others congratulations.

That night, Bloomfield and Maxine Champion celebrated their victory in a hotel ballroom filled with lobbyists. The event, called the Bryce Harlow Dinner, honored Anne Wexler of Wexler Group as the "lobbyist of the year." Harlow was a lobbyist, first for the White House and then for Procter & Gamble Company, helping to establish the prototypical career path for the ideal corporate lobbyist: working initially in government to learn the ropes, then out to pay the rent. In his honor that night almost every lobbying shop in town was represented at the Capital Hilton Hotel. A special guest was Bryce Harlow's son, Larry, who at the time was chief lobbyist for the Treasury Department, and a close associate of Bloomfield's in the triumphant capital-gains fight.

Larry Harlow would soon follow in his father's footsteps and become a corporate lobbyist. But it was Bloomfield's star that shone brightly that night. Many of his colleagues went out of their way to shake his hand. They stopped by to chitchat. Some who usually thought of him only as an eccentric obsessed with capital gains were pleased to spend some time by his side. And, according to Champion, "he beamed."

Despite the success, though, Bloomfield knew his work was far from over. The next battleground was the Senate, and the chances were very good that he would win again. Still, he did not want to take any chances. Already he was planning Capital Gains Coalition meetings to assess the Senate vote count. "This is just the beginning," he said.

5

The
Feeding
Frenzy

On the sunny Friday morning after its big win in the House, the Capital Gains Coalition stopped celebrating long enough to go back to work. An expanded version of the core group gathered around the big oval table in the conference room of Walker Associates to plot its next moves. Strategy sessions like these usually were held in the sterile white plasterboard offices of Mark Bloomfield's American Council on K Street. But that space could not hold the crowd of more than a dozen people—from both inside and outside of government. So the group met in the grander, plushly carpeted conference room at Walker's place down the street.

Walker called the meeting to order. His cheeks were flushed from the success of the day before, and his eyes seemed to sparkle as he handed out congratulations around the room. Though he had not been a vigorous participant in the fight, he felt personally vindicated. Now that the big battle over capital gains was under way, his juices began to flow. And for the first time in years, he wanted to be part of it again.

But the self-congratulation did not last long. The group soon set about discussing where the votes could be found to get the job done in the Senate. The regulars were all there: Ed Hatcher of the electronics association, Allen Neece of the National Venture Capital Association, Steve Small of the Securities Industry Association, and Ken Hagerty, who was hired by a couple of groups.

Each lobbyist brought something of value to the table. Hatcher had the mailing list for the coalition's grass-roots lobbying drive. Neece and Small had access to gobs of money that helped finance that effort. And the bespectacled Hagerty brought an energy that was matched only by Bloomfield's. Hagerty was the coalition's clearinghouse for political information. He took charge of the faxing that kept everyone informed about the latest developments and delivered their marching orders. He also maintained a belief in the tax cut that bordered on zealotry. To him capital gains was a "Main Street issue" that only shortsighted politicians would oppose.

That morning Hagerty, who had once been a top lobbyist for the electronics association, was nearly jumping out of his chair with excitement at the prospect that his side might finally win. Many of the lobbyists in the room had been devoted to cutting capital gains for years, and they knew, almost by instinct, which lawmakers they could count on for a vote and which they probably could not. But until the vote in the House, all of their careful spadework and intelligence gathering was mostly a shout in a void. Now, however, their efforts took on a new seriousness as they moved closer to victory.

They knew that most, if not all, of the forty-five Republicans in the Senate were supporters of their effort. But which Democrats could be counted on? That was the consuming question. The lobbyists ran down the list, calling out lawmakers' names as if they were commodities on an auction block. There were sure bets like David Boren of Oklahoma, and there were more than a few likelies as well, such as Bob Graham of Florida and Alan Cranston of California. Each of them had sponsored their own capital-gains bills in the past. Some others were also possible, the lobbyists conjectured, like Max Baucus of Montana and even Thomas Daschle of South Dakota, both of whom also had the added virtue of being members of the Senate Finance Committee, where the bill would have to start.

But the lobbyists took nothing for granted. They determined that fifteen Democratic senators and all forty-five Republican senators favored some sort of cut in the capital-gains tax. That was more than enough to produce a majority in the hundred-member chamber. But what was the best way to get out the vote, especially in the face of active opposition by Majority Leader George Mitchell and Lloyd Bentsen, chairman of the Finance Committee?

For advice on that score, they turned to a special guest that morning: Russell Long. The ex-lawmaker was a member of Bloomfield's board of directors at the American Council for Capital Formation and had been an informal adviser to the capital-gains forces for years. He had retired from the Senate in 1986 after thirty-eight years there, declaring that the summers in his home state of Louisiana were too scorching to tolerate for another campaign. He also said he wanted to leave the Senate with his "garters snapping," not enfeebled with old age and an object of ridicule, as he had seen some of his colleagues go in the past. Long was legendary as a political operator, and his specialty was the politics of taxation, a genre he all but invented as chairman of the Finance Committee for fifteen years.

Nowadays, he was plying his expertise as a lobbyist. First as a highly paid member of a law firm, and then later on his own, Long commanded top dollar as a consultant to some of the biggest companies in the country. When companies needed to talk to the most important people in the Senate, Long guaranteed them a rapid entrée. And when companies needed advice about how to settle a legislative problem, Long told them how it all worked on the inside.

It was this insider's perspective that Long dispensed to the coalition, which sat in respectful attention. Ironically, Long's advice to his lawmaker colleagues had also helped keep tax reform on track in 1986. This time, Long's message to the lobbyists was that a capital-gains tax cut was possible, but only if the proposal was broad enough to benefit the many interests that were represented around the table.

President Bush's bill, he admonished, benefited only people who invested in the securities markets. According to Long, timber, real estate, and corporations had to be included in any congressional package. Senators will vote for the interests that elect them, he said, not for Wall Street moneychangèrs. "Their bill is a stock exchange bill," Long asserted about the administration's proposal. "If I'm just an ordinary member of Congress, the stock exchange isn't going to elect me dogcatcher. The people who are going to elect me dog catcher are the people in my own hometown and in my home parish." Given the right proposal, though, a winning coalition could be formed. It would be the task of the assembled lobbyists then to persuade the lawmakers that their constituents wanted the change.

The ex-senator sometimes rambled. Some of the lobbyists in the room were a little confused and perhaps a little concerned when his speech was over. Maybe a broad capital-gains cut was not the right choice, they thought. Certainly a capital-gains break for corporations seemed far afield from the goal of spurring investment by individuals. The electronics and venture-capital lobbyists in particular were hesitant about taking things too far. But the glow of the House victory was still bright, and the lobbyists left the meeting confident that they would find the votes to make their goal a reality.

That afternoon, Bloomfield and Maxine Champion left town for a weekend of well-deserved rest. They drove an hour out of Washington to a hotel and restaurant in Paris, Virginia, called the Ashby Inn. The spanking-white inn was known for its coziness, its good food, and its witty maître d' and owner, John Sherman, a former top staffer at the House Ways and Means Committee. After the 1986 tax act was passed, Sherman quit as Chairman Dan Rostenkowski's chief wordsmith and devoted himself to innkeeping and occasional speechwriting for corporate chief executives, including Boone Pickens of Mesa Petroleum and Rostenkowski's friend and Robert Juliano's benefactor, Jim Robinson of American Express.

The inn that night was filled with current Ways and Means aides who were also looking for a break. They gathered there regularly, as did many of the lobbyists who made their livings from Ways and Means work. Champion, who had been a Ways and Means staffer herself before becoming a lobbyist, was welcomed among the aides. Her relationship with the conservative Bloomfield was the subject more of humor than resentment in the group. And over dinner that night, Bloomfield was the butt of much good-natured teasing, even though he had just handed the Democrats who paid the staffers' salaries a major defeat.

Later, Bloomfield was able to escape the friendly gibes to have a more serious conversation on policy. Another diner at the inn that evening was, by sheer coincidence, Russell Long! Bloomfield sat down beside him and they continued to discuss the future of capital gains as if their meeting that morning had never ended.

· · ·

Work again reared its head on Sunday as soon as Bloomfield returned home. There on his telephone answering machine was a fresh message from Cody Graves, the tax aide to Democratic Senator David Boren of Oklahoma. Graves, a balding man with a scraggly mustache, asked if Bloomfield could stop by Boren's office that evening to discuss capital gains, and Bloomfield, of course, would never say no. He changed from his Top-Siders into something more suitable, and headed to Capitol Hill. At the meeting, both Bloomfield and Boren wore suspenders, an oddity for weekend work for most people, but Boren was every bit as finicky about his clothes as Bloomfield. Bloomfield joked that he was glad that at least they had not worn the same ones.

Boren looked more like a natty Pillsbury Doughboy than the Rhodes scholar he was. As one of the most pro-business members of the Finance Committee, he had undertaken the chore of devising a capital-gains plan and, in fact, had informed the Democrats on the panel that he had intended to offer it up for a vote. But Boren was still grappling with the same question that Russell Long had addressed. What should the proposal look like? Boren hoped to satisfy a diverse group of senators, ranging from liberals Alan Cranston of California and John Kerry of Massachusetts, who represented states with high-technology industries, to Sam Nunn of Georgia and Dale Bumpers of Arkansas, whose states had large timber interests. Freshmen senators such as Charles Robb of Virginia and Joseph Lieberman of Connecticut had also expressed their own interest in a cut.

To help devise his plan, Boren turned to Bloomfield. For most of that Sunday evening, Boren picked Bloomfield's brain about the best kinds of capital-gains tax cuts. Under Long's tutelage, Bloomfield pressed for one that was both deep and, unlike the one in Jenkins's plan, permanent. And Boren agreed. Bloomfield noted, though, that such a plan had some political shortcomings. But Boren stopped him. "Don't worry about that," the senator said, indicating that it was his job to keep an eye on where the votes were. Bloomfield was there to help with the content, Boren said, and the lobbyist could only smile. A few days later, his smile grew even wider when Boren published an op-ed piece in *The Washington Post* that called, in part, for "a carefully crafted and permanent cut in the capital gains rate to encourage long-term investment."

Meanwhile, the other members of the core group sprang into action. Ed Hatcher sent telegrams to electronics companies from Massachusetts to Washington State, asking for their "active support in lowering the tax rate on capital gains." The telegrams encouraged company executives to contact their senators to "make the following points: 1) Favorable capital gains tax treatment is needed to ensure that investors are willing to invest in, and stay invested in, young technology companies; and 2) Without a capital gains differential, young technology companies face an impossible task of attracting 'patient' capital—capital that focuses on long-term growth rather than short-term profits." The telegram added, "It is also important to add any personal experience you can to demonstrate the importance of a capital-gains differential."

In response to Hatcher's dispatch Bruce Murray, president of SeaFab Incorporated of Redmond, Washington, wrote to both of his senators. "On behalf of the 125 companies of the Washington Council of the American Electronics Association," he wrote, "I urge your support of a capital-gains differential." He referred the senators to Hatcher if they had any further questions. The senators from Massachusetts also got letters. "The House of Representatives' positive vote last week represents a significant step towards a permanent capital gains differential to encourage risk capital investment," wrote John J. Wallace, chief financial officer of Numerix Corporation of Newton. "Your anticipated cooperation is appreciated," he added.

· · ·

The startling vote in the House had more than electronics companies buzzing. Lobbyists all over Washington were aflutter with activity. Bob Juliano, for one, had planned to spend some time on the road after the House voted. As a hotel and restaurant workers' lobbyist, Juliano traveled well and often. His condominium in Washington contained ample evidence of that. The living room table was always stacked high with fine-living magazines, such as *Wine Spectator* and *Gourmet*. Boxes of wine purchased during his many trips were stacked in his kitchen and under the staircase to the apartment's second floor. Exotic wineglasses filled two cabinets, and at least one notable book was in ready reach. Called *The Edge of Everest*, it contained this inscription: "Merry Christmas, Happy New Year, Happy Holidays from Sue and Chuck Cobb," who were also listed on the inside of the cover as "Ambassador and Mrs. Charles E. Cobb, Jr., Embassy of the United States of America, Reykjavik, Iceland."

When Congress was in session, Juliano was always greeting and grabbing the members he knew outside the House and Senate chambers. But when Congress was out of session, Juliano was often out of town. He traveled to Chicago to see his grown son, Bobby, and mix in some union business along the way. Some of his other favorite stopping-off spots were California and Nevada (for the union) and New York City (for American Express). He also traveled abroad on behalf of a quasi-governmental group associated with the Commerce Department called the Travel and Tourism Advisory Board. He also went overseas on his own behalf, trying to organize an international lobbying network that could cash in on the unification of the European Economic Community in 1992.

But in light of the surprising vote in the House, Juliano was busy canceling trips. He had been scheduled to fly to San Francisco to attend a fund-raiser for Representative Barbara Boxer, who was thinking about running for the Senate. Afterward, he had intended to fly to Chicago for the thirtieth reunion of his class at St. Ignatius High School. But he jettisoned both of those plans to stay close to the Capitol to monitor the Senate's tax-and-budget debate.

"I'm too old to waste a weekend, but that's what I did," Juliano moaned. When he was not listening to the droning debate on the Senate floor from a seat in the gallery overlooking the chamber, he took up his post outside the chamber itself, hobnobbing with a staffer for Senator Joseph Biden of Delaware and exchanging a greeting with Democratic Senator Barbara Mikulski of Maryland. "These days," he explained, "anything can happen." And it was Juliano's job as a lobbyist to be there when it did.

Until the crushing defeat for the House Democratic leadership, the tax breaks that Juliano defended for a living—especially those that helped life-insurance companies and permitted taxpayers to deduct their travel and entertainment expenses—were considered safe. But now, it seemed, lawmakers were intent on fiddling with taxes. Surely if they could vote to cut the capital-gains tax after having voted to increase it just three years before, then anything could happen. And Juliano was leaving nothing to chance. "It appears as though the whole thing is wide open again," he said with a shake of his head.

The possibility that taxes were up for grabs was deliriously good news for many corporate lobbyists and, potentially, for their clients. Interest groups were lining up for the goodies all over Capitol Hill, and lobbyists were hauling in the fees. Wayne Thevenot's fellow real estate lobbyists were redoubling their efforts to ease anti-tax-shelter rules. Charitable groups were trying to reinstate the write-off for charitable contributions made by individuals who do not itemize their deductions. And heavy-industry lobbyists were quietly discussing the possibility of reinstating the investment tax credit. "There isn't any doubt that the thread of the '86 code has been given a mighty tug," Representative Thomas Downey said.

Lobbyist Lawrence O'Brien, the son of the former top White House lobbyist for President Kennedy, attended a hearing at the Ways and Means Committee where one special-interest pleader after another was allowed to make his or her case. O'Brien likened this new hunger for loopholes to "a Swiss cheese factory." And to lobbyists in search of work, he said, "the cheese smells pretty good."

In anticipation of a spree, groups were lobbying especially hard to make sure they were not left out of any giveaway package. Real estate interests, for example, were visiting dozens of Senate offices to protest what they saw as an omission in President Bush's original capital-gains proposal: The plan did not include a tax break for gains from the sale of real estate. "If there is going to be a tax scheme that contemplates lower treatment of capital gains, they certainly want to be part of it," Thevenot argued. At the same time, Sotheby's, the big auction house, was working to get its own special benefit. It sent a letter to congressional tax-writers asking that gains from the sale of collectibles be given the same preference. "Collectibles should continue to be recognized as capital assets," the letter stated.

Other tax benefits also were expected to be restored or created. The only obstacle was finding a way to pay for them all. Asked if the tax law was open game again, James Healey, a lobbyist for Black, Manafort, Stone & Kelly, said frankly: "A lot of us in town hope that it is." And one of the most optimistic people in town was Mr. Capital Gains, Mark Bloomfield.

Unfortunately for Bloomfield, Senator Bentsen had different plans. Even before the vote in the House, Bentsen had decided to take a stand against a capital-gains tax cut. He and Majority Leader George Mitchell agreed that cutting taxes for rich people was the worst thing their party could do. But how could they stop the capital-gains drive? In Washington, where interests vie against other interests, legislators could rarely beat something with nothing. So Bentsen devised a stratagem that at first seemed to make no sense, but that ultimately turned out to be a brilliant ploy.

He proposed to substitute one tax cut for another. Rather than reducing taxes on upper-income investors, he argued, the Congress should reduce taxes on middle-class people. Bentsen advanced a plan to bolster tax breaks for contributions made to Individual Retirement Accounts (IRAs) as a replacement for a cut in capital-gains taxes. Specifically, he proposed to give a 50 percent deduction for as much as $2,000 of IRA contributions made by people who currently did not qualify for any similar break. He also would have allowed penalty-free withdrawals from IRAs for expenses that intensely worried middle-class people—for example, higher education and first-home purchases—in addition to retirement.

In true Washington fashion, Bentsen recruited twenty-five interest groups, ranging from realtors and bankers to Catholic colleges, to support his IRA proposal. But he went even further. Behind the scenes, he deputized Democratic Senator David Pryor of Arkansas to undermine capital gains. The target: timber interests. Like Representative Beryl Anthony, his fellow Arkansan,

Pryor was a natural supporter of a capital-gains tax cut because timber farming was so important in his state. But the low-key lawmaker was eager to move up in the Democratic leadership in the Senate, and was willing to do what he could to help the political cause of his party. So in quiet consultations with fellow Southerners, he found a trade-off that helped timber farmers without tampering with capital gains: reestablishing a tax break called income averaging, which spread gains over several years.

Bentsen placed that provision into his starting-point proposal and with it won Pryor's vote against a capital-gains tax cut. He now had the hope that any capital-gains amendment would fail narrowly in his committee. But even more bargaining was needed before that was a fait accompli. Virtually every member of the panel had a wish list of narrow tax breaks, which Bentsen and his staff tried to accommodate in order to secure votes against the dread capital gains. As a result, the Swiss cheese factory of Washington was running full-tilt in the Finance Committee.

· · ·

On the night of Tuesday, October 3, the hallway outside the Finance Committee on the second floor of the Dirksen Senate Office Building was filled with lobbyists eagerly awaiting the outcome of their months of scheming and planning. Thevenot was there, informed about the timing of the drafting session by Bentsen's executive assistant, Gay Burton. He was hopeful that like-kind exchanges would be spared the ax; one of Bentsen's Finance Committee staffers had assured him that they would be. Jim Rock was there as well, waiting out the result of his effort to get a special break for the liquor stores that had hired his employer, Gold and Liebengood. Stuart Eizenstat, the R&D lobbyist, was there, too, and managed to exchange a few words with Bentsen in the hallway before the session began.

"We'll do what we can," the chairman told the dark-suited Eizenstat in hushed tones. That pledge repeated what he had told the lobbyist the evening before, when Bentsen strode by mistake into a meeting that Eizenstat and others were having with Senator George Mitchell about the R&D credit. "I'd like to do more," Bentsen had said at the time, but he indicated that at least something for Coretech would be in his bill.

Bloomfield was also in the hallway, though his mood was far glummer than his colleagues'. He had finally caught wind of Bentsen's plot, and it looked as if Boren did not have enough votes to win in committee. Bloomfield wore a tie that read DON'T LET THE BASTARDS GRIND YOU DOWN. Earlier in the day, a fax from Hagerty to the Capital Gains Coalition laid out the specter of impending defeat in the committee and the prospects after that:

> As of this morning, our best chance to secure a permanent capital gains reduction appears to be on the Senate floor. Senator Boren has announced that he or another Democrat will definitely offer a floor amendment to add capital gains.

But the bad news for capital gains was good news for the dozens of other lobbyists who jammed the halls. At the start of the drafting session, Bentsen handed out an eighty-four-page document labeled "Miscellaneous Tax Provisions" that, incredibly, listed more than fifty tiny exceptions and loopholes that corporate lobbyists all over town had fought to get into law for months and sometimes years. The list included tax subsidies for interests ranging from timber growers to oil drillers, from insurance companies to small businesses, from farm cooperatives to sports stadiums. The proposals also blew holes in the federal estate tax, which was paid by fewer than 100,000 of the nation's wealthiest people each year, and even allowed owners of crop-duster aircraft to apply for waivers from the gasoline tax. The total cost to the taxpayer: more than $4 billion over five years. The list was a lobbyist's dream come true.

The drafting session itself was carefully scripted. It began in the late afternoon and lasted well into the night. Before the basic bill was completed, Bentsen took time to vote on a capital-gains tax cut amendment, but not the one offered by Boren. Instead, Senator Bob Packwood of Oregon, the committee's ranking Republican, offered his own. It was ironic that Packwood would submit such an idea. He had been instrumental in ending the capital-gains benefit in 1986. What was more, his new proposal, not by coincidence, closely matched the wishes of Long and Charly Walker. Both lobbyists had been consulted by the senator from

Oregon. And Packwood's chief tax aide, Lindy Paull, had been in frequent contact with Bloomfield and sometimes even attended his coalition's meetings downtown. In the end, the Packwood plan was both broad and deep, cutting the capital-gains tax for both individuals and corporations. It also created a special, still-lower rate for individuals making profits on venture-capital investments. For good measure, it included a proposal by Senator William Roth to expand the tax advantages of IRAs, much as Bentsen's package had done.

Still, the Packwood amendment was defeated, though by the narrowest of margins, a 10–10 tie. Boren was the only Democrat to break ranks with the wily Bentsen to vote for a capital-gains cut.

After hearing the news, Bloomfield and his capital-gains cohorts slunk off to make plans for later battles. But theirs were among the few somber faces in the hallway. Thevenot left happily after confirming from conversations with aides in the hallway that the like-kind exchange proposals passed by the House had been omitted from the Finance Committee bill. Rock also had won the day: Liquor stores were given their break, thanks to Senator John Heinz of Pennsylvania. Riba Raffaelli, Heinz's tax aide, who was a regular on Rock's ski trips to Vail, came out of the meeting personally to show him that his provision had been included. Eizenstat too went home safe and secure after, lo and behold, the committee bill not only extended the R&D tax credit but made it permanent. For the first time ever, both the House and the Senate tax-writing committees were on record as favoring the permanent inclusion in law of a tax credit for increases in research-and-development spending.

Everything went smoothly for both the chairman and the lobbyists until, at about midnight, the staff informed the committee that about $500 million over five years was still available to be spent. A long silence ensued. Bentsen looked tired from the hours of debate and voting. He wanted to end the day. But he looked wearily around the horseshoe-shaped table that the committee sat behind and saw many eager faces. He began to call on members randomly. Aides scurried from their seats to bring up tax-break amendments, most of which had been drafted with the help of lobbyists who were standing outside the committee room.

For two hours, the Finance Committee indulged in an orgy of special-interest legislating the likes of which had not been seen in public for nearly a decade. Individual companies reaped substantial benefits. An amendment by Senator Tom Daschle of South Dakota gave a tax credit to a new ethanol-based gasoline additive, at a cost of more than $170 million over three years. Senators said the big beneficiary was Dwayne Andreas's Archer Daniels Midland Company, a major ethanol maker. Boren was the author of another amendment that gave tax relief to farmer cooperatives generally, but had as a major beneficiary the Farmland Industries co-op. The provision would have allowed Farmland to reduce its tax liability by millions of dollars by offsetting, with tax losses, a gain from its sale of an oil refinery.

Thanks to Senator Pryor, timber farmers actually got two benefits: income averaging and special relief from the anti-tax-shelter rules that curbed the use of passive losses. Other tax benefits were sprinkled from Hawaii to Pennsylvania. Hawaii's Democratic Senator Spark Matsunaga helped restore to pineapple and banana growers the ability to use a special method of agricultural accounting called the annual accrual method, which had been available since the year before only to sugarcane growers. And Senator Heinz won an amendment that allowed rental tuxedos to be written off for tax purposes in two or three years, rather than the existing five years. Pennsylvania made more tuxedos than any other state in the union.

When the extra money was all used up, and the drafting session was forced to end, an obviously pained Senator Bill Bradley— a principal architect of the 1986 tax reform act that had eliminated many of these same special breaks—said he would vote to send the measure to the Senate floor, but only reluctantly. Ruefully, he added: "The bill has become increasingly more troubling; there are many, many aspects of the bill now that are of real concern."

For his part, Bentsen said that he was proud of the overall package. He said he wished there had been fewer narrow amendments, but, he explained, "that's the way the process works." In the meantime, tax aides poured out of the hearing room to inform their lobbyist friends in the hallway what bounty they had reaped from that process.

· · ·

The victories were short-lived, however. Even in a town accustomed to lobbyist-led legislation, the Finance Committee bill was excessive. The next day Pryor confessed on the Senate floor that the session had turned into "a feeding frenzy" that needed to be reconsidered. The senators realized that their gluttony could not be sustained. Newspaper articles and editorials lambasted them for their special-interest greed. On Thursday, October 5, Senate leaders took the floor to strip out all of the bill's revenue-losing provisions.

Confusion reigned. One of the tax breaks taken out of the bill was Coretech's R&D tax credit. It was not one of the more controversial tax breaks, but it was a tax break nonetheless. So out it came. Eizenstat tried to be philosophical; he likened lobbying to being in a boat at sea during a storm. He also tried to make a jest about "the shortest permanent tax credit in history." But he and Ken Kay were deluged with phone calls from companies wondering what they could do. And their answer was, in short: Not much. Not only was the chance for a permanent credit out the window, but there was a decent chance that the credit could be gone entirely.

Coretech lobbyists held strategy sessions, trying to make sense out of the situation. Ultimately, they concluded that they needed to raise the visibility of their issue, reminding lawmakers just how popular a provision it was. They sent letters and made telephone calls. They even joined a coalition of groups that were lobbying for extensions of other soon-to-expire tax provisions. The group was headed by William Signer, the former aide to Representative Charles Rangel who now lobbied to extend his old boss's pet tax break, which subsidized the hiring of economically disadvantaged workers.

Kay referred to the Signer group as "the ugliest coalition ever devised," and imagined as he sat through its meetings in Signer's office that he was "in a funeral home with ten caskets open"— one for each tax break that was about to expire after the first of the year. But Signer argued, and Kay grudgingly agreed, that by pooling their information and sending a joint letter to lawmakers on the Hill, the various coalitions enhanced their strength as a lobbying force.

Still, the feeding frenzy had caused events to spin out of the lobbyists' control. Who knew what might happen next? So, in defense, they could leave no avenue unexplored. Coretech even tried to make allegiance with the one lobbying group it had shunned the longest: the Capital Gains Coalition.

Far from giving up because of the setback in the Finance Committee, the capital-gains forces were pushing even harder. Hagerty faxed a "revised target list" of Democratic senators to contact and of "Republicans to bolster." And he also communicated encouragement that he had received from White House lobbyists. On the night of the stripping exercise in the Senate, his faxed message read: "While the parliamentary situation surrounding the tax bill is confused for the moment, our coalition has received the following guidance: 'The President and senior advisers continue to believe that restoring the capital-gains differential is a high priority. They are working actively to secure it.' "

At around this time, Eizenstat placed a telephone call to Walker. According to Bloomfield, Walker was not in at the time, so the call was transferred to the American Council, where Bloomfield took it. The conversation was not friendly. There had been bad blood between the two men. Bloomfield thought Eizenstat was a sourpuss, and resented the fact that, even though he was a lobbyist, he did not always return telephone calls. Bloomfield remembered that Eizenstat had tried to defeat the capital-gains tax cut when he was a White House adviser in 1978; as a lobbyist, he seemed just as unsympathetic. To the capital-gains crew, that position was unconscionable, since a permanent R&D credit was as much a part of the Jenkins plan as was the capital-gains break. "They tried to play both sides of the street," Bloomfield complained.

To make matters worse, Eizenstat insisted on calling Bloomfield "Mike" during their conversation. Bloomfield listened quietly as Eizenstat asked if Bloomfield could help place the R&D credit into Boren's capital-gains package, which was expected eventually to come to a vote on the Senate floor. Then, after reminding Eizenstat that his name was Mark, Bloomfield said politely, "You must have misunderstood." The Boren package, he explained, contained only a capital-gains tax cut and an expansion of IRAs, and was not as comprehensive as the Jenkins plan in the House. The discussion ended quickly after that. The two sides would continue to go their separate ways during the many legislative battles to come.

. . .

While the R&D lobbyists thrashed about and the capital-gains people tried to regain their footing in the Senate, lobbyists for utility companies were winning big in the House. Their eventual victory there against Representative Robert Matsui was a textbook-perfect example of one of the lobbyist's most basic tools: campaign contributions.

Back in 1985, Matsui had inserted an obscure provision into the tax-reform bill that was worth billions of dollars to telephone, electric, and gas utilities. In return, the utilities rewarded him with more than $60,000 in donations for his 1988 reelection campaign. And he was not alone. The utilities discreetly pumped some $8 million into the campaign treasuries of the lawmakers who decided their issues.

But by 1989, Matsui had been stung by negative publicity about his 1985 action, and he switched sides. He did not want his campaign for the Senate to be marred by this one big mistake, he thought. So he took on the utilities. At issue was revenue that the utilities collected from customers to pay for future taxes that, because of the 1986 legislation, were no longer owed. The 1986 bill dropped the top corporate tax rate to 34 percent from 45 percent, leaving $19 billion of deferred taxes that would not have to be paid to the government after all. The question then was whether the money should be paid back quickly to consumers or, as the utilities preferred, over decades.

Perhaps as much as half of these so-called excess deferred taxes were owed to business customers, but residential customers were also owed a lot. The typical residential customer probably should have gotten $100. Ordinarily, state regulators would have forced rapid refunds, perhaps over two or three years. But the regulators could not do that because of Matsui's insertion into the tax-reform bill: section 203(e), which provided that the refunds be paid over a longer stretch—thirty years in some cases.

Matsui said he took up the utilities' cause in 1985 after having championed an earlier and, he contended, more justifiable tax break of theirs at the behest of two Pacific Telesis lobbyists from Sacramento who were friends of his. "It was a question of friendship; it wasn't a matter of money," he said. He embraced the utilities' claim that section 203(e) would save customers money in the long run.

During the scramble to finish the tax bill then, neither Matsui nor anyone on the committee seemed to have thought deeply about the utility-refund matter. Lobbyists for consumer groups said they were caught completely off guard; there were no public hearings and they did not find out about the Matsui provision until it was too late to protest. The result was a windfall for utilities.

But a few weeks after the break was enacted, opposition began to form. Representative Byron Dorgan of North Dakota introduced a bill he called the Utility Ratepayer Refund Act, and he lined up forty-eight other Democrats and nine Republicans as cosponsors. Some labor unions and consumer groups got behind his measure, but the main push came from state regulators. "It has frustrated many of us to know that billions upon billions of dollars of those benefits are beyond our grasp," said Bruce Hagen, president of the National Association of Regulatory Utility Commissioners.

Then the utilities counterattacked. The U.S. Telephone Association, representing telephone companies, listed defeat of the Dorgan bill as its top legislative goal, and brought waves of telephone-company executives to Washington to try to influence their state delegations. Telephone, electric, and gas utilities, meanwhile, stepped up political contributions. A computer-aided tabulation by *The Wall Street Journal* showed that during 1987 and 1988 some 198 political-action committees sponsored by the utilities and their trade associations gave more than $5 million to House members.

The utility lobby also paid honoraria to scores of representatives and senators for speaking before various industry groups— $2,000 per appearance, in many cases. The telephone association alone paid $129,250 in 1987 and 1988. During the same period, American Telephone & Telegraph Company paid $64,500; the Edison Electric Institute paid $56,000; and BellSouth Corporation paid $39,500. In all, utility companies and trade associations opposing the Dorgan bill spent $446,000, according to a tabulation made by Mead Data Central at the request of the *Journal*.

"It's the way you do business in this town," said Robert Martin, a lobbyist for Pacific Telesis. "We're not trying to buy votes; we're trying to get our point of view across. It takes a long time . . . and sometimes we need a member's undivided attention."

To help focus their attention, the utilities lured lawmakers to some luxurious vacation spots. Democratic Representative Butler Derrick of South Carolina cosponsored the Dorgan refund bill in 1987. Then the telephone association flew him to Naples, Florida, for a three-day vacation and paid him a $1,000 honorarium, of which half went to charity. The following February, the same group paid Derrick $2,000 and expenses for a two-day trip to Palm Springs, California. Derrick also got $22,500 in utility PAC donations. He said he supported the bill originally at the request of South Carolina utility regulators, but was not cosponsoring refund legislation in 1988 because "no one has gotten in touch with me from back home." The money and trips, he said, had "nothing to do with" his change of heart.

Democratic Representative Terry Bruce of Illinois also cosponsored the Dorgan bill, but later signed a letter arguing against it. Bruce received a $1,000 honorarium from the telephone association on January 28, 1987. He received another $250 honorarium from Edison Electric Institute three days before the letter. On April 9, he took the unusual step of rising on the floor of the House to ask permission for his name to be removed from sponsorship of the refund bill. The next month he got a $2,000 appearance fee from Illinois Bell, followed, in August, by $1,000 from Pacific Telesis. And before the end of his successful 1988 reelection campaign, he got from the utility PACs $28,158 in political contributions. Bruce denied the campaign donations and honoraria had influenced him.

In all, nine of Dorgan's original cosponsors, including six of the eight Republicans, formally repudiated his bill before it died without a vote in the Ways and Means Committee at the end of 1988. Of the nine, all but one received campaign donations from the utility PACs, averaging $13,057 each. The power of money politics was making itself felt.

Meanwhile, Matsui had come under fire at home for his pro-utility stance. He began to ask the utility companies for more information of the sort he could use to defend himself from criticism. Instead, he got only offers to raise more campaign donations, a temptation that he would later liken to a bribe. "I had at least three or four meetings with the utility coalition and asked them to provide me with an analysis about why their position was proconsumer. Each time, they would say they would try to come up with something, and on the way out someone from the USTA [U.S. Telephone Association] would want to talk to me about fundraising," Matsui said. "The first time I kind of sloughed it off; the second and third time it got to be a little trying."

While Matsui switched sides and took up against the utilities, most of the movement in Congress went the other way. One of the utilities' major backers was Dan Rostenkowski, who for twenty-five years has been a friend of James J. O'Connor, the chairman of Chicago's big electric utility, Commonwealth Edison. Rostenkowski also received $48,600 in campaign donations from utility PACs for his lightly contested 1988 reelection race, including $2,000 from Commonwealth's PAC. In addition, two former Rostenkowski aides, including his former top aide, Joseph Dowley, were hired by utilities to lobby against refund legislation.

Matsui knew that his chances of success against such potent opposition were slim. "I have been told a number of times by [House] members whom I have sought as cosponsors that my bill makes good policy sense but dangerous political sense to them," he said. "Rich in honorariums and campaign contributions, their [the utility lobbyists'] talk is pretty loud in the halls around here."

On Wednesday, October 11, Matsui learned just how loudly the money talked. The Ways and Means Committee soundly defeated his proposal to speed refunds in overcollected federal taxes. The vote was a lopsided 22–13.

The utilities prevailed after their political-action committees had poured at least $610,000 into the campaigns of Ways and Means Committee members between January 1, 1987, and the day of the vote. Those contributions were part of $10.3 million given by those PACs to all House and Senate candidates during the same period. "It's disappointing," Matsui said. "But it wasn't any surprise to me."

. . .

Few lobbyists entered the fray of Washington without first making sure they had a ready hoard of dollars to spread around. PAC and personal political contributions were expected of anyone who wanted to get his point across. Though money rarely bought votes outright, it did buy a lobbyist the chance to make his views known, a chance not everyone had. Access to the powers that be was rationed, and the size of one's political pocketbook was important to making the cut.

The importance of money in politics was openly acknowledged by both the lawmakers who took it and the lobbyists who doled it out. "Money is power," said Democratic Representative Bill Alexander of Arkansas. And the lobbyists who were able to provide money were able to wield more than their share of power. "Access to Congress can't be bought, but it can be acquired with the help of campaign contributions," said Democratic Senator Brock Adams of Washington State, in a marvelous example of doublespeak.

The influence of money was directly related to the central imperative of all elected officials: remaining in office. Washington insiders loved to recount the probably apocryphal tale of the senator who asked a lobbyist if he knew what the three most important things are to a member of Congress. The senator answered his own question: "Number one is getting reelected. Number two is getting reelected. And number three is getting reelected." Whatever a lobbyist could do to help the lawmaker stay in office, the lesson went, was certainly worth the effort.

One of the chief things a lobbyist could do was raise money for campaigns. The reason: Getting elected or reelected was astronomically expensive. Hundreds of thousands of dollars were needed just to win a seat in the House; millions of dollars were necessary for a Senate race, even in small states. And the only place to get that much money with relative ease was from political-action committees and Washington-based lobbyists.

Would-be lawmakers were taught this harrowing lesson openly in a seminar conducted by the House's Democratic Congressional Campaign Committee. According to a *Washington Post* article by Steve Sovern, a candidate for the House from Iowa, aspiring lawmakers were instructed that the only way they could win their elections was to join the campaign-money circuit that lobbyists controlled. At a seminar for candidates that Sovern attended during the 101st Congress, campaign consultant Frank Greer of Greer, Margolis, Mitchell advised, "The game of raising PAC money here in Washington will make the difference. Understand how the game is played. It's crucial to your being one of the few that will win."

Sovern was horrified when it was also made clear that the candidates had to do something in return for campaign contributions. Sovern quoted Democratic Representative Peter Hoagland of Nebraska as saying that a "business relationship" was formed between the PACs and the lawmakers they contributed to. What kind of relationship? "When you take PAC money," explained George Gould, a lobbyist for the letter carriers' union, "you are saying you're their friend."

Another way to look at campaign giving was that it placed lobbyists on an even plane with the lawmakers' own constituents. The people from back home did not need to give their lawmakers money. They could purchase their attention with the prospect of delivering votes. Washington-based lobbyists, in contrast, could not vote for legislators themselves, but they could provide the funds that bought the advertising and campaign support that got out the votes. Campaign contributions, in effect, permitted the lobbyists to buy their way into legislators' offices.

"A foot in the door" is the way former Democratic Representative Michael Barnes of Maryland described what campaign contributions offered to lobbyists. "It's a big factor in this town in terms of access," agreed lobbyist Tommy Boggs in an interview with *The New York Times*. "In terms of knowing what's going on, you've got to participate in the fund-raising side of town," he added. To that end, his firm, Patton, Boggs & Blow, assigned three or four junior partners to run computer programs to try to match members of Congress with campaign contributors.

In John L. Zorack's *The Lobbying Handbook*, Boggs elaborated on the value of campaign giving: "Attending fund-raising activities increases access. If you expect a member of Congress to give you a few extra minutes, spend some time raising money for him.

Members keep track of contributions, the companies that contribute and the lobbyists who help. Lobbyists should not just mail money; they should attend fund-raising functions, even if they don't stay long."

And woe be to the lobbyist who does not contribute. "Contributions are more a defensive than an offensive tool," Boggs said. "In my case, if I don't give money to a member, his or her attitude is, 'Why did you contribute to Senator X and not to me?' You must contribute enough so that some members won't complain that you're not participating. Then, even if you don't give enough to be recognized as one of the inner circle, you won't be treated like an outcast, either."

Senator Adams, who also contributed to the handbook, went so far as to suggest that a lobbyist needed to give money to have any chance of being heard. "Some lobbyists make a good living organizing fund-raisers, and volunteering for every member's fund-raising steering committee to develop access," he said. "Lobbyists arriving in Washington must either compete with those who already have access and proven track records or tie themselves to experienced lobbyists who are known and trusted and have probably been involved with political activities and fund-raising."

Some lobbyists believed that the constant pressure to give money amounted to nothing short of extortion. One lobbyist complained, "There are some congressmen you have to buy your way in. If you pay 'em, they'll see you; if you don't, you don't get in."

But that kind of extortion was a necessary evil. In *The Lobbying Handbook*, longtime lobbyist Joseph S. Miller is quoted as saying: "Because members and staff have their tin cups at the ready for campaign contributions, I often feel that they look upon me as a dollar sign, not as a person." But the pressing need for campaign money, he added, "means that those who can give money get access and are in a better position to move bills than those who can't."

In an interview, ex-Senator Long made clear that giving campaign money was an essential part of the Washington scene: "Members aren't going to have much time to visit with people who can't be bothered to attend a fund-raiser, who don't find it convenient to make an appropriate campaign contribution or urge a principal to make a contribution. They've got a word they use in the [lobbying] fraternity: They refer to people as players. All of the more effective lobbyists are known as players. The most effective tend to work on a bipartisan basis and contribute to campaigns. A lobbyist attends fund-raisers because he needs access, he needs to communicate with these people. He'll have a lot better chance to communicate if he's a player than if he's not a player."

Money, therefore, brought clout, as lobbyist Miller starkly recounted. In a paraphrase of Senator Long, Miller said: "The shades of gray are many between bribery and a contribution, and . . . it is difficult to determine whether money was given to support a campaign or because the contributor expected something in return. Neither party may state what that 'something' is, but both parties understand what's expected. We have come a long way since giving cash was the norm, but few people today doubt that strings are attached to campaign contributions."

Representative Alexander of Arkansas, for one, was not shy about acknowledging that he owed a debt to the lobbyists who contributed to him. "Because helping someone who helps you is common sense, a lobbyist who raises funds for a member's reelection automatically increases his access to him and is in a position to talk with him about a problem," he is quoted as saying in the handbook. And Republican Representative Bud Shuster of Pennsylvania admitted, "A member naturally has a warm spot in his heart for anyone who supports his fund-raising efforts, because the most difficult and distasteful part of being a member of Congress is raising money for campaigns."

For lobbyists, therefore, the ability to carry PAC contributions to fund-raisers was an important part of their job. For Thevenot, the $250, $500, and $1,000 checks he toted to fund-raisers, usually drawn on the National Realty Committee PAC, were proof that he was a member of the club, someone to be listened to by the people he lobbied. And being listened to was virtually his entire stock-in-trade. His philosophy, he said, was "let them see your face, chat with them a little so that you become familiar to them. Let them know that the industry you represent is supporting them financially." Access, and maybe influence, surely would soon follow.

Experience had proved this to be the case. Back in 1987, Thevenot was seeking help for the real estate industry from Representative Beryl Anthony. In response to the request, the congressman handed the lobbyist a list of names to call for campaign contributions. According to an account in *Business Month* magazine, Thevenot took the list and then tried to start explaining what the industry wanted. But Anthony stopped him short and told him to leave a memo. Later, when Thevenot retold the story, Anthony replied, "Yeah, and if you hadn't made the calls, I wouldn't have read [the memo]."

Throughout Washington there were hundreds, even thousands of Wayne Thevenots, distributing millions of dollars in PAC contributions each year in quest of being heard. One of them was Clifford Gibbons, a lobbyist at the law firm Hogan & Hartson. "The PAC, let's face it, gives you more visibility in a town with very, very competitive interests," he confessed to the *National Journal*. If a lobbyist doesn't help a lawmaker raise money, he added, "chances are you are not going to get your phone calls returned. Maybe once, but you are not going to be on anyone's short list." Another lobbyist put it this way: Members of Congress might forget who gave to their last campaign, but "their schedulers don't."

This fact of life was reflected in Washington's ever-burgeoning world of campaign giving. A study of campaign reports filed with the Federal Election Commission showed that from 1972 through the end of 1989 members of the Senate alone raised more than $158 million in PAC donations. During that period, seventy-eight senators raised more than $1 million each, with five Democrats and five Republicans in the top ten. In 1988 alone, PACs contributed $31.9 million to the winners of Senate contests and $86.1 million to winners in the House. In 1989, the giving continued apace. According to *The Washington Post*, PACs contributed more than $57 million, 90 percent of which went to incumbents.

Fund-raising of one kind or another had become virtually a way of life for both lawmakers and lobbyists. Members of Congress, even those with safe seats, spent hours trying to shake the money tree. Boulder County, Colorado, Commissioner Josie Heath, a candidate for the Senate, told the *Post*: "You're just sort of shamelessly begging. That's what federal politics is about." And lobbyists devoted many of their work and after-work hours to either delivering checks, trying to get other lobbyists to deliver checks, or explaining to lawmakers why they couldn't deliver checks.

There was so much giving that lobbyists had to come up with inventive ways to collect more and more money. Increasingly, the nearly five thousand registered PACs built their coffers through "checkoff" programs, which allowed people to contribute automatically through payroll deductions. And once the money was collected, lobbyists spent morning, noon, and night distributing it. Charles Babcock and Richard Morin of *The Washington Post* followed George Gould of the letter carriers' union, which was 1989's biggest PAC, as he attended as many as eleven fund-raisers in a single day. "If I drank," the lobbyist confessed, "I'd be incoherent by eight."

Few lobbyists attended that many fund-raisers, but almost all lobbyists were campaign givers, often through, or with the backing of, a PAC. Thevenot's National Realty Committee PAC, or REAL–PAC, gave $48,250 to fifty-one candidates during the 101st Congress. Juliano's Hotel Employees and Restaurant Employees International Union PAC, called TIP–PAC, gave $230,225 to more than two hundred candidates. And Ken Simonson and Tom Donohue's American Trucking Associations PAC gave $300,040 to 284 candidates. Even Eizenstat's and Kay's law firms established PACs that became major contributors. Eizenstat's firm's PAC gave $131,790 to 167 candidates in 1989 and 1990, and Kay's PAC contributed $91,106 to 142 candidates. In other words, they all covered a lot of ground.

Fund-raising was not confined to PAC contributions. A lot of campaign money came right out of lobbyists' own pockets and the pockets of their clients as well. The *Los Angeles Times* and Common Cause found that seven individuals, in fact, had contributed too much, exceeding the $25,000 legal limit in 1988. These included corporate-buyout specialists Henry Kravis, Ronald O. Perelman, and Harold Simmons, as well as Dwayne Andreas, the chairman of Archer Daniels Midland, and Andreas's wife, Dorothy Inez.

Sometimes individuals grouped together—without the benefit of a PAC—to make sure their voices were heard. Under instruction from Washington-based lobbyists, dozens of lawyers and labor leaders from around the country gathered in a drab hotel not far from Capitol Hill in November of 1987 to contribute more than $80,000 in one sitting to the campaign of Democratic Senator Howard Metzenbaum of Ohio. The send-off was in thanks for Metzenbaum's unswerving support for an eighty-year-old law, the Federal Employers' Liability Act (FELA), that made the lawyers rich and the labor leaders happy. FELA compelled railroad workers who were injured on the job to sue their employers for damages rather than use worker's compensation. With contributions like the ones made that evening, "you get people's attention, and make people aware of what's happening," said Richard Kilroy, chairman of the Railway Labor Executives' Association and an organizer of the event. "That's the most important ingredient."

Most lobbyists could not unleash that much money by themselves. But sometimes they did give personally. During the 101st Congress, Juliano shelled out at least $10,600 to candidates, in addition to the thousands he gave to the hotel workers' PAC. According to FEC records, Eizenstat contributed nearly $4,000 in addition to his contributions to his law firm's PAC. Thevenot, by comparison, gave only $1,200 or so of his own money, and mostly to a fellow Louisianian, Senator John Breaux. Kay gave about $3,500, $2,000 of that to Senator Baucus, his patron, which was certainly a small price to pay.

· · ·

Often political money worked for lobbyists in subtle ways. It was not just a way to buy access and win friends; it also was the ticket to some of the biggest lobbying fests in Washington: political fundraisers.

Thevenot found himself at one on Tuesday, October 24, the gala of the Democratic National Committee at Washington's historic Pension Building. The cavernous yet elegant structure is lined with three-story pillars, and that night it was packed to the rafters with black ties and glittering dresses. Lawmakers by the dozens and lobbyists by the hundreds mingled and chatted. The lobbyists paid $1,500 a head for the opportunity to do this hobnobbing, and the event cleared about $2.5 million for the Democrats' coffers. It was so crowded that the bars ran out of glasses during the cocktail hour, and security guards had to be called in to help close the bars down.

Thevenot made the best of his time there. In his wanderings through the throngs, he ran into Representative Norman Dicks of Washington State. Thevenot knew the congressman from when they both were Senate staffers, and they had stayed in touch through the years. Dicks asked Thevenot what he was up to, and the lobbyist happily explained his new Maglev coalition. Surely, Thevenot thought, a congressman from a region dominated by the Boeing Company would like to know about a new mode of transportation for which the aircraft maker might someday make components.

The table where Thevenot sat had been purchased by the PAC of one of his partner's clients, Wheelabrator Corporation, at the request of Senator Wyche Fowler of Georgia. It was the custom at these functions for lawmakers to contact potential contributors, often Washington lobbyists, and persuade them to buy a table where the lawmaker could sit. This time Thevenot's partner Bill Boardman was tapped. Thevenot himself had been contacted by other senators who had asked him to buy a table. But, he had to explain, a lobbyist could do only so much. His lobbying firm already had bought an entire table, and it was a good thing too. Thevenot's main corporate backer, the National Realty Committee, contributed to individual lawmakers and not to political parties.

Strategically situated then, Thevenot went about some serious schmoozing. A fund-raiser, he explained, "is an opportunity for people in my business to meet a lot of people, see a lot of people, be seen not only by members of Congress, but by potential clients who see you moving with the glitterati of the party. They observe how many of them you seem to know or seem to know you. The facility with which you move around in these circles makes an impression on them. It's kind of nice when you are standing there and someone whom you might want to, at some point, represent, sees a member come up, put his arm around your shoulder, and say, 'Wayne, how are you doin'?' That is part of the reason why you attend these things."

Thevenot found that he too was the object of lobbying. During dinner, Grace Bender, who once worked for Thevenot as an office manager, but had since become a Democratic party loyalist and fund-raiser, reminded him about a fund-raiser she was throwing in six days for Senator Jay Rockefeller of West Virginia. Thevenot agreed to attend. Saying no without good reason, he said, could be dangerous:

"A lot of it you do because you are asked to do it. A member calls you up and says, 'Will you do this?' and you say, 'No'? I'm not sure what kind of reception you would get if you were one of ten people asking to see him that week. Who would get the nod? It's a hell of a risk to take. And we're part of the process. I don't write the campaign-financing rules. But it's the system, and I'm not going to play the martyr and try to change it single-handedly. I'm just going to play it until they change it."

Notably absent from the gala that night was Juliano, who was usually a mainstay at Democratic functions of all sorts. The omission did not go unpunished. About a week before the event, someone from the Democratic National Committee had telephoned Juliano's boss at the union, Edward Hanley, and pointedly asked why the union had not yet purchased a table. Hanley's secretary had called Juliano, who was both wounded and angered. "Listen, let me tell you what happened," Juliano recalled explaining to his superior. "I'm getting tired of using the union's money, which belongs to the members, for fucking functions which do absolutely nothing for anybody. It's gotten to the point where there are no benefits. It's a fucking given that you're expected to do something. And it's like if you don't, we're going to call you. I'm at the point where, Jesus . . . The number of calls you get from people for money—unbelievable!"

· · ·

Meanwhile, the legislative process dragged on without a clear resolution. A breakthrough finally came on the day after the Democratic gala, Wednesday, October 25. That evening Bloomfield was exercising at his usual spot, the University Club on 16th Street. He stepped away from the equipment at about seven-thirty to check his answering machine. There was a message from Larry Harlow, the Treasury lobbyist. "I want you to know that the Packwood proposal has been offered to the Rolland bill," Harlow said into the tape. Sipping a Diet Coke, Bloomfield wondered, "What's the Rolland bill?"

Also on the tape was a call from Ken Hagerty, so Bloomfield decided it would be better to make a few phone calls before he showered. First he tried Harlow. No luck. Finally he reached one of Harlow's assistants, Mary Sophos. "What's going on? What's this Rolland bill?" he asked.

"It's 'Poland,' " she replied, explaining that Packwood had attached his capital-gains plan to a bill authorizing aid to Poland and other Eastern European countries.

"What can I do to help? Should I go up to the Senate?" Bloomfield inquired, feeling more than a little embarrassed.

Sophos said she would check and call back. In the meantime, Bloomfield watched "The MacNeil/Lehrer NewsHour" on the television in the exercise room. By the time Sophos called back to say there would be no further action that night, Bloomfield had decided to telephone coalition members anyway.

He started with Hagerty, but Hagerty was already fully up to speed. A White House lobbyist named Brian Waidmann had alerted him earlier, and he had been following the Senate debate live on C-Span. Bloomfield kept calling, using the telephone numbers he always kept with him in a little notebook. But mostly he reached answering machines and five-year-old children who said their daddies were not home. At about eight-forty-five Bloomfield stopped, ate a tuna fish sandwich, and finally took a shower.

The next morning he was hungry for more information, and knew where he could find it. Representative Michael Andrews of Texas was having a breakfast fund-raiser at eight-thirty at La Colline on Capitol Hill, and Bloomfield attended so he could work the crowd. More than one lobbyist there congratulated him for his clever strategy on the Senate floor the night before. And Bloomfield was honest enough to say he had had nothing to do with it.

Bloomfield came to the event empty-handed. But Thevenot had not. He not only brought a $500 check from the National Realty Committee PAC, but he had persuaded several other real estate lobbyists to contribute as well. Thevenot was a member of Andrews's steering committee, and was responsible for coaxing about $6,000 worth of contributions from groups that ranged from apartment builders to shopping center developers. He had done the same thing earlier in the year for another Ways and Means Democrat, Sam Gibbons of Florida.

Bloomfield and Thevenot spoke briefly at the breakfast event. Over the years, Bloomfield had tried to enlist Thevenot's aid in persuading Trammell Crow Corporation, a big Texas-based real estate developer, to become a member of the American Council for Capital Formation. That morning, Bloomfield informed Thevenot that Trammell Crow had finally joined. "He was rather proud of that," Thevenot recalled. Indeed, Bloomfield was happy to have the entire real estate industry on his side on capital gains. But the two men did not discuss that. Bloomfield was in search of information, and Thevenot did not want to antagonize him by relating his own misgivings about pushing capital gains too hard.

Bloomfield left without learning much. No one in the restaurant—and maybe no one in Washington—knew when or whether the capital-gains tax cut would be enacted. The Poland bill effort, it quickly became apparent, was mostly a symbolic gesture. It would not be the vehicle to carry the issue to victory. So the capital-gains lobbyists continued to plot. At 10 A.M. the coalition gathered at the American Council's office to go over its lists again and make assignments. The White House's Brian Waidmann was there along with members of Bloomfield's core group of lobbyists. The Venture Capitalists agreed to talk to Senator Lieberman; the electronics association took Senator Cranston; and the timber lobbyists agreed to reach Senators Richard Shelby and Howell Heflin of Alabama and Senator Nunn of Georgia. Bloomfield made calls to aides in Senator Bob Graham's office and elsewhere, and sent fact sheets to Republican Senator Connie Mack of Florida. "We still have a majority in Congress and there's still a way we will prevail," Bloomfield asserted. "It's not over."

On Friday, October 27, Hagerty faxed some encouraging news to the coalition. Bush had been meeting personally with members of the Senate to encourage their support, and the White House's best count was that a capital-gains tax cut had fifty-four or even fifty-five votes. "Home owners that want to sell their houses some day and investors all over the country have been looking forward to capital-gains relief. It will not be easy for Senator Mitchell to persuade his colleagues to ignore their constituents—if they are hearing from them," Hagerty wrote. "It is important to remember that a majority of the House, a majority of the Senate and the President all favor this cut."

But on Halloween, Tuesday, October 31, Bloomfield paid a visit to Representative Ed Jenkins to discuss what both men knew in their hearts was an uphill battle. The congressman was more anxious than usual that afternoon, but not because of capital gains. The rigors of the year—first his failed race for majority leader, and then his surprise victory with capital gains in the House—had left him weary. He was having trouble shaking a cold, and three days earlier he had stopped smoking—a habit of decades—in hopes of improving his health. At his meeting with Bloomfield, he was breathing easier but suffering serious nicotine withdrawal.

On this day, most of the talk was not about policy, but politics. The capital-gains forces were increasingly concerned that the Democratic leadership in the Senate might try to block them by using the arcane procedures of the chamber to require them to get sixty votes, rather than a simple majority of fifty-one. And Senator Mitchell, by pressuring his Democratic colleagues to vote against capital gains, appeared to be gaining the upper hand.

"The assumption is that there's forty-four out of forty-five Republicans that will be okay. Some of the members think you're at fifty-one altogether, and it just keeps going back and forth," Bloomfield said, attempting to be conservative in his vote count. But then he added ominously, "If it's a procedural vote, we lose because members can justify voting with the leadership on a procedural vote. They will say that it was not a vote on capital gains."

Bloomfield also expressed his unhappiness that some elements of the business community were not backing the crusade. He said he had been asked by the publisher of *Forbes* magazine if business groups were actively involved in the effort. "And I said some are, but it is not a bottom-line business issue. It is a business issue because it affects your cost of capital, and they should be more involved. That is one of my disappointments."

The rest of the conversation put aside such worries and dwelt on what both men believed was the solid support for their effort, both in Congress and in the electorate. Jenkins said: "I spoke to a group this weekend who were salesmen for a company based in my district. All they wanted to talk about was capital gains. That's because they get some stock every year from the company as a bonus and they sit on it and hold it. And at some point they want to sell and that's the reason."

Jenkins added that he had seen Senator Shelby of Alabama

over the weekend, and he had expressed support for Jenkins's capital-gains plan. "Is that what he told you?" Jenkins asked.

"Yes," Bloomfield replied, and added, "Judge Heflin is on board, too," referring to the other Alabama senator.

"Now I think that there's enough momentum that whatever happens—if they kill us or delay us—we'll send over another bill at the first of the year," Jenkins said. "I think it ultimately will pass. Keep plugging."

"Thank you again," Bloomfield responded. "I appreciate everything you've done. We'll hang in as long as you hang in."

• • •

In the end, though, a majority was not enough. Mitchell and Bentsen had maneuvered the situation so that at least sixty votes were needed for capital gains to prevail. In effect, the Democratic majority was so determined to block the cut that it resorted to a device designed to protect the minority: the filibuster. No matter how the Republicans tried, Mitchell vowed that they would face a sixty-vote hurdle, the number needed to force a vote on the most contentious issues the Senate faced. And this was certainly one of them.

Mitchell had waged a two-tiered campaign against the President's priority. Publicly, he argued that the cut was unfair and fiscally irresponsible. Privately, he demanded the personal allegiance of his fellow Democrats, using procedural votes on capital gains as a test of their loyalty. "This vote is for me!" he told them in seemingly endless meetings in his office. He also played hardball partisan politics, asking some wavering colleagues, "Do you want to be the one who gives George Bush a victory?"

The capital-gains lobbyists tried to fight back. Ed Hatcher's electronics association mounted yet another letter-writing campaign. Letters were dispatched to Graham of Florida and Robb of Virginia from electronics executives in their states. The New England Council of the association held what it called a CEO breakfast with Kerry of Massachusetts to urge him to vote for capital gains. But to no avail. On Thursday, November 2, the Republicans threw in the towel, realizing they could not get the requisite sixty votes. In order to get on with more-important deficit-reduction efforts, Minority Leader Robert Dole agreed to set capital gains aside—at least for the time being. "Lightning might strike, perchance," said House Minority Leader Robert Michel. "But I couldn't conceive of it before the end of this session."

. . .

During that same autumn week, Chairman Dan Rostenkowski traveled halfway across the country to deliver a special dose of reality to a group that had agreed to pay him a few thousand dollars. The group was the American Trucking Associations, which deeply opposed the gas-tax increase Rostenkowski favored. Rostenkowski's message was this: All this fooling around in Washington could not be sustained. Meaningful deficit-cutting would soon be on the way, and the truckers, like every other interest group, had better be wary. Rostenkowski addressed a packed auditorium at the truckers' annual meeting in a Chicago hotel. The truckers' Tom Donohue introduced the chairman with glowing praise and only an oblique reference to his support of the dreaded gas tax. But Rostenkowski did not pull his punches.

"Our refusal to attack the deficit would be comic if it were not so irresponsible," he said. "We simply refuse to pay for the government services that we demand. The result is a debt that grows by fifty million dollars each and every day. Our willingness to saddle our children and their children with this debt is an outrage. . . . Let's stop pretending that taxes should not be part of this debate and start talking about the fairest and most efficient way to raise needed revenue. It's no secret that I have advocated an increase in the gas tax as part of a large and balanced deficit-reduction measure. I know that's not a popular stand in this room and I respect the association's position. My point today is that we're afraid to admit that any new taxes are needed, much less [discuss] what they should be. If we are ever going to put our fiscal house in order, we've got to get our heads out of the sand. . . . My first rule in approaching all of these issues is that everything has to be on the table. All taxes and all spending. No sacred cows. We may disagree, but we have to start working."

The warning was chilling to both Donohue and his economist, Ken Simonson. But they did not panic. Rostenkowski had pushed a gas-tax hike before, and nothing had happened. And in this slide-by year of 1989, big-ticket taxes like that one clearly were off the table. Maybe next year, they thought—and then again, maybe not. At least they would be ready. Thanks to the Rostenkowski address that they had solicited, they at least had been forewarned.

• • •

Back in Washington, with capital gains effectively laid aside, legislation of all sorts began moving more freely. Coretech also began to have more luck, and surely it needed some. Its R&D tax credits were scheduled to disappear entirely at year end.

On Friday, November 10, Senator John Danforth's tax aide, Tracy Kaye, telephoned Coretech's Ken Kay at his office. The two had been in steady contact because of their mutual interest in tax breaks. The aide was calling this time to inform Coretech that her boss was planning to offer an amendment on the Senate floor on Monday at 2 P.M. that would extend all of the expiring tax breaks, including Coretech's. She urged the lobbyist to "rally the troops" and assist her in finding other senators who would support Danforth's effort.

"We'll do what we can," Kay replied eagerly, and hung up the phone. He drafted a memo to Coretech companies, telling them about Danforth's amendment and asking for help in finding co-sponsors. He faxed the one-page note to the activists in his group, knowing they would probably find it as soon as they came in to work on Monday and began making calls.

But when Monday arrived it was Kay's own phone that was ringing. His members were worried that the Danforth amendment might prove to be more of a problem than it was worth. None of them knew for sure whether there were enough votes to support such an effort. If there were not, they would be reluctant to lend their support.

After considering the issue, Ken Kay called Tracy Kaye. "Some of our people are worried that there might actually be a negative vote," the lobbyist said. "If we take a 'no' vote it's worse than not having one. What are we really going to do?"

"Don't worry," the aide replied. "We won't let ourselves get in a posture where we're going to lose a vote. If we think we're going to lose, we won't offer it."

At that moment, Kay recalled, "that's when I sort of became

confident that they would offer it and withdraw it"—and that was precisely what happened later that day. The Danforth effort, like the Packwood ploy on the Poland bill before it, was designed primarily to demonstrate the importance of the issue, rather than to force an immediate resolution.

In the meantime, the Maglev issue was rapidly coming to a head; this was an especially important development for Thevenot, since, by his own choosing, his work with the National Realty Committee would conclude at the end of the year. After much prodding, Thevenot and Boardman met with the head of the Federal Railway Administration, Gilbert Carmichael. The get-together was a hopeful sign that some funding might be forthcoming.

Carmichael was a blustery, white-haired man who once sold advertising space for *The Wall Street Journal*. But he quit that job after hearing the company's chief executive say that only newsmen—and not business-side executives like Carmichael—would ever be allowed to run the corporation. Feeling personally slighted, Carmichael chose instead to become a car dealer in Mississippi, a vocation he found was a more than ample substitute. A failed political career later in life qualified him for his current position, a midlevel patronage job in the bowels of the Transportation Department.

Carmichael was no fan of government funding for such fancy technology as Maglev. A true believer in the hands-off, private-sector-first philosophy of the Ronald Reagan era, he would have preferred to give strong words of encouragement rather than U.S. taxpayer dollars to almost anything that fell under his purview—anything, apparently, except his travel budget, which was ostensibly the reason for his meeting with the lobbyists in November. In his thickly carpeted office, Carmichael briefed Thevenot and Boardman about his recent trip to Germany and the Maglev system he saw there.

Such a courtesy probably would not have been extended to the lobbyists had Carmichael not crossed swords with Senator Daniel Moynihan the week before. At a meeting of the High Speed Rail Association at the Mayflower Hotel in downtown Washington on Thursday, November 9, Moynihan had delivered a blistering critique of the government's inattention to Maglev. Moynihan had recalled Carmichael's recent testimony before the Senate Commerce Committee as a particularly flagrant example of this foolish neglect. He even called Carmichael a "boob."

"Carmichael is a classic man," Moynihan had begun. "He said, 'I had a chance to be in Russia and look at their system on Maglev and to sign an agreement for swapping technology. And their research-and-development man said they had four thousand people in their department. I believe our fifteen people over here are doing some great work to match any work they can do.' Fifteen Americans, four thousand Russian slobs. This man was a used-car dealer in Mississippi before he lost an election, or something like that. I don't know him. I don't want to be disparaging of him, personally. But anybody who would say that is a boob. Right? . . . That's the sort of man that loses wars. Make him a general, and you lose the war."

At the moment those lines had been uttered, a Carmichael aide who was stationed in the audience had dashed to a telephone. Carmichael was scheduled to speak next, and the aide had wanted to be sure Carmichael knew that the audience had been expecting to hear a "boob." At the meeting in Carmichael's office a week later with Thevenot and Boardman, Carmichael was still hesitant to commit much, but at least this time he was listening.

Carmichael was forced into action soon, however, when Thevenot's lobbying at La Colline earlier in the year began to bear fruit. A $1 million appropriation for a Maglev study by the U.S. Army Corps of Engineers was passed in a bill that bore the fingerprints of Senator Bennett Johnston, whose aide Thevenot and Boardman had lobbied over lunch. Not wanting to be outdone, Carmichael's Federal Railway Administration sought and got its own appropriation of $500,000 for a separate Maglev study. In bureaucracies, turf is all-important, and Carmichael did not want to lose any of his to the Corps of Engineers—even if the matter was one to which he was not wedded. It was a small start, but at least it was a start. It was also more than enough for Thevenot to prove that Maglev USA was a coalition with a future.

. . .

Despite being blocked in the Senate, the capital-gains lobbyists had not given up completely. They still believed that they had a majority of votes in the Senate, and they wanted to prove it. The

Bush administration also was still eager to flex its muscles over the issue. A cut in capital-gains taxes was, after all, the President's top domestic priority. The White House began a new drumbeat to develop and mobilize support. To do so, officials reached out to the corporate lobbyists in town.

In the late afternoon of Monday, November 6, lobbyists from all over town were summoned to the Roosevelt Room at the White House. Bloomfield had not expected to go anywhere that day and was wearing a tweed jacket, a sweater, and a green tie with the words CAPITALIST TOOL written on it. Usually he would have gone home to change his clothes, but he decided that his colleagues thought of him as a daffy professor anyway. So he left for the meeting at about 5 P.M., dressed as he was. To his distress, his gray-suited friends poked fun at him as soon as he arrived.

The jollity ended when three Bush administration heavyweights marched into the room: Treasury Secretary Nicholas Brady, White House Chief of Staff John Sununu, and Budget Director Richard Darman. Brady was the first to speak, and his message was simple and straightforward: The administration remained committed to lowering capital-gains taxes. "The real question," he said, "is 'When is the vote?' "

Darman then made a pitch for help. He conceded that Senator Mitchell would continue to win as long as he insisted on a sixty-vote hurdle. But he said that there were probably twenty-two Democrats who were strong prospects to support a capital-gains cut. Of those, only seven were needed to assure a majority vote. "The private sector needs to deliver," he said, and he listed some good candidates whom the lobbyists should try to win over: DeConcini, Graham, Heflin, Boren, Baucus, Bryant, Lieberman, and Shelby, among others.

Sununu took the floor to assert that there might be a chance for a vote on capital gains that required only a majority to win. He joked that one such opportunity might come on the motion to adjourn for the year. So strong was the lawmakers' interest in starting their vacations before Thanksgiving, Sununu said, that they would accept anything that allowed them to leave on time.

It would not have been a laughing matter if a capital-gains bill got less than a majority, however, and Hagerty gave voice to that nagging fear. "Could we pull back" if a loss seemed imminent? he asked. Darman assured him that they could. But the lobbyists had the best chance of stirring enough interest in the bill to avoid that outcome, Darman said, by generating letters from back home to lawmakers.

After the meeting a few of the capital-gains stalwarts stayed behind to talk to Fred McClure and Brian Waidmann of the White House lobbying staff. There Bloomfield spoke frankly in a way that he felt constrained from doing in front of the other lobbyists. "I haven't heard anything here today which changes the equation," he complained. So why, he wondered, should he have to go back to senators he had been bugging for weeks to ask for their votes again? What was the point? "If you are below fifty-one, there is no way it is a victory," he recalled saying. "If you are at fifty-one, I'm not sure what you gain. And if you are at fifty-four, I'm not sure what you gain either, especially given the price of getting there."

Still, the lobbyists gamely went through their lists again and decided to focus their attention on Lieberman, DeConcini, and Baucus. Someone would try to speak to each of them. As a reward for their assistance, Waidmann treated the lobbyists to a tour of the Oval Office.

A week later, on Tuesday, November 14, the Capital Gains Coalition hovered around the Senate chamber, hoping to catch a last-minute word with senators. During part of the debate, though, Senator Dole's tax aide, Carolyn Seely, escorted some of them to what is known as the wives' gallery in the Senate chamber itself, where they sat for a while. This gallery, on the east wall of the chamber, is where senators usually situate their family members— or special friends—until they can go off the floor to talk to them in person. But this day it was also home to the capital-gains lobbyists.

When it came time for the vote, the lobbyists migrated back down to the Senate reception room and watched a television tuned to C-Span. No one knew for sure how the vote would come out. There was still the worry that Mitchell might even prevent them from getting a majority. But a cheer went up from the group when first Lieberman and then, as a surprise, Johnston of Louisiana voted against Senator Mitchell and in favor of capital gains. Johnston's vote, it was said later, had as much to do with a tiff he was having with Mitchell at the time as it did with his backing for capital gains. But no matter, it was the vote the lobbyists needed to score a face-saving win.

"Although we were not able to end the filibuster today, I am heartened by the strength of the vote," Senator Packwood said afterward. "This vote proves that there is a majority in the Senate that supports a reduction in the capital-gains tax. You can be sure that we will push this again and again next year. In the end, we will win this battle."

Hagerty dispatched his own, slightly hyperbolic memo of praise as well: "Our coalition just scored a major psychological victory by garnering an absolute majority of the Senate on the first of two cloture votes. . . . The unexpected strength of our votes, against the intense, personal lobbying of Senator Mitchell now shifts the momentum on this issue back to the President and the pro-capital-gains forces."

In truth, the victory was dangerously thin—51–47. Only six Democrats broke with Mitchell. In addition to Lieberman and Johnston, there were Boren, DeConcini, Heflin, and Shelby—all prime targets of the lobbyists. Rather than feeling ecstatic, many of the lobbyists were simply relieved.

After the vote, Dole came out to the reception room to thank the lobbyists for their efforts. "Meet some real taxpayers," Dole quipped to a couple of other senators who were standing with him. "Keep up the good fight," he added, shaking hands all around. "We will win this thing together." But to some of the lobbyists, the words did not ring true.

A similar encounter was played out later in Secretary Brady's conference room at the Treasury Department. "We surprised a lot of people by coming as far as we had," Brady said to the assembled lobbyists. He then began to talk about next year.

• • •

On the same day that capital gains was officially stopped, the R&D credit was officially revived. The long-suffering aid-to-Poland bill was finally passed by the Senate and sent to the House with a six-month extension of all of the expiring tax breaks attached to it. The House had quietly approved temporary extensions of the expiring provisions already, so it was now up to House and Senate negotiators to find a compromise.

Kay and Eizenstat were hopeful that the R&D credit would be extended somehow. But for how long, and in what form, was a complete mystery. Indeed, it was still unclear where the money to pay for the extensions would come from. After all, the point of the entire budget exercise was to *reduce* the deficit, not *enlarge* it.

But Kay counseled patience and minimal action. "Part of what we do as counselors is to avoid having the group burn up its chits where it's not going to have a lot of utility," Kay said. In the capital-gains fight, for example, the issue's "visibility was so high . . . that discretion was the better part of valor." Repeatedly, Eizenstat and Kay had advised their clients to stay out of that fight, so as not to risk angering Democratic leaders. "We should pick our shots carefully," Kay told them.

Mostly, then, Coretech sat and watched. Some small precautions were taken; for example, telegrams from Coretech, signed by its chairman, Roland Schmitt, were sent to high administration officials. And James Burke, the chief executive of Johnson & Johnson, was asked to contact Treasury Secretary Brady again, as he had done earlier in the year, just to remind him of the credit's importance. As Thanksgiving neared with no clear signal about the fate of their provisions, Kay did begin to panic, and he gave serious thought to mounting a full-scale mailing to Congress and the administration.

But by the week before Thanksgiving it was clear that the credit would be part of the final budget plan. Tax-writers had agreed with the White House that the package should include a net increase of about $6 billion in tax revenue in the fiscal year that began October 1. The net figure in the package, which was part of a broad deficit-reduction measure, would result from $7.9 billion in tax increases and $1.9 billion in tax cuts—primarily the extension of tax breaks. Another nearly $10 billion was raised in fiscal 1990 through spending restraint.

The taxes were raised mostly through obscure tax-law changes that included increases in some excise taxes and the modest restriction of tax benefits for corporate leveraged buy-outs. One not-so-obscure provision was a back-door increase in the Social Security payroll tax. Several provisions were essentially gimmicks, one-time revenue raisers that simply sped up the collection of such items as the payroll, gasoline, and airline-ticket taxes, rather than increasing them outright. Indeed, the measure's biggest revenue-raising provision—accounting for $2.45 billion in the first year—forced major corporations to speed up their payment of payroll taxes to the federal government. Another notable tax increase was the one authored by Ken Kies, which dealt with cellular telephones.

One of the last decisions the lawmakers made was on the length of the extension for the expiring tax breaks. Everyone seemed to agree that they should be extended; they were sweeteners that could help pass the politically painful deficit-cutting package. Bill Signer, the lobbyist who headed the "ugly" coalition that was fighting to extend the provisions, stood with reporters in the hall outside the Senate chamber late on the night the final terms were decided in Mitchell's office. Nine months was the verdict, and Signer had to shake his head. Why not a full year? he wondered. The answer, lobbyists were convinced, had a lot to do with capital gains. Republicans, still eager to cut capital-gains taxes, thought an autumn deadline for the popular credits would force an early tax bill in 1990, to which they could attach the ever-present capital-gains cuts.

The result was clearly a disappointment to Coretech. "We came within a hair's breadth of getting permanence," Kay said. "Were it not for another set of lousy circumstances, we would have gotten it." But at least the R&D credit was still alive. Nineteen ninety would provide another, and perhaps better, chance for a permanent extension. "Our basic posture is to go back and work harder; it will get us over the hump," Kay said hopefully. But he added with a sigh, "It's a lot of work for a little credit, isn't it?"

• • •

The year did not come to a close until yet another lobbying-related scandal had hit a high point in Congress. Throughout the year, revelations had dribbled out about influence-peddling at the Department of Housing and Urban Development during the Reagan administration. And in November, as Congress prepared to close up for the year, the Justice Department was preparing to appoint an independent counsel to investigate charges of criminal fraud against Samuel R. Pierce, Jr., the former secretary of HUD.

In the months that preceded this development, three congressional committees had held eighteen hearings with testimony from thirty-nine witnesses about the HUD mess. A major focus of the inquiry was the way that former Reagan officials and other prominent Republicans were able to use their pull to win huge federal housing subsidies for their clients. In exchange for obtaining this special treatment, the lobbyists hauled in for themselves some $6 million in lobbying fees, which congressional Democrats asserted were little more than political payoffs.

Many of the abuses occurred in the Section 8 Moderate Rehabilitation Program, which was designed to repair privately owned housing so that it could be made available to low-income families. Poverty-stricken individuals were the ultimate beneficiaries of the program, but the wealthy developers who owned the properties also gained handsomely. In exchange for the renovations, the program guaranteed the developers fifteen years' worth of federal rent subsidies.

It turned out that getting the grants, which totaled hundreds of millions of dollars a year, was often as much a matter of political favor-giving as of need. A report written by HUD Inspector General Paul A. Adams concluded that deciding who got the grants "was based on the perception and reality of favoritism." Adams testified that seventeen well-connected individuals benefited financially from about fifty-five HUD-subsidized projects, and that as a result, only ten states got 51 percent of all of the subsidized housing units funded by the department.

The list of those who received the favors was a compendium of Republican insiders. Former Interior Secretary James Watt was paid more than $420,000 in consulting fees. Frederick M. Bush, a longtime aide to President Bush (but not a relative), and his firm grossed more than $600,000 from HUD-related business. And Paul Manafort, a big-time GOP political consultant and lobbyist, collected $326,000 for getting HUD to help a New Jersey project that local authorities called "a horrible waste of taxpayers' money." Manafort conceded that he had engaged in political influence-peddling, and both Republicans and Democrats expressed outrage. "This is a smelly system," accused GOP Representative Christopher Shays of Connecticut.

There was nothing new about Washington's revolving door. Former insiders had been going on to lobby for corporate interests for many years. What was startling about the HUD scandal was that it involved a bureaucracy that most people thought was lobby-proof. It also appeared to be part of a pattern that infected the entire eight-year Reagan administration.

In December of 1987, Michael Deaver had been convicted of perjury relating to testimony about his lobbying activities. The former deputy chief of staff, a longtime close aide to President Reagan, was ordered to pay a fine of $100,000, was placed on probation for three years, and was required to perform 1,500 hours of community service. He was also prohibited from lobbying the federal government for profit, which was a major loss for him.

Before his fall, Deaver "was part of a growing cadre of ex-officials who were cashing in on their government relationships," according to a report issued in 1989 by Whitney North Seymour, Jr., the independent counsel in the Deaver case. It was not hard for Deaver to find lobbying business. As a lobbyist, he made contacts with his old pals in the administration on behalf of TWA, Smith Barney, Boeing, and Rockwell International, among others, for fees ranging from $100,000 to $250,000 a year.

"Access" lobbying like this was harshly criticized by Seymour. "The problem can be stated simply," he said in his report to Congress. "A small group of highly-paid consultants is able to gain special privilege for its clients because of personal and political ties to senior staff members in the White House and other executive agencies, including most major departments and key independent agencies in Washington. These consultants have direct 'back channel' access to decision-makers in the Executive Branch that is not available to citizens at large."

The independent counsel's top recommendation to close this "back channel" was to end the secrecy that pervaded Executive Branch lobbying. He said:

> Secrecy is important to successful Executive Branch lobbying from two points of view: 1) For business reasons, the client does not want publicity about its high-fee lobbying with government officials. 2) For political reasons, the Executive Branch official does not want publicity about his accessibility to high-fee lobby-ists. From the standpoint of public interest, lobbying is most

dangerous when it is carried on in secret, with no one representing the citizen-taxpayer or the public at large.

In addition, Seymour suggested the closing of several loopholes in the Ethics in Government Act. A major one was the way in which the White House was "compartmentalized" into separate agencies so that former high government officials such as Deaver could lobby most of their former colleagues with impunity soon after leaving the public payroll. Seymour also found that the law was so loosely written that former officials could still have "social and informational" visits with former colleagues, which was usually what lobbying was about anyway. Another gaping hole was that former Executive Branch officials could talk with their successors about issues that were not before the agency at the moment.

"Present-day lobbying of the Executive Branch of the federal government," Seymour concluded, "is an unregulated, freewheeling, essentially lawless activity that is damaging to public confidence in the government, and potentially harmful to the integrity of the governmental process."

By the end of 1989, Seymour's views were adopted by a powerful lawmaker, Senate Appropriations Chairman Robert Byrd. In addition to reacting with disgust to the HUD revelations, the West Virginia Democrat had gotten his own taste of lobbying, and it did not suit his palate. During the summer, a delegation of officials from West Virginia University had arrived for a meeting in Byrd's office, accompanied by lobbyists whom they had hired. Byrd coolly directed the lobbyists to wait while he met privately with his constituents. Behind closed doors, the gray-haired lawmaker vented his resentment and outrage. "Why do you waste your money on a lobbyist when I'm being paid to be your senator?" he asked. "I'm on the Appropriations Committee—if I can't do it, nobody can."

The fiery encounter led eventually to the loss for the university of $18 million in federal funds for a research center, and to a decision by Byrd that lobbying needed to be reined in. One of the chief targets of his anger was Cassidy & Associates, a rapidly growing lobbying firm in Washington that was West Virginia University's lobbyist. Headed by former Senate aide Gerald Cassidy, the company specialized in obtaining federal research projects for universities. Its one hundred clients included forty colleges, and its billings in 1988 had hit a whopping $15 million.

All of this was too much for Byrd. So he attached a tough anti-lobbying amendment to the spending bill for the Interior Department. It required anyone who received large federal contracts, loans, grants, or loan guarantees to disclose the identity of lobbyists they paid to help them obtain the money. The reports had to specify how much money the lobbyists earned, what actions they took to earn it, and the source of the compensation. Recipients of federal funds were expressly prohibited from using any of that money to pay for lobbyists.

The goal of the Byrd amendment was to put a chill into the kinds of influence-peddling that were made famous by the HUD scandals, and, he thought, in a smaller way, to end lobbying in his own office. "We've seen what happened on the HUD cases," said GOP Representative Ralph Regula of Ohio, a leading House supporter of the Byrd amendment. "We don't want to be embarrassed again."

Congress also enacted other reforms that made clear that for at least one year, and in some cases two years, high-level executives from the government could not come back to lobby their old friends and colleagues. Congress stopped the executive office of the President from "compartmentalizing," and widened the number of former officials who were prevented from lobbying through government's revolving door. Congress imposed similar restrictions on itself as well. It barred members and officers of Congress from lobbying their own, legislative, branch of government for a year after they left office. And for a year after they left the government payroll, former congressional staffers were prohibited from lobbying the member, office, or committee for which they had worked. The new restrictions passed easily with bipartisan support.

By giving the public these new lobbying laws, congressional leaders believed they had the leeway to give something to themselves as well. Jim Wright had ruined their chances early in the year of getting a 51 percent pay raise. But maybe a 40 percent raise was more doable, they thought, and at the very end of the session they moved quickly to make it law. To help ease public outrage over the pay raise, they also proposed to either ban or reduce the amount of special-interest honorarium money they could keep.

On November 18, Congress cleared a measure that increased salaries of House members to $96,600 in 1990 and $125,000 in 1991 from their existing base of $89,500. Senators' salaries were set to rise to $98,400 in 1990, but they balked at approving the heftier second phase of the increase. Instead, they voted to increase their pay only with the rate of inflation in 1991. Honoraria were slated to be banned completely in the House and reduced in the Senate.

Fred Wertheimer, president of the "citizens' lobby" Common Cause, hailed the legislation. The trade-off of more taxpayer-paid salaries for limits on honoraria and ethics-law changes, he said, "could well spell the beginning of the end of the anything-goes ethics era that has dominated Washington in the 1980s."

But Ralph Nader of Public Citizen said the size of the raise was unconscionable, and he vowed to try to roll it back. Rather than proving that corruption was abating, Nader implied, the pay raise was yet another sign that Washington was rotten to its core. Only in official Washington, where even young lobbyists and lawyers routinely made more than $100,000 a year, did $89,500 seem like a pittance.

6

The
Fly-In

Robert Juliano did his work with great subtlety. He would rarely
confess to applying any pressure on anyone. But a small window
onto his mysterious ways was opened on the evening of the first
day of the second session of the two-year 101st Congress, Tuesday,
January 23, 1990. At his favorite watering hole, Giorgio's, near
Georgetown, Juliano hosted a birthday party for Illinois Representative Marty Russo and about thirty of his well-placed friends.

Originally the party was planned for only twenty-four people,
mostly lawmakers and lobbyists. But others invited themselves,
and Juliano, the ever-gracious host, could not say no. So, to give
everyone enough room to eat and be merry, the restaurant manager put an extra, circular table at the end of the long one he had
already set.

One of Juliano's first conversations of the evening was with
Representative Barbara Kennelly, a Democrat of Connecticut and
a member of the Ways and Means Committee. She also was one
of the most outspoken members of Congress on the taxation of
insurance companies, because so many of them were headquar-

tered in her state. Juliano did not discuss insurance taxes with her directly that evening, even though he lobbied for the stock-insurance side of the business. Instead, he worked to get on the congresswoman's good side. He told her that someone who worked for Bruce Morrison, another Connecticut lawmaker, had telephoned him to ask for a campaign contribution for his impending race for governor. But before he contributed, he said, he wanted to make sure that Kennelly had no interest in running. Obviously impressed by the deference he showed, she moved with Juliano to the bar to talk some more—until they were interrupted by Vincent Reusing, one of the leaders of the mutual life-insurance companies, the sworn enemies of Juliano's stock companies.

The hyperactive Reusing brazenly sat down next to Juliano and Kennelly and insinuated himself into their conversation. After a while the rarely rude Juliano simply exploded in disgust. "They're all in the other room," he said indignantly, as a way to get rid of Reusing.

But Reusing could not be stopped from lobbying. When Representative Tom Downey, his wife, and their two children arrived later that evening, they all sat next to Juliano at the circular table, which they quickly dubbed the children's table. For a while they chatted amiably. But in the same way that Juliano was a light touch, Reusing was a sledgehammer. Downey was the champion of the mutual life-insurance companies, and Reusing could not stand the thought of a lobbyist for the rival stock companies having the lawmaker to himself for so long. As a result, Reusing again intruded. First, he got down on one knee to talk to Downey. Then, when someone got up to go to the bathroom, he took the vacated seat and would not give it up. Even when Juliano finally told him to go back to the other table, Reusing would not relent. He tried to wedge another chair next to the helpless Downey.

"Crazy Vince Reusing," Juliano said later with a shake of his head. "He basically has lost it." But the lobbyist's ungraceful actions illustrated the intensity of the fight ahead between the stock and mutual life-insurance companies, the biggest tax-lobbying gravy train of 1990. Hundreds of millions—and maybe billions—of dollars were potentially at stake, so entire platoons of lobbyists were hired by each side. So numerous were the lobbyist minions on the issue that it was sometimes more useful to think of official Washington as divided not between Republicans and Democrats, but between stocks and mutuals.

In the volatile world of Washington lobbying, victory was sweet but chaos was sweeter. For a lobbyist, nothing was better than a long, even bitter, legislative battle, and nothing was worse than a final resolution. Constant conflict was what kept coffers brimming. Peace meant only poverty. In that sense, the battle between the stock and mutual life-insurance companies was a classic.

The issue was simple enough: How should the federal government tax these two different types of business enterprises? The two types of life insurers sold the same products: life insurance, annuities, and health insurance. But because their corporate structures were different, they paid taxes in different ways. Mutuals were owned by their policyholders and could deduct some of the dividends they paid out. Stock companies, on the other hand, were owned by their shareholders and could not deduct their dividend payments. The bottom line, stock companies complained, was that mutuals got away with paying less in taxes. And this created what each side called a serious competitive problem. It was a disagreement that had been raging for more than eighty years—since the very inception of the federal income tax—and the lobbyists were happy to keep the pot boiling.

In 1990, Congress was preparing to take another crack at addressing the dispute, but no one in the lobbying community was worried that it would actually be resolved. "There is no way you can get the right answer," William Harman, the lead lobbyist for the stock companies, said confidently. "You can get only an approximately correct answer." Harman, for one, had been working on the stock-mutual conflict since 1958, when he was a junior aide at the Treasury Department.

The warring sides arrayed themselves in full battle regalia. Each was equipped with Republican and Democratic lobbyists, and with House and Senate lobbyists. There were company and industry association lobbyists and even lobbyists for factions. The smaller mutuals hired a lobbyist to protect them from the big mutuals. Each side was spending millions of dollars, and the result was clear: Everywhere lawmakers went, life-insurance lobbyists were there.

They were at fund-raisers. The stocks and the mutuals held separate fund-raisers for congressional tax-writers. They convened breakfasts, lunches, and dinners for the legislators and their staffs. They paid honoraria when they could to attract lawmakers, and when they could not, they paid for everything else—during lobbying weekends at exotic or fun places ranging from New York to New Orleans and from the Homestead resort in Virginia, to Kiawah Island, South Carolina. One mutual company even sponsored a lobbying event in December in Des Moines, Iowa, presumably to avoid being accused of trying to bribe congressional staffers with irresistible junkets.

So essential to the industry was this effort that the lobbying was not left to the lobbyists alone. The companies resorted to using *real* people, too. Well, almost real. Washington lobbyists flew out to the districts of pivotal members of Congress to recruit insurance salespeople and train them on how to make their case. Their message was usually delivered personally, during brief encounters with lawmakers that the industry called "meet-and-greets," and was later reinforced in letters the agents wrote at the behest of Washington lobbyists.

The most important part of all of this was that neither side should ever be outdone. The mutuals took this creed to the maximum. No doubt in order to cement relations with their chief House sponsor, six mutual companies contributed a total of $100,000 to a charity function organized by Representative Downey's wife, Chris. Another organizer of the event called the contributions coincidence, but in the world of lobbying such coincidences were usually well planned.

• • •

On the chilly afternoon of Monday, February 5, 1990, the stewardess in the first-class cabin of Delta Airlines Flight 701 dispensed some extra packets of peanuts. One of her passengers was Mitchell Kertzman, a man who liked to munch as he pondered the challenges he was about to face. The chubby and charming Kertzman ran his own software company, called Computer Solutions Incorporated, later named Powersoft Corporation. But this day he was flying to Washington from Boston to sell not floppy disks, but an idea: cutting capital-gains taxes.

For the next two days, Kertzman and a dozen fellow chief executive officers of electronics companies would serve as corporate lobbyists. They each believed deeply that reducing the tax would help spur investment, particularly in fast-growing cutting-edge businesses like their own. But they also knew that their argument had a weakness: as top executives, they made too much money to avoid seeming grossly self-interested. Any capital-gains tax cut would surely help make them richer. "These are dangerous times on Capitol Hill," Kertzman asserted. "People say, 'Hey, you're a CEO, what are you complaining about?' "

Still, the "CEO Fly-In," as the event was called, represented the year's first major salvo in the renewed fight for a capital-gains tax reduction. Lobbyists well understood that many of the old fights from the previous year were about to be revived, and that capital gains would be first among them. But many, like these electronics executives, sensed that they had better start preparing their best case for what they suspected would be a big year.

The CEO Fly-In was sponsored by the American Electronics Association, of which Kertzman was chairman. And it was an example of a growing number of working visits to the capital by the nation's corporate chieftains. By virtue of their hands-on experience in business, chief executives were regarded as the most effective kind of corporate lobbyist, more potent even than the hired guns who usually trolled the halls of Congress on their behalf. But in the case of the capital-gains tax cut, even the CEOs had their work cut out for them.

The situation was a running joke with the garrulous Kertzman. Before he left for Washington from his teal-and-gray offices overlooking the Route 128 high-tech corridor in Burlington, Massachusetts, he told his chief marketing executive, Robert Roda: "I'll be lobbying for tax breaks for the rich. Maybe we'll get more that way." And as soon as he arrived in Washington, he suggested to the other CEOs that they form a new trade association, to be called NARP: the National Association of Rich Persons.

The electronics association did not think that was so funny. As its briefing papers for Kertzman made clear, capital gains needed to overcome the stigma of being a rich person's tax break. That, indeed, was what the visit was all about. "We need to get across that this is not a 'fat cat' issue but a 'jobs issue,' " the document stated. Emphasizing how a lower capital-gains tax would encourage long-term investments "has worked especially well with Democratic members of Congress," it added.

For the next two days, the CEOs fanned out on Capitol Hill to press the case with their local lawmakers. Kertzman also had an additional assignment. He was slated, and for good reason, to focus on Democrats, no matter where they were from. Unlike most of the other CEOs, the forty-one-year-old entrepreneur was a Democrat. And he was not shy about using that fact to curry favor. It even tickled him to refer to himself as the "Sandinista in pinstripes."

The lobbying began on Tuesday, February 6, with a breakfast meeting that featured Ed Jenkins, who was ready again to push his capital-gains package through the House. The session was held in the sparsely furnished conference room next to a bank of elevators in the Rayburn House Office Building. Kertzman and six other CEOs took turns regaling Jenkins with tales about opportunities they had lost because of their lack of financing. Until things got better, complained Robert Gilbertson of the Connecticut-based Data Switch Corporation, he would have no choice but to print his business cards in both English and Japanese, and he displayed one to the group.

As the leader of the group, Kertzman had the job of saying thank you to the congressman. "Washington is a place with large but sensitive egos," Kertzman explained later. "If somebody's carried your water, it's important to acknowledge that as part of this whole process." But the executive laid it on thick. When Jenkins predicted lightheartedly that any new capital-gains law would surely be more "perfect" than his own proposal, Kertzman gushed, "There aren't any flaws in your proposal." He then mistakenly called Jenkins "Senator."

After the meeting with Jenkins, the CEOs trekked across the Capitol grounds through the winter air to meet with Senator Joseph Lieberman of Connecticut, one of the few Democratic senators who had voted for a capital-gains preference in 1989. In a chandeliered room off the Senate floor, Lieberman seemed as interested in thanking the CEOs as they were in thanking him. One of the executives, Papken der Torossian of the Silicon Valley Group of California, personalized his pitch for capital gains by announcing that he wanted to buy part of an ailing electronics company in Lieberman's home state, and thought the tax break would help. Lieberman responded with a broad grin and said, "Would it be inappropriate if I rushed over and embraced you?"

But Lieberman was cautious about the outlook for capital gains, and implored the CEOs to maintain their vigilance. "I'm encouraged, but I'm not overly confident. There's a lot of work yet to be done," he said, and added that the work the CEOs did was particularly important. "Your influence is considerable," he said, and urged them to meet with and write to as many lawmakers as they could.

"Capital gains will be portrayed as helping the wealthy," Lieberman warned. "But we have to continue to make the point that that's not the point. The point is that the capital-gains cut creates an incentive for the people who have the capital to put it places that benefit society. Without the lower cost of capital, without some sort of incentive, we're not going to be viable, we're not going to be able to employ people. You can't just say that it helps a few rich people. You can't have a successful capitalist system without a few successful capitalists."

• • •

One way the electronics association tried to gain access to lawmakers was to play the home-state card. Each meeting on Capitol Hill that day carefully included at least one CEO from the lawmaker's own region. But that was not possible in the case of their next scheduled encounter, with Senator Max Baucus: There was no association member in his state of Montana. Instead, the association's entrée was based on money—or so the leadership thought. The association "was key host for a Silicon Valley CEO fund-raiser on his behalf last year," according to its briefing papers. But Baucus missed the meeting anyway.

That evening the CEOs tried to lure even more lawmakers by holding a reception in the Capitol in honor of Kertzman. More than thirty lawmakers showed up, but few of them seemed to know—or care—much about the businessman-lobbyist. Representative Jake Pickle of the Ways and Means Committee draped his arm around Kertzman and inquired about "Route 130" (instead of Route 128). Democratic Representative Austin Murphy of Pennsylvania was even more befuddled. "I have nothing else to do but go to receptions at night," he admitted, wineglass in hand. "I didn't know what they are here for."

"Some people come here for the industry," Kertzman said. "Some people come for the cheese."

Other members of Congress knew exactly who was sponsoring the event, and were eager to butter up what they thought was a well-heeled business group. GOP Representative Toby Roth of Wisconsin handed his business card to Kertzman and to other electronics-association officials who were standing nearby. "I'm going to need some help from some of these fellows," he said frankly.

"It's frustrating," Kertzman concluded. "It makes you wonder whether you want to be part of that cynical and manipulative process." But, he added, "I've come to understand it as a game."

Indeed, the power of persuasion was not the only weapon corporate chiefs brought to Washington lobbying. They also wielded considerable sway over the campaign funds given through corporate and trade-association PACs. The power that these CEOs held in this area was brought up only obliquely with lawmakers— if at all—but the CEOs and the lawmakers knew it was always there, beneath the surface, all the same.

The electronics-association PAC was not a major contributor to congressional campaigns, but some of its member companies were, a fact that Kertzman knew was important to certain lawmakers. He once had a meeting a few years earlier with then-Senator Chic Hecht, a Nevada Republican. "We told him about our issues," Kertzman said. "He told us about his reelection and his need to raise money."

On the morning after the reception, Wednesday, February 7, Kertzman was slated to have a series of one-on-one meetings with House Democrats. And he intended to press the case that, contrary to conventional opinion, capital gains could be good for their party. His first meeting was with Representative Norman Mineta of California, in the Members' Dining Room. "As you know, many in our industry are hidebound conservative Republicans," Kertzman confessed over a bagel and cream cheese. But supporting a capital-gains tax cut, he asserted, was a way for the Democratic party to build a new constituency—"a tremendous opportunity for the Democrats to do something not Democrat-like." In saying this to Mineta, though, Kertzman was preaching to the choir: The congressman's district included California's Silicon Valley, and Mineta said he had already planned to vote for a capital-gains tax cut.

Kertzman's next visit was not so easy. It was with Representative Edward Markey, whose district included Kertzman's own company in Massachusetts. But the dreaded fat-cat problem came to the fore nonetheless. During an otherwise congenial meeting in Markey's office, the congressman leaned over to Kertzman to say that President Bush's capital-gains tax cut "smacks of a campaign payback . . . to everyone in the country clubs." To which the beleaguered Kertzman replied: "I don't belong to a country club." Clearly, Markey was not convinced.

The rich-man argument, Kertzman concluded later, was capital gains's "Achilles' heel." Another problem, he acknowledged, was the huge revenue loss that the cut would cause the federal government over time. His own preference would have been to "carve out" a special low rate for gains in stock from start-up companies— a proposal that would have been relatively inexpensive, and also seemed to Kertzman to be more justifiable on policy grounds. But when talking to Markey, he held his tongue. The electronics association was, after all, a member of Mark Bloomfield's Capital Gains Coalition, which took a broader view of what the cut should look like.

• • •

By 1990 it was nothing new for chief executives to come to Washington. Organizations such as the Business Roundtable and the American Business Conference had for many years brought corporate chieftains there to express business's views on the great issues of the day. But executives had usually shunned lobbying on narrower issues of more specific importance to their own companies, viewing that as a distasteful task better left to unseen hirelings. Now, though, many chief executives argued that government policy was so entwined with the well-being of their companies that "lobbyist" had become an unwritten part of almost any CEO's job description.

"The biggest single change in management in my forty years in the game has been the revolution of the involvement of the American business people in the government process," said Edmund Pratt, chief executive of Pfizer Incorporated, the New York–based pharmaceutical company. "What government does is at least as important these days as what your competitor does." What's more, he added, "politicians obviously have concluded that business was too important to leave to the businessmen. We've come to the offsetting conclusion: Politics is too important just to be left to the politicians."

Asked why he lobbied in Washington, Robert Malott, chief executive of the FMC Corporation of Chicago, cited the comment of Reginald Jones, a former chief executive of the General Electric Company: "I can do more for General Electric by spending time in Washington and assisting in the development of responsible tax policy than I can by staying home and pricing refrigerators."

But the value of lobbying was even more than that, Malott said: "When I entered the business world I felt that business controlled its own destiny, and that maybe five percent of your future was determined by the political environment. That's changed dramatically. Regardless of how smart you are, regardless of what your products are, you just have to recognize the political process is important. You've got to establish an interface both with public-policy think tanks and those that are responsible in government. You have to come down and establish relationships here; you have to make a contribution. It's part of a CEO's job these days."

A chief executive's visits to Washington were usually more than one-shot affairs. They were geared toward establishing ongoing relationships with the people in power. "Down here people tend to stay in office a pretty long time, so building up a relationship and maintaining a relationship is important," said John Creedon, chief executive of the Metropolitan Life Insurance Company of New York. "Some of the visits are relationship visits rather than trying to influence a specific piece of legislation."

As chairman of a major trade association, Kertzman came to Washington about twenty times a year, and believed the experience benefited not only his industry, but his company as well. By focusing on national issues, he said, he had become intensely aware just how weak the economy had become; so he was able to trim his expansion plans earlier than he might have otherwise, and thus to avoid a costly mistake.

Experience showed that a chief executive's intervention in the legislative process could make a difference. In the early 1980s, when the Chrysler Corporation was seeking its government bail-out, lobbyist Tom Korologos put the company's CEO, Lee Iacocca, to work making telephone calls to members of the House Banking Committee. Iacocca had missed one particular lawmaker in his office during the week, and called him at home on Saturday. The lawmaker again was out, but Iacocca struck up a conversation with the lawmaker's wife. In the midst of their talk, the congressman finally came home, and the wife handed him the phone. "Honey," she said, "this is Lee Iacocca. You're voting for his bill, and I bought a car."

For their part, Washington-based lobbyists viewed chief executives as invaluable weapons in their lobbying arsenal. "There isn't anyone as effective as the CEO," asserted lobbyist Mark McConaghy of Price Waterhouse & Company, who coordinated a highly successful group of pro-tax-reform CEOs in 1985 and 1986. Members of Congress and high government officials tended to treat CEOs as equals—or, in some cases, as celebrities. When chief executives asked to see a lawmaker or a decision-maker, they were rarely refused, and in Washington, access was the key to influence.

The CEO Fly-In had been organized by Ed Hatcher of the electronics association. The young lobbyist hovered in the background during almost every meeting Kertzman conducted and, as the principal author of the event's briefing papers, quietly guided the executive's rhetoric. But Hatcher knew the words were more persuasive when they came from Kertzman. "I would rather have one well-versed CEO lobby on capital gains," Hatcher said, "than ten Washington lawyers." And his judgment was confirmed by Jenkins. "A [Washington-based] lobbyist is a hired gun and can take either side of an issue, like a lawyer," the congressman said. "A CEO has more than a fleeting interest in an issue."

But the chief executive had plenty of frustrations as well. Foremost was the knowledge that he or she represented just one of many interests vying for attention on Capitol Hill, and that his or her views might not prevail. "They give you a badge with your name on it, and you feel pretty important," Kertzman said, "until you see there are a dozen other people with badges from other groups."

Another frustration was the relative inexperience of the ever-important congressional staffs. "Washington is being run by kids," Kertzman said. "It's a frustrating experience for a CEO to be lectured by a kid."

CEOs did not always enjoy the process of lobbying. "Most of them do come," Creedon said. But, he added, "I don't know that they like it. There can be a high level of frustration with the process. In business, usually you can decide to get something done, and do it. In Washington, it's difficult to get something done that you think should be done."

"Do I look forward to going to Washington? I wouldn't put it that way," agreed John Young, the chairman of Hewlett-Packard. "The problems these people [in Washington] are wrestling with are tremendously challenging. I learned pretty quickly if you go in as a simple advocate for your own position, you don't really get very far. Most of these people have very complex agendas. If you see a way of helping put a compromise together, you always have a bigger impact."

Not every CEO was as wise in the ways of Washington as Young was. As a result, not every lawmaker welcomed every CEO with open arms. "They're the parsley on the platter of fish," said Democratic Representative Pete Stark of California. "If I have a word of advice to chief executives, it is to stay home and let the pros do it."

For most routine visits, the CEOs did exactly as Stark counseled, and left the lobbying to their lobbyists. At best, the CEOs could only be part-time lobbyists, and Washington required full-time attention. So CEOs relied on the people they hired in town for day-in, day-out contacts. And the CEOs, for the most part, had only good things to say about the "Washington types" they hire. Malott, for one, referred to his company's capital office as "excellent," and said that any major corporation needed to have one in order to keep a constant vigil over the odd ways of Washington. "It is beyond comprehension," he said. "You can read about it, you can be told about it, but you have to live it. The process in

Washington is not like the one we're used to. Problems are not addressed head-on. There are trade-offs that often don't have very much to do with the issue at hand. Some people don't have the tolerance, and I must admit, it's tested mine."

David Roderick, the chairman of USX Corporation, agreed. "I don't see how you can operate a large company today and not have a communication vehicle in Washington to clarify different issues that are emerging and to communicate with committees on specific issues and be a party to the process. I just can't imagine any major company with a diverse commercial market presence being able to function without having some liaison—maybe a better word than lobbying. If you didn't have people there you'd have to have people going back and forth all the time between there and our headquarters [in Pittsburgh]. We'd make USAir rich. People can be more effective if they're located there, and work at it eight or ten hours a day. That's the reason we have our Washington office."

• • •

In early 1990, much of the talk in Washington offices of major corporations focused on the size of the still-looming budget deficit and the daunting deficit-reduction targets that Congress had set for itself under the Gramm-Rudman law. The deficit cutting in 1989 had been small potatoes compared with the size of the deficit problem, and it looked as if 1990 might be the year, finally, when a serious attempt would be made to stanch the red ink.

The Gramm-Rudman Law mandated that Congress write laws to bring the fiscal 1991 deficit to $64.7 billion, give or take $10 billion. That might seem like a pretty large deficit. But for the same fiscal year, the deficit was expected to reach at least $100.5 billion without any deficit-cutting, according to the optimistic estimates of the White House's own budget office. The nonpartisan Congressional Budget Office estimated the real number to be about $60 billion higher than that.

This vast spread between where the deficit was, and where it was supposed to be, gave policymakers cause to believe that President Bush might be forced to abandon his anti-tax-increase rhetoric and get down to the business of tackling the budget problem. But his initial budget proposals cast doubt on that prospect. They embraced an overtly rosy forecast and purported to get fully one-third of their "revenue increases" (Bush still refused to use the word "taxes") anomalously, from a tax cut—in capital gains.

In the meantime, the budget squeeze had lobbyists hopping, Coretech, the R&D lobby, in particular. As the President's budget proposal was being devised, word had reached Stuart Eizenstat that the $800-million-a-year 861 provision was not included in the R&D section of the budget plan. The reason for the omission, the R&D lobbyists heard, was Eizenstat himself.

In December, an increasingly anxious Eizenstat had telephoned White House Budget Director Richard Darman to find out how the R&D issues were faring. But Darman had refused to call Eizenstat back, despite repeated attempts to reach him. During budget deliberations in 1989, Darman had perceived that Eizenstat and Coretech had switched sides, turning their influence against the President's chief domestic initiative, capital gains. That rankled the budget director, and he had chosen to punish the lobbyist by declining to give him even the courtesy of a returned telephone call.

Finally, after the dogged Eizenstat had called so many times that it had become embarrassing, Darman picked up the phone. Like Eizenstat, Darman was not known for his social graces, but he nonetheless felt guilty about snubbing Eizenstat, with whom he had worked, on and off, for many years. But when he got on the phone, Darman did not mince words. He told the lobbyist that he was "extremely disappointed" in Eizenstat's opportunism on capital gains, and, according to Eizenstat, implied that 861 was in danger of not being included in the President's final budget plan.

"If, as is likely, R and D makes it," Darman had concluded, "it will be because I like it on the merits, not because of any lobbying by you."

Darman was a believer in the need for research-and-development funding. After all, he had been the main speaker when Coretech was first created several years before. But as White House budget director, he had no choice but to juggle around items that cost money—like R&D tax breaks. In tight fiscal times, he was always fighting, as he liked to say, to find ways to "square the circle"—to manage to keep everything within budgetary limits. One option throughout his deliberations was simply to exclude, either partly or completely, proposals to extend soon-to-expire tax breaks like the R&D credit and 861.

Darman did not see the life or death of 861 as an event of earth-shaking consequence. Its biggest beneficiaries after all were drug companies, which already had plenty of government assistance of one kind or another. Besides, almost no one among the general public knew or cared about how multinational corporations allocated R&D expenses between their domestic and foreign subsidiaries. But Eizenstat and his client, Coretech, were in business to care a lot about 861. The big companies for which 861 made millions of dollars of difference a year were the bedrock financial backers of the Coretech operation. So when they were upset, Eizenstat and his sidekick Ken Kay were deeply concerned as well.

At this first inkling of trouble for the 861 extension in December, Kay had initiated a "fire drill." Letters were written and telephone calls made, basically to everyone in sight. Eizenstat got on the phone to Kenneth Gideon, the top tax-policy official at Treasury, and Roger Porter, the President's chief domestic-policy adviser. Despite their fancy titles, neither man had much influence on administration policy. Darman and White House Chief of Staff John Sununu were the real power brokers. But the lobbyist took what opportunities he had to make his point. "This business is a cumulative business," Eizenstat said about lobbying. "It's a whole lot of raindrops that you hope will fill a bucket up. And one never knows what one thing will fill it."

During his phone calls, Eizenstat had stressed the importance to the R&D community of the 861 allocations. He had argued that there was "very strong" support in Congress for the provision, and said that the President's failure to back 861 would be "a stark reversal of administration policy." For the companies involved, he said, the loss of the allocation rules "would have had at least as great, and in some cases a greater financial impact, as the loss of the R and D credit itself." He also noted that the companies for which he lobbied were responsible for one-third of the total $60 billion worth of corporate research and development in the nation.

Individual lobbyists whose companies belonged to Coretech also had made major efforts as part of the fire drill. Foremost among these lobbyists was Catherine Porter, a former tax aide to Senator John Chafee of Rhode Island and now a lobbyist for Hewlett-Packard. At Kay's suggestion, she had importuned her old boss to write a letter to Darman about the importance of 861.

Porter was Coretech's main conduit to Senator Chafee. For years, she had been the senator's diligent and loyal staffer. Together they worked for tax reform in 1986, and they rarely backed the most onerous of tax breaks that benefited the wealthy and the privileged. The exceptions to this were the R&D credit and 861. Partly because of Porter, Chafee became one of the main sponsors of 861 legislation in the Senate. And her request that he write the letter to Darman was only the latest 861-related effort he had agreed to make at her urging.

In effect, the ever-affable Porter—and the respected Eizenstat—were the main engines that propelled Chafee's support for 861. Porter sent Chafee a draft letter that served as the starting point for the senator's own letter to Darman. Earlier, she also had written what became the basis for the statement he had delivered on the Senate floor when he introduced the 861 legislation in 1989, and a draft of the letter he had sent to his colleagues soon afterward, asking for their support for the bill.

She was able to do all of this because she retained, even as a private lobbyist, the complete trust of her old boss—a trust she guarded jealously. She also benefited from a greater-than-usual allegiance on the part of the senator's new tax aide, and for good reason: The young lawyer had been hired by Chafee on her recommendation. Such ties are one of the reasons that lobbying works so well for the nation's corporations.

"I do have a sense of personal loyalty to Senator Chafee," Porter said. "I wouldn't ask his support if I thought it would be detrimental to him [or] inconsistent with his views. I just wouldn't go to him and talk him into something that would be an embarrassment to him."

Chafee also maintained a strong loyalty to Porter and to Eizenstat, with whom he had worked closely during the Carter presidency. "Every dealing I ever had with him when he was in the White House," Chafee said, "he was a square shooter, a man who knew what he was talking about, and somebody I could trust. Likewise, obviously, with Catherine Porter. I have tremendous respect for them, I have confidence in those people. I believe them. They are serious people who aren't coming in to waste my time. They wouldn't come here unless they thought it was a serious matter. They aren't traipsing in just to run up a fee. That's where the trust comes in. They give us supporting documents. They're giving me the straight information. And, importantly, they have a good product to sell."

The 861 lobbyists got what they wanted but not necessarily because of what Chafee did on their behalf. Although the senator sent the letter about 861, as Porter had suggested, Darman did not even see it. One of his underlings intercepted it before it got to his desk. In any case, Darman had already found enough revenue to pay for both the R&D credit and 861, and had included them both as permanent parts of the tax code in the President's budget. All of the last-minute lobbying, he claimed, had no effect on him at all. But who can know for sure? Had there not been similar fire drills in earlier years, there might never have been an R&D credit or 861 provision at all.

Still, Kay saw the last-minute scramble as "a wake-up call" that needed to be answered. In the meantime, on Thursday, February 15, he went on another of his "thank-you" runs, this time to Austin, Texas. There, at a luncheon attended by more than 150 people in the elegant Four Seasons Hotel, he presented an award to Representative Jake Pickle. Most of those in the audience were electronics-company executives whose interests Pickle had long served as the chief House sponsor of the R&D tax credit.

"Mr. Pickle does an awful lot for the high-tech community," Kay recalled saying, praising the cantankerous lawmaker, "and I don't think the people in Austin realize that. I have worked with him for five years. He was always available to us; his door was always open. The really amazing thing about him is that he is extremely tenacious; he just won't give up. He also has extremely good political judgment and is not bashful about giving it to us in no uncertain terms. We follow that advice and we've always benefited from it, which is the way it should be."

After the address Pickle walked up to Kay and said, "You really said an awful lot of very nice things."

"I meant every word of it," Kay replied.

. . .

To no one's surprise, the President's budget proposal also included a cut in the capital-gains tax rate. But its shape was different from that of a year earlier, and not by accident. One influence on the change was the lobbying team of Mark Bloomfield and Charly Walker. As the Bush administration was deciding on its capital-gains proposal, the two lobbyists contrived to help it along. At the end of 1989 they had devised what they called their "Game Plan for Capital Gains in 1990," and many of their ideas were adopted in the final plan.

The "game plan" was usually labeled "confidential" to add an air of importance to the document, even though it had been sent to several fiscal-policy advisers. The plan, part critique and part recommendation, was written with the confidence of the insiders that both men essentially were—at least when it came to capital gains.

"When the bell rang a few weeks ago," the document began, "supporters of a capital gains tax differential experienced a TKO. But, with the House of Representatives on record . . . and with a majority of the Senate also having voted . . . for a capital-gains tax cut under the most difficult political circumstances, a presidential win on this issue appears to be in the cards."

The eleven-page memo detailed how best to win the proposed cut. It made clear that the effort a year earlier had been a flop, and for good reasons. The Jenkins plan, which was only a temporary cut in capital-gains taxes, was decried, in ever-wise hindsight, as "yo-yoism" and "hard to justify on economic grounds." Bush's original plan to give a preference only to stocks and bonds was derided as politically naive. A broader capital-gains tax cut would be better: "Inclusion of timber and other assets," the document stated, would bring the "timber industry, agricultural interests, heretofore reluctant small business organizations and others into the private-sector capital-gains coalition." Pitches also were made to place real estate and even corporations into the types of assets that would get preferential tax treatment, and to use a "sliding scale" that would grant a bigger tax break the longer that assets were held.

The game plan even urged the Bush administration to be more solicitous of the Capital Gains Coalition. The White House staff was supposed to be prohibited from managing the lobbying efforts of outside groups. But that rule was routinely broken, and the Bloomfield-Walker memo pleaded for even more guidance. "Give specific marching orders to the organized core of the capital-gains coalition," it said. "They need it. They welcome it. If treated nicely, they can be a big help."

At least in the area of substance, the memo clearly had had its impact. The President's proposal in 1990 was nothing like the narrow, securities-only proposal of the year before. It was a permanent tax cut that worked on a "sliding scale"—just as the memo suggested. The top rate on profits from the sale of assets held for at least three years was set to fall to 19.6 percent. Assets held for two years would drop to a top rate of 22.4 percent; and for assets held one year, the top rate would be 25.2 percent. The preferential treatment would go not just to securities, but also to real estate, timber, and most other assets, except for collectibles such as antiques.

Walker and Bloomfield did not get everything they wanted. Only individuals and not corporations would get the preferential treatment. That was a loss to the lobbyists and to the companies that paid their salaries. And something else was also lacking. Bloomfield and Walker sensed a lack of enthusiasm from the White House on the thorny capital-gains issue after the political beating it had taken from the Democrats in 1989. They wondered whether the President was only paying lip service to capital gains. Still, at least for now, the lobbyists' favorite tax break was back in play.

· · ·

While Bloomfield thrived, Jim Rock, Jenkins's former aide, suffered. By mid-February he had decided it was time to find a new job and, ultimately, he joined Concord Associates with Wayne Thevenot, the Maglev man. Job switching was a frequent occurrence in the mutable lobbying trade, and Rock had gotten caught in one of the periodic upheavals of the industry. But with his background as a Capitol Hill aide, he landed solidly on his feet and was already helping to attract new clients, including the mutual life insurers.

At the end of 1989, Rock's career had not looked so promising. His lobbying firm, Gold and Liebengood, had succumbed to the latest rage in Washington influence-peddling—the merger—and Rock had not been pleased with his part of the deal. Lobbying-access companies like Gold and Liebengood were being gobbled up by bigger public relations and advertising companies on a regular basis. And when it was Gold and Liebengood's turn to be bought by Burson-Marsteller, Rock demanded, but failed to get, an equity stake that would have given him a share of the $4 million transaction.

It seemed as though Rock had been one of the last people in the firm to learn about the nearly year-long courtship between the two companies. "I asked someone what the fuck was going on," Rock recalled. And the person replied, "Oh, you don't know about this?" Rock had been expecting to win a partnership interest in Gold and Liebengood early in 1990—after a couple of years on the job—but the merger had made that impossible. In December, he had had a two-hour meeting with several of the firm's principals to discuss the situation. "It was obvious to both sides that things would not work out," he said. "They looked after their best interests and I looked after mine." So he quit, informing them of his decision on December 15. "I was very comfortable and very sure," Rock said.

Sue, his wife, was not as sure. "This is the worst possible time to drop this on me!" she scolded. The family was about to go on vacation to her parents' house, and Jim had no plans about how to get another job. He had left Jenkins's office at the end of 1987 to nearly double his pay, to the $100,000 level. Now he had only the small retainers of two clients, the Georgia Power Company and the American Resort and Residential Development Association, which even together got him nowhere near that amount. Still, the confident Rock went on vacation anyway, and returned after the holidays to set himself up, at least temporarily, in the Capitol Hill office of John Winburn, a lobbyist for Philip Morris Company, among others. Winburn was a close friend of Rock's old boss and patron, Ed Jenkins. Surely something would turn up, Rock thought.

The tumult that Rock was suffering was part of a larger trend in Washington. While the urge to merge was waning on Wall

Street, it was growing on K Street. And like the corporate world of the mid-to-late 1980s, the lobbying business was going through a transformation: Big lobbying conglomerates were devouring littler ones with increasing frequency, and controversy.

The concept behind it all was the widespread belief that Washington lobbyists could no longer get things done by themselves. The job of lobbying had grown more complex. Lobbyists could not just rely on friendships or even on rational debate to win their case. They had to persuade politicians that the voters were with them, too. "We've moved a long way toward plebiscite democracy," Charly Walker said.

True, much lobbying continued to be done by law firms. But they no longer held a monopoly. The business of influencing government was becoming an increasingly sophisticated, multidisciplinary exercise, and in order to compete for big corporate clients, firms were moving toward placing more and more of those skills under one roof. And that had spawned the merger mania.

Hill & Knowlton Public Affairs in Washington was the model for diversified lobbying of this kind. In its 180-person office overlooking the Potomac River, H & K wielded almost every tool in the modern lobbyist's arsenal. It had traditional lobbyists who contacted lawmakers and Executive Branch officials. But it also had researchers, economists, political analysts, publicists, graphic artists, speechwriters, and managers of campaign contributions. It trained executives how to give press interviews and when to avoid them.

Hill & Knowlton also housed an entire electronic broadcast studio. It produced radio and television spots of varying lengths ranging from brief video press releases to entire documentaries extolling a client's cause. It even broadcasted its own "news" programs, including a monthly "magazine radio" show called "Washington Spotlight," and a shorter radio program, called "Capitolink," which it sent via satellite to 4,400 radio stations five days a week and which, it said, was regularly used by about a thousand of them, often during prime drive times.

By far the largest Washington acquirer of lobbying skills of this diverse kind was a deceptively quiet foreigner, WPP Group PLC, the British advertising and public relations giant. It even owned the massive H & K. Without fanfare, it had purchased all or part of the lobbying-related firms headed by some of the best-known names in the Washington establishment, including William Timmons, Charly Walker, and public relations executives Jody Powell and Robert Keith Gray.

The WPP octopus grew in Washington like this: In June 1986 Ogilvy & Mather bought Targeted Communications Corporation, a direct-mail firm specializing in ginning up letters from home to lawmakers. Then, in July of the same year, Ogilvy agreed to purchase a 30 percent stake in Walker Associates. In June 1987, WPP agreed to buy JWT Group Incorporated, which already owned both Gray & Company and Hill & Knowlton Incorporated. Then in May 1989, WPP also bought Ogilvy, having already added to its stable of companies Reese Communications Companies, a direct-mail, marketing, and polling firm, and Timmons & Company, a lobbying specialist.

Not to be outdone, other communications companies were fast on WPP's heels. The purchase of Gold and Liebengood by Burson-Marsteller was just the latest example. Earle Palmer Brown, the Washington area's largest advertising agency, bought the Madison Public Affairs Group, a lobbying and public relations firm. And other mergers would soon be consummated. Black, Manafort & Stone would be bought by Burson-Marsteller. Anne Wexler's firm would be purchased by WPP. And even the law firm Arnold & Porter would eventually sell its lobbying subsidiary, APCO Associates.

Lobbying firms that wanted to be bought—and there were few that did not—carefully made themselves bipartisan and bicameral in their ability to gain access to lawmakers. Gold and Liebengood's employees included two former Republican aides to Senator Howard Baker of Tennessee, a former tax aide to Democratic Senator David Boren of Oklahoma, and former Democratic Representative William Ratchford of Connecticut.

Critics charged that the creation of mega-lobbying firms disadvantaged the public interest by concentrating too much power in the hands of the big-money interests who could afford to hire the firms. "Ultimately, it's the public who gets squeezed every time," asserted Ellen Miller of the Center for Responsive Politics. And even lobbyists complained. All in all, the takeover trend "diminished the quality of lobbying services," asserted Bob Juliano, and he was probably right. Before the year was out, Hill & Knowlton Public Affairs was beginning to fall on hard times, amid complaints of too-high fees and mediocre service.

Widespread consolidation also produced the likelihood that conflicts of interest would arise between rival corporate factions within the firms. The issue was apparent with even a cursory glance at WPP Group's Washington clients. Hill & Knowlton Public Affairs Worldwide Company worked for Mazda Corporation, while its sister company, Timmons & Company, represented Chrysler Corporation. Former White House spokesman Jody Powell's Ogilvy & Mather Public Affairs Incorporated occasionally represented whiskey maker Seagram's, while its affiliate, Walker Associates, worked for beer maker Anheuser-Busch.

For their part, the lobbying firms did not see a conflict. They contended that each WPP unit operated independently, giving any corporation leave to hire a WPP division and not worry if a competitor hired a separate one. By maintaining such distinctions, WPP believed, it could attract many more clients and also add "marketing panache," said Robert Dilenschneider, the chief executive of Hill & Knowlton Incorporated, New York. "The separation gives WPP a chance to show more than one face to the potential customer," he said.

There would always be room for small, specialized lobbying firms as well as the Hill & Knowlton–style lobbying supermarkets. But, according to Thomas Bell, Jr., the vice chairman of Burson-Marsteller, "the growth will be in the firms that can do it all." Indeed, corporate lobbying in general, which had grown dramatically over the last decade, was likely to continue to grow for a long time to come. "I don't see any way to stop Washington growth," said Robert Gray of H & K. "I've never seen it decline."

• • •

The prospect of steady growth in lobbying was good news for Jim Rock. From his temporary perch in John Winburn's office, he had begun to call around, and quickly got some positive reaction. Jeffrey DeBoer, a real estate lobbyist and hockey-going friend of Rock's, had suggested that he call Thevenot and his partner, Bill Boardman. Rock was attracted to the idea of joining a firm with just two other people. He was, understandably, bitter about the

Burson-Marsteller purchase, and had wanted to find work at a smaller, more collegial place. "You lose your entrepreneurial edge, which is what it's all about," he claimed about buyouts of small companies by bigger ones. Rock was still in his mid-thirties with a long career ahead of him, a fact that Thevenot and Boardman recognized immediately. They also saw in him something Concord Associates lacked: a strong tie to the House. So, after just a few conversations, in February Rock moved into suite 560 of the Willard Office Building, as the newest member of the firm.

Concord Associates, in reality, was more of a loose collection of lobbyists than a formal partnership. They marketed themselves individually or as a group, depending on what would sell best. Boardman was the anchor of the organization; he held the lease. As an enticement to Rock, Boardman allowed him to occupy his office space free of charge, and also to keep for himself the small retainers from Georgia Power and the resort-development association. Any business he brought in later would be split, two-thirds to Rock and one-third to Boardman, mostly to cover the cost of overhead and clerical help. And soon new clients did come to the group. All three lobbyists, in fact, managed to get contracts with the mutual life-insurance lobbying team. Boardman, Thevenot, and Rock were each put on retainer, and together brought in more than $200,000—win or lose.

So many people had been hired by either the stocks or the mutuals that lawmakers had gotten used to visits from one side or the other. One lawmaker who was certainly no stranger to such meetings was Representative Sam Gibbons of Florida, whose son, Cliff, was a lobbyist for a mutual company. For the elder Gibbons, serving in Congress was a family affair. His wife, Martha, was active in running his congressional campaigns. And Cliff, Sam's eldest son, did a lot of his father's fund-raising. "They have an interest in this job, in my work, and they all have some expertise in it," the ruddy-faced lawmaker said.

But Gibbons took this closeness to an extreme. He was the second-ranking Democrat on the Ways and Means Committee, and was chairman of its trade subcommittee. The thirty-nine-year-old Cliff Gibbons was a corporate lobbyist and registered foreign agent who represented his firm's clients not only before his father's committee but also, occasionally, before his dad. And to the horror of some of his more ethically minded colleagues, Gibbons was introduced by his son to James Farley, the chief executive of Mutual Life Insurance Company of New York (MONY), during a lunch in the members' own special dining room in the Capitol Building itself.

The arrangement was cozy even by Washington standards, under which it was not unheard-of for close relatives of important people to lobby. Offspring of two previous House speakers, of a former House majority leader, and of the current Senate minority leader, Robert Dole, were Washington lobbyists. But these children of politicians generally declined to bring clients to their parents.

The Gibbonses did not have such reluctance, as the meeting with Farley amply proved. During their lunch, Representative Gibbons interrupted his conversation with the chief executive to introduce him to another chief executive who happened to be sitting at the next table: President George Bush. It was mere coincidence that Bush was eating in the Capitol that day. But it was no coincidence that Farley was with Representative Gibbons. The lawmaker had agreed to meet him at the request of Cliff, who was one of the company's paid lobbyists.

The policy stands taken by Representative Gibbons, and the interests of the groups that retained his son were rarely distinguishable. Unlike other lawmakers, Gibbons had no technical staff in his personal office to help him with the wide array of issues that came before him. One sure way to determine Gibbons's position on any matter was to check which companies or countries Cliff represented.

That was the case in 1984 when Cliff's firm, Hogan & Hartson, was a registered congressional lobbyist for Mercedes-Benz of North America Incorporated, which was fighting a proposal to reduce tax write-offs for luxury automobiles. Representative Gibbons took the company's side. Since 1987 Cliff Gibbons's firm had been working for the Province of Ontario's Ministry of Industry, Trade & Technology. In 1988, Representative Gibbons was in the thick of pushing a free-trade agreement with Canada, which that ministry dearly wanted. And in 1989, Hogan & Hartson advocated the position of the Coalition of American Steel Using Manufacturers, which resisted the extension of voluntary restraints on steel imports. Representative Gibbons, one of the Congress's foremost free-trade advocates, stood with the coalition, and, along with it, did not oppose the short-term extension it won as a compromise in the end.

And as the Ways and Means panel pondered changes in the taxation of stock and mutual companies, Representative Gibbons was considered an ally of mutual life insurers such as Farley's MONY. The lunch with Farley was one of a series of meetings Farley had that day with tax-writers and their staffs "to introduce the new chairman of Mutual of New York and to express how concerned we are as to the ultimate disposition of the stock-mutual controversy," according to Lee Smith, a MONY vice president. And the congressman's son? "To the extent that Cliff has contacts in the Washington area, and through his father by virtue of where he works, that's very important," said Valerie Kilhenny, MONY's director of government relations. "You use connections where you can."

. . .

At the American Trucking Associations, Tom Donohue and Ken Simonson were doing their best to show a united front against gas-tax increases. Their efforts were expended in two directions: public relations and economic analysis.

On the public relations front, Donohue went out of his way to make the truckers appear to be good guys in the eyes of what he understood to be a basically hostile and disbelieving public. Prior to the turn of the year, he had invited reporters to a small private dining room in the National Press Club to highlight how committed his industry was to safety and to the elimination of drugs from the trucker's cab. "We at ATA are proud of the energy and money we spend on safety," he had told the reporters, and then screened a brief film giving motorists tips about how best to maneuver around trucks on major highways.

He went on to introduce the newest members of what he called "America's Road Team" for 1990. These were eight men and one woman who were chosen from among truckers around the country to spend five days a month lecturing about highway safety. The latest winners were seated in the front row, wearing blue blazers specially designed for the occasion. The message they would bring over the next year was summed up by Pete Salberg, a particularly articulate trucker from the Road Team of 1987 who was on hand for this event. "We have families, we are humans, we are not monsters," he said. He then concluded: "Remember: buckle up, slow down, practice courtesy, and God bless you."

Afterward, Donohue declared the event a success and placed it in the context of the looming tax battle that he feared might result in higher gasoline levies in 1990. He knew that lawmakers and their voters disliked trucks. They were big and they were dangerous on the roads. But if, maybe, the public started to like truckers a little better, they might be less inclined to punish the industry with higher taxes. "When I first came here I got letters saying, 'Your safety record is terrible, so we're going to raise your taxes,' " he said over a fancy lunch at the nearby City Club. As a result, he explained, "safety is essential to everything else we do."

The other essential element of the truckers' no-tax campaign was led by Simonson. It was his job, often under the aegis of CART, to make sure that no one ever forgot how regressive excise taxes were, and how difficult it would be to repair the damage to poor people if those types of taxes were ever raised. He also wanted to find ways to communicate how difficult it would be for truckers to continue operating with higher costs.

Donohue and Simonson took this message before the Ways and Means Committee on Wednesday, March 14. The subject of the hearing was environmental taxes, and Donohue was scheduled to testify at about ten-thirty. But it did not turn out that way. "Hey, come on!" he grumbled when the lawmakers continued to ask questions of earlier witnesses. By twelve-ten, when Donohue's turn finally came, only one lawmaker, Sam Gibbons, was still in the room to ask questions. Still, Donohue, unfazed, took his seat at the witness table facing Gibbons. Simonson sat dutifully behind him in one of the seats that were usually reserved for witnesses' staff.

After being welcomed by Gibbons, Donohue launched into a litany of reasons for not raising fuel taxes. Higher taxes would weaken the economy, hurt tourism, and burden poor people, he asserted. And when he was through, he seemed pleased.

From the chairman's seat, Gibbons scowled. "Is there anything you can do to get these buses to turn off their engines around the Capitol?" the lawmaker asked, incongruously, referring to the tourist buses that were perennial street-cloggers on Capitol Hill. "That's one of my pet peeves," he said.

Donohue managed to keep his composure. "Maybe we can take care of some of your pet peeves," he replied smoothly, but the problem with bus fumes was not one of the them. He patiently explained that he represented the trucking industry, not the busing industry. And trucking was plenty big on its own: 200,000 companies and 7.5 million employees. Besides, Donohue said, a tax on diesel fuel would not be the answer to Gibbons's complaint, since diesel contributed very little to the atmosphere in the way of either carbon dioxide or other pollutants.

But Gibbons would not relent. "Does that take care of the black belching smoke I breathe?" he asked.

"There are very few trucks belching smoke," Donohue answered.

"Where do you live? Do you live in Washington? It's so bad going home you can't see," Gibbons said.

"It's not diesel trucks," Donohue insisted.

"It *is* diesel fuel," Gibbons said.

"Trucks have significantly reduced their contribution to the pollution," Donohue said. "We are caring for the good of this society."

"They usually pass me like I'm standing still," Gibbons persisted, and ended that line of questioning.

Another witness before the committee, sitting with Donohue, was a representative from a taxpayer group who insisted that trucks should pay more in taxes because they are a major cause of potholes. And to this Donohue nearly exploded. He said the charge was untrue and probably inspired by the railroads. With only a 2 percent profit margin, he argued, most trucking companies would be thrown into the red if fuel taxes were raised significantly.

Truckers don't get federal subsidies, Donohue insisted, but "railroads are subsidized more than a billion dollars a year."

"Next time we do this," Gibbons responded, "let's get the railroads and the trucks together." Then the lawmaker asked Donohue, "Got any shots you want to take at me?"

Donohue replied that he did not, and even professed to have "enjoyed" the sparring.

· · ·

In addition to drafting testimony before congressional hearings, Simonson had spent the first few months of the year preparing yet another study by the accounting firm Peat Marwick. The newest results were unveiled on Thursday, April 5, a few weeks after Donohue's close encounter with Sam Gibbons. On that morning Donohue made his way once again to Room EF-100 of the U.S. Capitol to tell anyone who cared to assemble there just how bad raising excise taxes would be.

"I want to make a few points," Donohue began in the harried manner of someone who had done it all before. "First, these are very, very regressive taxes. Lower-income families pay five times as high a share of these taxes than [sic] upper-income families do. Even Social Security taxes are far less regressive. The second point is the federal income-tax system has gotten worse over the past decade, and the burden on the wrong end would shoot up even more if excise taxes were increased."

"What is the relevance of all this? How does it fit into the political picture?" he asked rhetorically. "Well, an excise-tax increase would severely worsen this problem."

As had not been the case during the lackadaisical press conference of the previous year, Donohue got some tough questions from the audience this time. The first was "Who should be taxed, if not you?"

Donohue's answer was that the pain should be spread around and not just placed on his industry alone: "If there is to be a tax to resolve our deficit problems, all of the companies and all of the citizens should share in that. It's expediency that allows people to consider excise taxes. And when we take that expediency route it hurts the people who are least able to pay. It's important for somebody to speak up and say it's an easy way, but what you are doing is hurting a select group of industries and the end product is that you are hurting those [who] are least able to pay. A member of Congress ought to stop and think who's being hurt."

Donohue promised to circulate his study widely, and to meet with lawmakers to make sure they understood the point. "We haven't come this far to sit on our laurels," he concluded. "We intend to raise the matters in this study and the matters I've discussed today to the greatest visibility. We don't want to lose this deal." He then referred any questions to the representatives of Peat Marwick, who were sitting nearby.

. . .

When most people think of lobbying, accountants do not usually come to mind. Influencing government officials is supposed to be racier than accountancy. In fact, though, the hottest tactic in lobbying pitted corporate technicians for hire, like those at Peat Marwick and its even more prominent competitor, Price Waterhouse & Company, against the government's own technicians. And increasingly, the government was simply outmatched.

"We have an advantage" over government staffers, asserted Bernard (Bob) Shapiro, forty-eight years old, who headed the Price Waterhouse national tax practice with Mark McConaghy, forty-nine. "We may take two months to do an estimate that sometimes they have to do in one week. We have the time and resources to collect the data."

Shapiro and McConaghy were former staff directors of the Joint Tax Committee, Congress's repository of tax information and analysis. As Price Waterhouse partners in 1983, they began to build, for the benefit of corporations, a staff that mirrored the multidisciplinary structure of the highly regarded staff they headed on Capitol Hill: lawyers, accountants, economists, revenue estimators, and experts on every cranny of the federal tax code.

By 1990 the still-growing Price Waterhouse operation dwarfed the Joint Tax Committee staff; it employed 123 professionals compared with forty-five at Joint Tax. What began as a four-person operation in the corner of the seventh floor of a K Street office building was now about to take over the entire forty-thousand-square-foot floor.

Size was only part of the story. Price Waterhouse had become one of the first places top tax staffers turned when they decided to leave government—often when they were in need of more income. The firm's nickname among lobbyists was "Joint Tax West," and it was virtually a shadow federal government without the politicians; its employees included a former Internal Revenue

Service commissioner, a former deputy comptroller of the currency, and the former head of the IRS office of mergers and acquisitions. It had also begun a budget practice, with a former senior aide to both the House and Senate budget committees.

Other big accounting firms were also beefing up. Touche Ross hired a former congressman, Hal Daub of Nebraska, to run its Washington office. A former deputy staff director of the Joint Tax Committee, Randall Weiss, moved to Deloitte, Haskins & Sells. And Peat Marwick had bought a revenue-estimating and consulting firm formed by a former top Treasury economist. It was this group that did the CART study.

As they grew, the accounting firms gained detractors. Because many of their employees had only recently left government, the firm's employees sometimes tried to present themselves not so much as corporate hired hands, but rather as senior statesmen of a sort. "We feel close to the process," Shapiro contended. "We want to work in it, not against it." But that line rarely sold, at least among the people who still worked in government. On Capitol Hill, Rob Leonard, the staff chief of the Ways and Means Committee, said, "People who read their studies do so with some caution, realizing they are commissioned by companies and industries that have a financial stake in what the study proclaims."

More traditional lobbyists, such as lawyers, also complained. They claimed the accountants were encroaching on their turf, yet rarely registered as lobbyists. In addition, lobbying accountants faced conflict-of-interest problems within their own firms. Any time they advocated the view of any single client, they risked angering other clients of the firm who might have benefited from a different stand. And the companies that hired them for Washington lobbying work were often the same companies for which they functioned as "independent" auditors.

Peat Marwick had gotten into the middle of a revenue-estimating controversy a few years earlier when Congress and the Executive Branch were trying to shut down tax shelters used by Alaska natives. The Alaskan Indians were selling tax losses that corporations could use to reduce their tax liability. In this case, the private companies that bought the tax shelters had the advantage: They had the private data that the government did not have. The official estimate for revenue gained from the closing of the loophole was modest. But then Peat Marwick produced its own data, based on information supplied by its corporate clients, to show in fact that many millions of dollars were involved. The move was meant to help the companies. With the extra money that Peat Marwick had uncovered, Congress paid for generous "transition" relief to the corporations while still meeting the modest revenue-raising goals it had sought. The government had gotten the revenue it wanted, but so did the companies. Many of them were even allowed to keep their tax shelters—all thanks to the lobbying skills of accountants.

· · ·

Wednesday, April 25, was another Lobby Day for Coretech. On this go-round there were more scientists than ever. To be precise, 108 scientists from thirty-nine states descended on Washington to meet with lawmakers and their staffs on behalf of the R&D tax credit. By design once again, the lobby group's agenda was carefully structured to include an effort to increase federal funding for college research as well as to extend the corporate tax breaks.

At an 8 A.M. breakfast briefing, Ken Kay gave his troops their instructions. This time the breakfast was held in the starkly modern conference room directly across the hall from Senator Baucus's office in the Hart Senate Office Building. There were plenty of donuts to go around, just as there had been the year earlier. But this time the scenery was much more interesting. In the previous year, the lobbyists-for-a-day had been cooped up in a windowless hearing room. In 1990, they could look out panoramic windows into the building's eight-story atrium, which featured a huge black metal sculpture and mobile by Alexander Calder that was supposed to resemble a mountain with a cloud hanging overhead.

Kay once again asked the college professors to speak on behalf of corporate researchers, and vice versa. He also told them to emphasize that they were scientists, not lobbyists. "But let me warn you, please, not to spend fifteen minutes doing that," he said. "One of the tests is to look at the other person's eyes, and as soon as they start to glaze over, back off." Another warning was to avoid overkill, a piece of advice that Kay had trouble taking in his very first meeting of the day, with Representative Tom Downey.

The Coretech delegation to Downey's office was so heavy

with Cornell University professors from his home state of New York that the congressman actually got visibly irritated. "It's not by coincidence that you decided to tap my natural inclination toward my alma mater," he said sarcastically. "I appreciate being appreciated."

The lobbyists-for-a-day needed all the sympathy they could get, but even their friends offered words of caution. "It's this overall deficit," complained Representative Mike Andrews during one group's visit to his office. "All too often these issues are driven by revenue; the merits of the issue are secondary."

Stuart Eizenstat had tried to lay the groundwork for Lobby Day with staffers on the Hill a few weeks earlier. Over Cokes and sandwiches in a basement conference room of the Hyatt Regency on Capitol Hill, he had delivered a fact-filled address to a seminar sponsored by the nonprofit Tax Foundation. The audience, which included many tax aides, heard him extol the virtues of more research spending and the need for the federal government to inspire more of it.

"We don't do nearly the amount of R and D we must," Eizenstat asserted. "We spend less than our competitors on civilian R and D. American companies are leveling off and the Japanese companies are rapidly increasing theirs. The rest of the world must be laughing as they pass us by."

He then delivered a blur of statistics that compelled at least two people in the audience to take notes. They were Tracy Kaye, Senator Danforth's tax aide, and Tim Vettel, who was the tax staffer for Senator Baucus. "This is great," Kaye whispered to Vettle. "This is great data for us." And before Eizenstat completed his part of the proceedings, he went out of his way to mention, and compliment, them both. He called the two aides "very important to the effort."

A similarly good feeling was evident at the end of Lobby Day in April. The researchers had met with no fewer than 150 lawmakers and a hundred congressional aides. One of the last meetings of the day was with Lloyd Bentsen, and the visitors got as warm a reception as they could have hoped for. "I'll do everything I can," the Finance Committee chairman told them, as he posed for the photographer they had brought. "You really know how to get to a guy."

But Coretech had heard those words before. No promises were made, and none had been expected.

· · ·

Buoyed by their successes from the year before, Wayne Thevenot and Bill Boardman began to give Maglev a higher profile. When they were able, they testified on behalf of their pet project before congressional hearings. Such hearings were mostly hot air. But for lobbyists, hearings were also proof to clients that they were doing something for a living. Thevenot and Boardman were not above that kind of showmanship, especially with so fragile, even flaky a concept as high-speed rail. But they did not stop at testifying. They coupled their public displays with private lobbying, sometimes arm-in-arm with their legislative patrons.

That was what happened on Wednesday, April 25, the same day as Coretech's Lobby Day. Unlike Coretech, the two lobbyists did not stride down the hallways of Capitol Hill with constituents in tow. They had an even more potent door-opener: a member of Congress. They were part of a lobbying effort launched and directed by Representative Robert Mrazek, Democrat of New York.

Mrazek was the House's version of Senator Daniel Moynihan when it came to Maglev. Mrazek's Long Island district was near the headquarters of Grumman, where his own father had once worked. The aerospace company was one of Maglev's biggest boosters and was a member of Boardman and Thevenot's fledgling Maglev USA lobbying coalition. The wild-eyed Mrazek was as excited about Maglev as anyone. He was a dreamer, unafraid to tackle schemes that others saw as outlandish. His risky real estate hunches had earned him hundreds of thousands of dollars over the years. Once, he even persuaded some of his colleagues to buy a tropical island with him, though the investment eventually soured. In Maglev, however, he saw enormous possibilities, and enlisted the lobbyists' aid.

At Mrazek's urging, Boardman had already appeared once at a press conference in the Rayburn House Office Building to promote legislation sponsored by Mrazek that would have created a Magnetic Levitation Transportation Administration within the Transportation Department. The bill envisioned a nearly billion-dollar commitment by the United States to design and build a prototype Maglev system.

Boardman was more than happy to help. He read a statement for the press that thanked "Mr. Mrazek for his leadership in encouraging a renewed federal commitment to Maglev development" and pledging "full support in demonstrating the renewed commitment of U.S. industry to this vital national effort." At the same time, though, he knew that his words, like the Mrazek plan, were mostly fluff. As he placed copies of his statement on the press table he confessed: "This is what you do when you don't have approval from your board to say anything—pure flimflam."

More serious efforts had been under way elsewhere. On April 3, the Senate Commerce Committee had voted to create a new high-speed-rail office in the Transportation Department and to authorize $100 million over two years for matching grants to U.S. companies researching Maglev. On April 24 the Senate Public Works Committee had voted, at Moynihan's urging, to allow Maglev projects to be built on federal highway rights-of-way. And inside the Bush administration, a special interagency group had been formed to coordinate efforts, which it formally called its "Maglev Initiative." President Bush had singled out Maglev as an "emerging technology" in his fiscal 1991 budget, and had recommended spending $9.7 million—more than quadruple the currently available sum—to study the system.

Now Mrazek was leading his own delegation of lobbyists to promote the effort some more. They met with the House lawmakers who held sway over how much Maglev could be funded. His team included executives from Grumman and General Dynamics, as well as Maglev USA's Thevenot and Boardman. They visited three Democrats: Representative William Lehman of Florida, who chaired the House subcommittee responsible for transportation appropriations; Representative Norman Mineta, a senior member of the Public Works Committee; and Representative Robert Torricelli of New Jersey, a senior member of a science subcommittee, whose fiery style gave him the nickname Torch.

The lobbyists tagged along to prove that American companies indeed wanted to build Maglev. Lehman and Mineta listened intently to their spiel, but wondered aloud where all the money would come from. And at first, Torricelli did the same. But after five minutes, the Torch ignited with enthusiasm. "I want the biggest, finest dog-and-pony show ever!" Mrazek quoted him as saying. "I want video displays and charts and everything. How soon can you do it? Sixty days? I want it June first," which was right before he hoped to hold a hearing on Maglev.

The delegation was a little taken aback by Torricelli's outburst, but they were gratified nonetheless. They agreed to meet his deadline. "It's a natural," Mrazek said. But questions, especially the ones asked by Lehman and Mineta, still remained.

• • •

The trucking associations were not taking Maglev for granted. Simonson had been reading about the new rail technology, and he was intensely curious and suspicious about it, as he was about all railway initiatives. To find out more, he sent a spy to watch how it all was going.

He assigned one of the junior economists he supervised, Dennis Monts, to attend a two-day "Government/Industry Forum on the Federal Maglev Initiative," held by the federal government in early May at the Embassy Row Hotel in Washington. Speaking there and, for a while, sharing the podium, were Senator Moynihan and Gilbert Carmichael, the Transportation Department's railroad administrator. By then, Carmichael had come around to believe that it was an important part of his job to oversee the study of Maglev in the United States. He even delighted in speaking publicly about how much he enjoyed "gliding along in comfort at over two hundred miles per hour in the prototype Maglev" in Emsland, West Germany.

Moynihan was at least polite about Carmichael's newfound interest. Looking out at the packed audience, the senator said he was witnessing "a moment that I didn't know that I'd ever see: a transition of this subject from a legislative initiative to an executive program." He then bowed toward Carmichael and the commandant of the Corps of Engineers, who were sitting to his right. This new stage in the development of Maglev, he said graciously, was "greatly due to the persons present here on the platform."

Moynihan would not leave it at that, however, and said he felt compelled to add "a measure of candor." "I am not very optimistic," he said. "You don't build bridges by wishing the structure," and the Maglev program, so far, comprised good intentions and not much else. "I don't want to travel to space," he implored. "I would like to get to New York City." He shook his head, left the conference room, and returned to Capitol Hill.

Simonson's spy correctly conveyed the flavor of the event. In a memorandum to Simonson, Monts wrote, "The forum provided a meeting ground for those government and industry groups interested in the success of a Maglev transportation system." But then Monts quickly added: "The group lacked clear objectives that could be understood and shared by all involved. The success of a Maglev system depends on industry initiative coupled with the federal government's willingness to develop a long-range strategy."

Even with these large doubts hanging over the concept, Simonson was not willing to ignore Maglev. "I see Maglev as a big threat," he concluded after reading Monts's memo. "It will take a hell of a lot of money and a hell of a lot of it may come out of the Highway Trust Fund. That would hurt trucking." But the trucking associations refrained from taking any official position. Moynihan was an important member of the Senate's Public Works Committee, which helped oversee the industry, and the lobbyists were loath to oppose his pet project. Still, Simonson was careful to keep his employee assigned to his surreptitious research.

As the Maglev incident proved, trucks and trains did not get along. They were competitive modes of transportation, and they competed for favorable legislation in Washington as well. Donohue had once warned the railroads: "If I find them walking on our lawn all the time, I will turn on the sprinklers." He did more than talk. He laid plans.

At the associations' headquarters, he assigned staffers to dig up dirt on railroads wherever they could find it. "ATA needs to counter railroad attacks," a senior aide advised him, "and to launch some of our own." The result, according to the *National Journal*, was a draft proposal called a "program of railroad reform," which really was a proposal to strip the railroads of some of their federal subsidies.

Donohue did not intend to launch such an attack. But when it came to the railroad lobby, the truckers were always working to gain an advantage. Donohue found one such opportunity on the evening of Wednesday, May 16, at a very prestigious locale: the White House. That night he was invited to a state dinner to honor the President of Tunisia, Zine al-Abidine Ben Ali. Considering the occasion, Donohue donned his tuxedo and took his wife, Elizabeth.

Making it onto the guest list of such a dazzling affair was always a prize. And that night the guests were more eclectic than usual. They included the actress Linda Evans of the television series "Dynasty," a model from the Victoria's Secret underwear catalog, and Don Rickles, the comedian. Also there was White House Chief of Staff John Sununu.

President Bush quipped to his Tunisian guest of honor: "You keep track of your cabinet personally with a home computer. Your home computer is called an Apple. Mine is called John Sununu." And it was Donohue's intention to store a little data in the President's computer that night about motor-fuel taxes. When he had the chance he sidled up to Sununu. After some pleasantries he said, "When you come to the point when the things I'm concerned about are in play, I respectfully request twenty minutes so we can present you with our side."

Donohue was able to talk to another guest at greater length: Bill Diefenderfer, the deputy director of the White House Budget Office. "Listen, I'm an advocate, you're a deal maker," Donohue recalled saying. "If I were in your shoes, I'd do things differently." He then commenced to try to tell Diefenderfer how to conduct his business. Mostly his advice boiled down to refraining from raising the motor-fuels tax. Donohue suggested that they meet again sometime soon.

· · ·

Truckers and railroaders might not have liked each other much. But in 1990 the conflict between stocks and mutuals was becoming a war. When the stocks said, "Black," the mutuals said, "White." And white was the topic on the afternoon of Friday, May 18, when the entire contingent of Concord Associates made their way by cab to the Senate side of the Capitol. They met with Senator Bob Dole's tax aide, Carolyn Seely. She was an old hand at such meetings. Before joining Dole's staff she had worked as an assistant to Eizenstat at his law office. She had also been Thevenot's compatriot in days gone by, when they both lobbied for real estate interests.

All of this made the meeting congenial, or at least as congenial as a discussion about stocks and mutuals could possibly be. It was an example of the reason why the lobbying of staff had become so important in Washington. The details of the proposed legislation were far too complex for busy lawmakers to digest; they were left to the staff. So when Boardman, Thevenot, and Rock wanted to lobby Dole on behalf of the mutuals, they talked to his staff. The group met in a reception room just outside of Dole's own office.

"You do have better digs than most of the people we visit," Thevenot began lightheartedly. But then the hard slogging started. Referring to the tax-code section dealing with life-insurance companies he said, "You've heard about 809 ad nauseam. We've been retained to bring a non-barnacle-encrusted view to this. We've been visiting with your peers. We've been trying to boil this down to its essence. Eight-oh-nine is unworkable and untenable. If there is an additional amount of money to be taken from the mutuals, so be it. We want to see that this industry is taxed fairly." From then on most of the exchanges were jargon-laden grunts and talk of revenue estimates. Rock did most of the talking; Seely asked highly technical questions. And somehow the two understood each other completely.

In the course of the conversation, it became clear that the lobbyists were worried that Dan Rostenkowski's preference would be to hurt the mutuals more than stocks. The powerful chairman had said he wished that the Treasury, which was known to have sympathy for the mutuals' position, could become more influential in the House proceedings. "Maybe your boss and Senator Packwood would have something to say about that," Rock suggested. But Seely did not reply.

Thevenot raised the prospect of the biggest danger of all: that both the stocks and the mutuals would get stuck with a big tax increase for deficit-reduction purposes. "When those bears emerge from hibernation," Thevenot said, referring to lawmakers who wanted to reduce the deficit, "they'll be looking for something to eat."

The meeting broke up without any resolution, but only a good-natured warning from Thevenot. "Thank you," he said as Seely showed them to the door. "You should beware of anyone who comes and says he understands it."

· · ·

By springtime, Rostenkowski had had enough. Lobbying continued apace all over town, in anticipation that something major might happen. And Rostenkowski was determined to make it so. Ever restless and always eager to write new laws, he had finally tired of stalemate and decided to take action. His number one concern had for a long time been the budget deficit, even though he seemed to worry about it in virtual isolation among the top policymakers in town. Publicly, at least, President Bush was still unwavering in his no-new-taxes stand, and the Democrats were loath to challenge him. Rostenkowski had a different idea, and pursued it.

With the help of his staff—and with some input from former staffers who were lobbyists—Rostenkowski put together his dream plan: a deficit-reduction package so audacious that it would wipe out the entire deficit in just a few short years. The ideas in the package were far from new. In fact, its basic framework had been revealed in November 1988 by John Salmon, a former top aide to the chairman who was then a lobbyist for the law firm Dewey, Ballantine, Bushby, Palmer & Wood. At the annual conference of the Tax Executives Institute in Maui, Salmon predicted that "a major budget bill is inevitable," and he knew what he was talking about. Even though he was a corporate lobbyist, he continued to toss around ideas with the people who became the primary authors of the ultimate Rostenkowski proposal: Wendell Primus, a senior Rostenkowski aide, and Salmon's eventual successor as Rostenkowski's top aide, Rob Leonard.

Before Rostenkowski unveiled his plan, he traveled to the White House to brief Richard Darman and John Sununu about its details. And in the first signal that the President might be willing to raise taxes to fight the deficit problem, neither man objected to its release. They also agreed not to dismiss it out of hand. In fact, Rostenkowski's bold move presented them with the opportunity to move on the deficit issue without appearing to move first.

"The Rostenkowski Challenge" was first unveiled in a column

under the chairman's byline in the "Outlook" section of *The Washington Post*. Later, on Thursday, May 10, 1990, he presented its full justification and details to a packed audience at the National Press Club in downtown Washington. It was a slash-and-burn performance of the first order, which sent tremors through the lobbying community.

In a blow to the capital-gains forces, Rostenkowski proposed to eschew all tax cuts and, instead, raise the top individual tax rate to 33 percent from the existing 28 percent. He also threw down the gauntlet to CART by proposing to increase virtually every kind of excise tax, including those on gasoline, beer, wine, and cigarettes. He also proposed to freeze most federal spending programs, including Social Security, for one year and to cut military spending by 3 percent from existing levels. The goal of his five-year proposal, he said, was to reduce projected deficits by a staggering $511.6 billion and eliminate the annual budget deficit entirely by the end of fiscal 1994.

"In years past," Rostenkowski said, "I have come to the National Press Club whenever I had an ambitious project in mind. I appeared here in 1985 to talk about my commitment to tax reform. By the end of that Congress, we had enacted the most comprehensive income-tax reform in America's history. I returned here two years later to talk about the need for trade legislation that was strong enough to help force open foreign markets, but fair enough not to trigger a political trade war. The omnibus trade legislation enacted in 1988 ultimately met both objectives. I learned my lesson. Apparently, when someone at the Press Club talks, people listen. And act. This time the mere announcement of my speech may have been enough to get the deficit-reduction ball rolling. I'm here today to talk about my plan to eliminate the federal budget deficit, reduce our dependence on foreign investors, restore our international competitiveness, and revive the reputation of our government as a positive force in our society. I'm here to ask you to embrace my budgetary challenge of substantial tax increases and essential budget discipline."

In his plan, Rostenkowski sought to balance the need for deficit reduction with a desire to help people with low incomes—in line with the rhetoric of his party. His one-year freeze on federal spending, for example, would have exempted programs aimed at poor people. And just as Simonson had predicted the year before, Rostenkowski sought to offset the regressivity of his proposed increase in excise taxes with a 20 percent increase in the earned-income tax credit, the law that allows people with low incomes to receive direct payments in the form of tax refunds.

Specifically, Rostenkowski proposed to increase the federal excise tax on gasoline by 15 cents, to 24.1 cents a gallon. That would have raised $12 billion the first year, after accounting for the increase in the earned-income credit. He also wanted to double the excise tax on cigarettes, to 32 cents a pack; double the beer tax, to 32 cents a six-pack; and double the wine tax, to six cents a 750-milliliter bottle. The change in beer and wine taxation would have raised $1.2 billion in the first year.

Notably, the Rostenkowski plan would have left unchanged the tax on distilled spirits. The ostensible reason for the omission was that the tax on hard liquor had just been raised in 1985, while taxes on beer and wine had not been touched since the early 1950s. But skeptics suggested another reason: that John Salmon had gotten special treatment from the chairman, with whom he was still very close. One of the lobbyist's longtime clients, Seagram's, was a major liquor producer.

In any case, after Rostenkowski's speech it was clear for the first time that some sort of big budget bill was at least possible in 1990. Coretech cheered, even though the chairman did not press for any tax cuts. The reason: A bill the size that Rostenkowski proposed would surely have room to extend its popular R&D benefits, maybe even enough room to support permanent extensions. The stocks and the mutuals feared that they had picked the wrong year to squabble with each other. And every other lobbyist in town was deciding how best to cash in. Micah Green, a lobbyist for the Public Securities Association, which worked to protect tax-free bonds, was way ahead of the crowd. From the trunk of his chauffeured sedan parked outside the Press Club building he distributed blue caps, made in China, that bore the inscription: TAKE THE ROSTY CHALLENGE.

So the stage was set for the huge budget battle to come.

7

An
Anchor
Windward

Traffic came to a complete halt along one of those endless highways that encircle sprawling Houston, Texas, and Sarah Hull had no choice but to call ahead with profuse apologies. She had flown in that day, Tuesday, June 12, to visit a handful of small businesses and persuade their owners to become part of a special network she was helping to construct. Her next appointment, for which she was a full hour late, would have to wait a little longer—at least until she could find a back-road route to get there. But get there she must. Her employers were not the kind of people to give up easily, and the situation demanded prompt work.

The twenty-eight-year-old Hull was a Washington-based operative for the National Venture Capital Association. And her quarry this day was a balding businessman named Reese Terry, Jr., whose small company, Cyberonics Incorporated, was housed in a tiny storefront in a rundown shopping center next to a Dairy Queen. Hull's mission was to enlist him in her client's newly stepped-up fight for a lower capital-gains tax. Traffic or no traffic, she was determined to win his assistance. When she finally reached her destination, she stepped out of her rented car, walked through the scorching heat into Terry's cramped office, and confidently handed him a black folder filled with documents.

"We are conducting a grass-roots campaign to lower the capital-gains tax," she told him. "Texas is important."

Indeed, almost every state was important now. As the result of Dan Rostenkowski's prodding, the Bush administration had finally begun to take its first, timid steps toward addressing the massive deficit problem. Not long before Hull made her journey to Houston, the White House, "without preconditions," had convened what it called a "budget summit" to test for solutions to the nagging deficit problem, which in the preceding weeks had gotten progressively worse. Twenty lawmakers and top Bush officials were designated as the chief negotiators.

By mid-June, the White House had hiked its forecast of the next year's budget deficit to $168.8 billion, which was more than two-thirds higher than its projection of just six months before. Unless a compromise was reached with Congress, Budget Director Richard Darman warned, automatic spending cuts under the Gramm-Rudman Law would be so deep that he would be forced to close airport control towers, cancel student loans, interrupt food inspections, and cut military forces in half.

With the prospect of these actions hanging like a guillotine over their heads, top-ranking Democratic and Republican lawmakers began to meet regularly with Bush advisers. At first the talks were unstructured, and White House Chief of Staff John Sununu publicly remained adamant that any significant tax increases were off limits. Democrats, for their part, countered that tax hikes were absolutely necessary to address the problem seriously, though Bush would have to make the first move.

In other words, gridlock still held sway. But some sort of arrangement was inevitable to avoid such harsh consequences, so lobbying groups remained prepared. The venture-capital association, in particular, made certain that it would be well positioned to push its views if the crunch ever came.

In the first several months of the year, the association, based in Arlington, Virginia, had spent a quarter-million dollars just on the "grass-roots" effort that Hull helped spearhead. Since February, she and an associate at the public relations firm of Robinson,

Lake, Lerer & Montgomery had scoured a dozen states to find and train homespun capital-gains advocates like Reese Terry. Their prime targets were, like him, founders of young, fast-growing companies who had struggled to scrape together enough capital to make a go of it—and for whom a lower capital-gains tax could credibly be translated into the creation of more jobs. From a politician's viewpoint, that was a relatively compelling story—more compelling, at least, than self-interested pleas from the money men who paid Hull to push for the capital-gains cut.

"It sure as hell beats running up to the halls [of Congress] and squeezing arms and throwing fat checks at them," contended Daniel Kingsley, executive director of the venture-capital association. By June, his group, with Hull's help, had pieced together a network of about 250 entrepreneurs, and intended to use them, as the need arose, to send letters to Washington, to write opinion pieces for local newspapers, and to meet with key lawmakers when they returned to their districts.

The investment of time and money had already begun to pay dividends. On March 20 Hull had mailed an urgent request to her recruits to write to Rostenkowski and nine members of his Ways and Means Committee. A model letter she had enclosed asserted that without a capital-gains cut "the entrepreneurial engine driving our economy won't just stall; it'll be running on empty." In response, forty business executives from Connecticut to California used the identical phrase in letters to the lawmakers.

In Houston that humid June day, Hull was attempting to expand the list of corporate executives in her capital-gains network. She met with much success. Terry, for one, readily agreed to help. So did shirt-sleeved James Pritchett, president of Trinity Computing Systems Incorporated, a maker of computer software for hospitals. "Be happy to," he said over coffee in his conference room, when she asked him if he would visit a local newspaper's editorial board. Hull also encouraged Pritchett to help lobby the main focus of her trip, Lloyd Bentsen of the Senate Finance Committee. "We want to get a letter to Bentsen from you," she said bluntly. She also asked the executive to meet with the senator. "That's something down the road we might want to organize." She got an affirmative answer to each request.

In the course of the trip, Hull did meet with some venture

capitalists—the people who were responsible for paying her salary. But mostly she used them to refer her to the hands-on managers they financed. They would be more credible to lawmakers. "We are trying to put a face on the issue," she explained at the time, and not the face of venture capitalists, who in Washington were sometimes derided as "vulture capitalists" because of the open opportunism of their profession. The case for the cut, Hull added, "is much more convincing when it comes from a businessperson."

To collect extra names, and advice about who might be most convincing, Hull lunched at the wood-paneled Century Club on the top floor of the First Interstate Bank building with David Hull, a principal of Criterion Investments Incorporated and no relation to her. With a spectacular view of Houston all around him, Mr. Hull suggested she visit the MIT Forum, in which start-up companies present their business plans for critique. "That's an audience that's easy to sell," he counseled. She promised to approach the group soon.

Sarah Hull worked hard to make it easy for the entrepreneurs she recruited to lobby. The documents in the folder that she gave them constituted a complete lobbying kit, much like the instructions many other professional lobbyists gave to their people from back home. Hull's folder included a sample letter to lawmakers that argued for a lower capital-gains tax, with a place reserved to "insert your own story about your company." Another document listed "talking points" that the executives could use to make the case for capital gains, including this debatable statement: "Lower taxes on capital gains will offer all Americans the benefits of a productive and more competitive economy."

The kit—and Hull, at each of her meetings—strongly recommended that the executives write editorials for local newspapers. Samples of such articles written by other business executives were included in the packet. She also told the executives that they need not worry about the wording of their columns. Her company in Washington could give them plenty of help with that: It kept three ghostwriters on its staff for that purpose.

Not everyone thought that manufactured sentiment of the kind Hull fostered would be particularly effective. Some of the doubters were among the lawmakers she hoped to influence. "It takes the spontaneity out of the process, and that is one of the things that has the biggest impact," complained Representative Mike Andrews of Houston, who was one of the lawmakers Hull mentioned along with Bentsen as a focus of her interest on the trip. Then again, Andrews did not need much persuading; he remained one of the Congress's firmest advocates for a lower capital-gains tax.

Bentsen also voiced doubts that he would be swayed by the efforts of the venture capitalists. "You can very quickly determine the difference between grass roots and AstroTurf," he said, trying to draw a distinction between letters written spontaneously by constituents and ones that were manufactured by Washington professionals like Hull. But those letters were read nonetheless.

· · ·

One of the fastest-growing businesses among Washington lobby-ists was the recruiting of non-Washingtonians to help them do their jobs. The reason was simple: It worked. Democratic Repre-sentative Byron Dorgan of North Dakota explained it this way: "Any lobbyist can get into my office in two minutes if he's smart enough to bring somebody from Grand Forks. And all of them are smart enough to do that."

Gathering that kind of home-state support became a sophisti-cated racket in the nation's capital. Rarely did it rise to the level of the venture capitalists' person-to-person assault. Usually it took place at arm's length. It often entailed the compiling of lists and the setting up of telephone banks that were used to reach out and persuade people back home to contact their Washington represen-tatives. In 1987, for example, Bonner & Associates, which jammed dozens of young telephone operators into two floors of a K Street office building, was paid $3 million for a month's work by the Pharmaceutical Manufacturers Association. The drug companies' trade group wanted to prevent a proposed expansion of Medicare coverage from turning into a kind of federal price-control mecha-nism on their products. So they paid Bonner to instigate nearly 100,000 letters and other messages to Capitol Hill. In the end, the drug provision that the organization opposed was softened in a House-Senate compromise.

Bonner was one of a handful of companies that adopted for private industry the methods that had long been used mostly by organized labor, consumer groups, and environmentalists. As a former staffer to Republican Senator John Heinz of Pennsylvania, Jack Bonner, the company's owlish president, learned firsthand what motivated a politician. "Basically the stuff in Civics 101," he said. "How many people know about an issue, and how many care, and how many care about it deeply." Those expressions of caring were communicated by "card, a call, a letter, or showing up at a meeting," he said. And getting constituents to do those things in the greatest possible volume was what his multimillion-dollar business was all about.

In Washington, where "eighty percent to ninety percent of all issues are decided on the basis of politics rather than the pure merits of the issue," Bonner argued, "there is a market niche to help industry generate support from home constituents who are outside of the industry." Bonner's most intensive labors were directed at convincing disinterested parties to contact their representatives to express his client's point of view. He actually charged higher fees for generating letters or calls from local ministers or community activists, whose opinions would be most highly valued by the lawmakers he sought to influence.

Sometimes Bonner cut out the middleman in this quest to get his clients' messages across. His computerized telephone system could switch callers directly to the offices of their members of Congress. Another organization with a similar system once did a lot of switching for the Tobacco Institute. Lawmakers from Texas, Georgia, and Florida reported a torrent of calls from constituents who opposed an increase in the cigarette tax. As it turned out, tobacco companies had provided the telephone bank with lists of known customers. When the people who were contacted agreed, their calls were switched directly into their lawmakers' offices, free of charge. "It overwhelmed our front office," an aide to Senator Phil Gramm of Texas told Roll Call, the Capitol Hill newspaper. "The calls came with such frequency that people with legitimate business couldn't get through."

Similar techniques also produced thousands of letters to lawmakers. In fact, in the spring of 1990 mail delivery to House members was running eight days behind, "because of the unprecedented and immense volumes of both constituent and special-interest group mail," according to the House's postmaster, Robert

Rota. He asked for forty temporary mail handlers to ease the burden. "My employees are suffering 'burnout' from hours of overtime and seven-day workweeks," he said.

This style of lobbying had its roots in Democratic politics. The godfather of Washington's fake-mail business was Matthew Reese of Reese Communications, who honed his skills as part of John F. Kennedy's groundbreaking victory in the West Virginia primary in 1960. Years later Reese applied similar methods to corporate causes, including a big one in the early 1980s on behalf of American Telephone & Telegraph Co. The telephone giant wanted to make sure that its upstart competitors would be charged access fees to use its long-distance lines. So it paid Reese to establish phone banks that were used to persuade voters to write their senators and representatives on behalf of AT&T.

Not every group was as well-heeled as AT&T, with a few million dollars to throw around. Instead, grass-roots lobbying was usually simpler, even routine for many companies. Tom Korologos of Timmons & Company called it the Utah-plant-manager method of lobbying. "Suppose we have a big issue boiling and bubbling in the Senate Judiciary Committee and we don't know how Senator Hatch of Utah is going to come out on it," Korologos said. "So we will fly in the Utah plant manager of a refinery in North Salt Lake, and go hat in hand to see Senator Hatch. And oh my goodness, Senator Hatch is on the floor with some highly brilliant, televised event. Well, ninety-nine times out of a hundred he'll leave those brilliant lights and cosmic issues, and come out and talk to his constituent. . . . Because if Hatch doesn't come out and see his constituent, the guy's going to go home and see his friends at church on Sunday or go bowling on Monday or Rotary on Tuesday and his friends are going to ask, 'Where were you last week?' and he's going to say, 'Well, I was in Washington, and the son of bitch wouldn't see me. He got up there in Washington and he forgot the folks who sent him.' "

When voters talked, the theory went, lawmakers had no choice but to listen. And lobbyists had few better devices to get a lawmaker's ear.

• • •

Lobbyists were so eager to please lawmakers that they, and their ready access to money, were sometimes abused. Such a case was on display on Tuesday, June 12, which by coincidence was the same day that Sarah Hull went looking for capital-gains supporters in Houston. In the high-ceilinged hearing room of the Senate Ethics Committee, Senator David Durenberger, Republican of Minnesota, started down the road to condemnation for his too-close-for-comfort dealings with lobbyists. In a rare public session, a special counsel to the panel recommended that Durenberger be denounced for "knowingly engaging in unethical conduct which has brought dishonor and disrepute to this institution." His offense: shaking down lobbying groups for extra money for himself.

Before a hushed hearing room, Robert Bennett, the counsel, methodically summarized the allegations against the fifty-five-year-old Republican, which proved to be eerily reminiscent of the accusations against Jim Wright. They involved a book-promotion effort for which Durenberger received $100,000 in an alleged scheme to circumvent Senate limits on honoraria, and a condominium partnership through which Durenberger may have improperly received Senate reimbursement for lodging expenses, even though he was really the owner of the apartment.

The book deal was the one most similar to Wright's case. Bennett alleged that the interest groups to which Durenberger spoke were referred for payment not to the senator's staff, as was customary, but to Gary L. Diamond, the owner of a small publishing firm in Minneapolis called the Piranha Press. "Honorarium" checks for 113 speeches were made payable to Piranha, which was the publisher of two of the senator's books, one on health issues, the other on foreign policy. In turn, Piranha paid Durenberger $100,000 in quarterly installments of $12,500 each from 1985 to 1987 as a "stipend" for promoting the books. "This very hungry fish, Piranha Press, was allowed to engage in a feeding frenzy on responsible organizations who thought they were sponsoring traditional honorarium events," Bennett said. "Unfortunately, the evidence shows that Senator Durenberger . . . allowed himself and the stature of his office to be used as the bait, and he got $100,000 for his trouble."

Durenberger was far from the only member of Congress giving paid speeches around the country. Though his colleagues did not try to manipulate the rules to put more than their share of fees into their pockets, they nonetheless took full advantage of rules that allowed them to be frequent fliers at corporate expense. In 1989 and 1990 members of the House accepted nearly four thousand trips paid for by corporations or trade groups. "Most of these trips are nothing more than lobbyist-funded vacations for the nation's lawmakers, a form of legalized bribery," charged Joan Claybrook, president of Public Citizen, Ralph Nader's public-interest group. "The trips allow well-heeled corporate lobbyists to hunker down with members of Congress over lunches or golf games for private tête-à-têtes about key legislative issues."

Even more galling was that lawmakers usually accepted speaking fees in addition to reimbursement for the travel and accommodations. Their destinations were some of the fanciest or most cosmopolitan places in the country, and their patrons were some of the most profitable corporate interests, including the Chicago commodity exchanges, the nation's cable and network broadcasters, Connell Rice & Sugar Company, and Textron.

California and Florida were by far the most popular destinations, accounting for more than a thousand trips. Resort spots such as the La Quinta Hotel in Palm Springs, California, where twenty-five House members flew in January 1990, courtesy of the Tobacco Institute, were particularly favored. The busiest months for corporate-sponsored flying by the lawmakers were also among the chilliest: January, March, and November.

Some House members bundled their travel together for especially long stays. In January 1990, for example, Republican Representative Bill Young of Florida, a member of the Defense Appropriations Subcommittee, had made stops in Los Angeles and Dallas. The Los Angeles leg was sponsored by eight companies, most of them defense contractors, which also gave Representative Young $16,000 in honoraria during his five-day tour. In Dallas, Young's trip was underwritten by four companies, which gave him an additional $7,000 in speaking fees.

At least in travel, Representative Patricia Schroeder, Democrat of Colorado, ranked first in the House during the 101st Congress: She logged a whopping ninety-eight trips. Next was Representative Bill Gray of Pennsylvania, the House's third-ranking Democrat, with seventy-four trips, and then Dan Rostenkowski, with fifty-three. Rostenkowski's itinerary in the winter of 1990 included two trips each to Maui, Palm Beach, and Palm Springs, as well as a visit to Scottsdale, Arizona. Corporate sponsors of these winter vacations included Merrill Lynch, the Futures Industry Association, and Philip Morris.

While Public Citizen was criticizing lawmakers for taking these free trips, the lawmakers were compelled to disclose the amount of honorarium money they had received in 1989. And even though the House had voted to end the practice of accepting speaking fees in 1990, a Mead Data Central computerized tabulation of honoraria carried in *The Washington Post* showed that the amount of honoraria in 1989 was still substantial: 2,696 groups paid almost $9.5 million to members of Congress that year. The total was a drop from previous years, in part because of the taint that scandals like Durenberger's had brought into the process. But lawmakers were still able—and willing—to accept free trips from corporate lobbyists, and that practice continued unabated.

Durenberger's ordeal ended quickly. He brought his hearing to a close the next day, Wednesday, June 13, by pleading for clemency. He apologized for his actions, asserting that he had tried to act "in good faith" and had not intended to violate any Senate rules. Later that summer, the Senate would meet and, after three hours of debate, vote 96–0 to denounce him.

· · ·

The anti-excise-tax lobby, in the meantime, decided to step up its efforts. It went more high-tech and high-powered. The corporate interests of CART decided to combine forces with organized labor to try to get their point across. Both CART and the unions, each for their own reasons, agreed that excise-tax increases were a bad idea. The corporations were opposed to a tax increase because it would lead to lower sales and profits. The unions did not want a tax increase because it would disproportionately hurt working people. So they chose their best argument against excise-tax increases—regressivity—and hammered it home by the best means they could think of—television.

Hard-hitting commercials were what the groups wanted, and

that was what they got in abundance from David Wilhelm, a political consultant with ties to the union movement. Wilhelm was a veteran of Democratic political contests, both electoral and legislative. He fought for tax reform as the executive director of the Washington-based Citizens for Tax Justice from 1985 to 1987. In 1987, he was for a short time Senator Joseph Biden's presidential campaign director in Iowa. And then he ran for Congress himself—unsuccessfully—from his hometown, Athens, Ohio. He moved to Chicago and established his own consulting firm, called the Strategy Group.

From his exposed-wall basement office, Wilhelm had directed election campaigns for local Democrats, including the new mayor, Richard M. Daley. But he was also willing to accept work from corporations when they found use for his particular specialty: a gut-grabbing appeal to populism. Though he personally had reservations about alcohol and tobacco products, he agreed to focus his polemics on the fight against raising taxes on the poor.

"Our point is not to defend alcohol and tobacco," he explained. "This is a tax-policy issue. How are we going to reduce the deficit in a fair manner? People bring up the health issue, the energy issue. Well, the genesis of the budget [negotiations] is not health policy or energy policy. It's the deficit, which was caused by huge tax breaks on the very rich. We ought to make the people pay who went to the party."

Earlier in the year, Wilhelm had discussed with the machinists' union the possibility that regressive taxes might be raised as part of the ongoing budget summit talks, and that something should be done to stop it. But then he took another step: He solicited money from major corporate interests. "What's different between this and other 'tax fairness' groups," he said, "is that we went out and raised the money for an ad campaign, as if it were a political campaign." Among those he got to contribute were the members of CART, including Philip Morris and the trucking associations. Donohue's trucking group ultimately coughed up $25,000 to help finance Wilhelm's commercials, and CART gave another $10,000. The total budget was about $750,000.

Wilhelm produced five commercials, each one hitting harder than the one before it. One ad showed tuxedo-clad men getting out of a very expensive automobile. "This is a Rolls-Royce Corniche convertible," the announcer said. "If you're a multimillionaire, you can buy one for $200,000." Then the camera turned to a bottle of beer. "Sixty-five cents," the announcer said. "Regular people enjoy them in their backyards on hot summer days. . . . Guess which one the government wants to tax now?"

A second ad pictured a balding man pumping gas into his own car. "I do this a couple times a week," he said. "This is how I get to work and my kids to Little League. Now I'm hearing that back in Washington they want to raise something called consumer excise taxes, which are really federal sales taxes on everything from cigarettes to beer and gasoline." The scene switched to the man dropping off his children at a baseball game, and he concluded: "I think gas taxes are high enough already, and there are a lot of families out here who just can't afford to pay any more."

Wilhelm's group tested the effect of the ads in six medium-size television markets, picking geographically diverse places where the airtime was inexpensive. They were Springfield, Massachusetts; Lincoln, Nebraska; Albuquerque, New Mexico; Little Rock, Arkansas; Scranton, Pennsylvania; and Flint, Michigan. The impact was impressive everywhere. Before the ads aired, 55 percent of respondents opposed a beer-tax increase; afterward, the opposition level rose to 66 percent. They were so powerful, in fact, that there were no plans to air them again. Just their threat had clout, both Wilhelm and Tom Donohue agreed. "There's no point in pissing on their legs unless you really have to," Donohue said.

• • •

Ken Kay, too, was worried about angering the people in power. He and Coretech had been stunned by the 861 scare during the President's budget deliberations at the end of 1989, and he did not want a recurrence. So by May he had plunged into serious consultations with the largest companies in his R&D coalition to determine what could be done. By early June they had made their decision: They needed to hire a well-placed Republican lobbyist to counterbalance the very Democratic Stuart Eizenstat. "Our perception problem was real, and we had to address it," Kay said, making sense in a way that only longtime Washingtonians would appreciate.

Kay wanted to be sure that the Bush administration was completely behind extending both the R&D credit and 861. The way to ensure that, he thought, was to hire a member in good standing of Washington's Republican network, and the person he thought would suit was Craig Fuller, a former aide to George Bush, and now a lobbyist with Anne Wexler's lobbying firm. Though he was not considered one of Washington's intellectual heavyweights, Fuller was one of the most thoroughly Republican lobbyists in town.

Fuller had long served Bush as his vice presidential chief of staff, and was a senior adviser to the 1988 presidential campaign. After the election, he lost out to Sununu in the contest to become the President's White House chief of staff, but he won the plum assignment of directing personnel selection for the new administration. Many of the people who got the highest jobs in government had Craig Fuller to thank—and that debt provided Fuller the ticket he needed to join the upper echelons of the city's lobbying crew.

Coretech lobbyists checked to make sure Fuller was still in good standing with his former colleagues. (He was.) But they also demanded that he prove he understood their issue. In early June, Fuller had managed to persuade them of that with a presentation at the Washington office of Pfizer, which was located just down the street from Fuller's old stomping grounds in the Old Executive Office Building.

Sitting calmly, but confidently, amid a handful of company lobbyists, Fuller had impressed the group immediately with his comprehension of the issue and its politics. He had told them he could remember well the internal White House discussions about the R&D tax credit, dating back to its inception in 1981. He had even recalled how close the credit had come to being made permanent in 1987. By the end of his talk, the lobbyists in the conference room believed him when he said he thought the R&D breaks should become a permanent part of the tax code, and that he was personally committed to making that happen.

Fuller was placed on a handsome retainer, and was ready to get down to business. So on Friday, June 15, Eizenstat, Fuller, and Kay met to begin what Kay hoped would be "the rehabilitation process" for Coretech in the eyes of the Republican White House. At the meeting in Eizenstat's office, the three lobbyists addressed the central question: how to persuade the White House that Coretech's issues were worth supporting without reservation. It was obvious by then that Coretech had gotten into trouble by trying to play both sides of the capital-gains debate. The coalition had received several warnings that Kay termed shots across the bow from a variety of people with Republican connections. And there was no doubting the fundamental cause of the warnings: They all stemmed from Coretech's refusal to actively support capital gains.

Kay wished that the White House would understand how difficult it was for Coretech's members to back a tax provision that was outside the group's research-based mandate. Supporting the capital-gains tax cut would complicate things with the Democrats. It also would place the highly paid chief executives of some Coretech companies in the position of lobbying for something that would benefit them personally—something they dearly wished not to do. "Why doesn't the White House understand?" Kay asked Fuller.

According to Kay, Fuller answered flatly: "I don't know. But I don't think it helps the issue a whole lot." He then became quite firm: "You do have a problem; you ought to do something."

The "something" they decided to do was a compromise. Coretech still did not wish to put its name behind an effort to cut capital gains. But Kay did agree to draft a letter to Richard Darman that pledged undying support for the President's proposal, and to get a dozen or so top executives from among Coretech's membership to sign it. If Coretech could not—or would not—make the endorsement itself, at least its corporate heavyweights should, they all agreed. The letter said, in part:

> We want you to know that you can count on our help in passing the reduction in the individual capital gains tax which President Bush, Secretary Brady, you and others in the administration have championed as part of a comprehensive budget and tax package. Just as we have long advocated greater incentives for American R&D to stimulate growth and investment, so, too, do we believe a lower capital gains tax rate will stimulate more general investment in our economy and more entrepreneurial activity. We look forward to working with you and the administration to secure a permanent R&D credit, a permanent

and fair solution to the Section 861–8 problems, and a reduction
in the capital gains rate.

Fuller took the letter to Darman, and sent copies to Brady,
Sununu, White House domestic adviser Roger Porter, and Darman's deputy, Bill Diefenderfer. By all accounts—especially his
own—it went a long way toward soothing their hurt feelings. "My
only regret," Kay said, "was that we didn't do it sooner."

• • •

As Coretech moved closer to the capital-gains lobby, Mark Bloomfield moved the capital-gains lobby farther to the right. For purely
tactical reasons, he decided to push a tougher version of the tax
cut than had been proposed by the President. He feared that
with the budget talks under way, the President's already diluted
position would be compromised even more. So he and Walker
decided to cast an "anchor windward," to prevent their position
on capital gains from drifting farther away from its home base.

"We think there will be a capital-gains tax cut coming out of
the budget talks," Bloomfield said confidently. "Our strategy is to
maximize the significance of that tax cut." His worry, he said, was
that the tax cut that came out of the talks "might be weak tea. . . .
What we worry about is ending up with capital gains in name
only."

So early one morning that spring, Bloomfield and Charly
Walker had one of their clipped telephone conversations. As they
had become accustomed to doing whenever they were about to
begin a new project, they tossed around names of lawmakers they
wanted to head their effort.

"How about Connie Mack?" Walker suggested, referring to
the young Republican senator from Florida, who was the gap-
toothed grandson of the famous manager of the Philadelphia
Athletics.

"Fine. I don't have any problem," Bloomfield said. "But my
concern is the bipartisan issue."

"Don't worry," Walker said, as he so often did to his high-
strung protégé. "We probably could find some Democratic cosponsors too."

Bloomfield already had been in pretty steady contact with

Mack's office. The senator had been a loyal backer of capital gains in 1989, and regularly came to Bloomfield for information. This had begun when the lobbyist returned to his apartment one night in the fall to find a message on his machine from Robert Mottice, Mack's tax aide. Bloomfield returned the call at eight-thirty the next morning and provided the data that Mottice had sought. Similar conversations had taken place since, and through them Bloomfield came to know how truly interested in capital gains Senator Mack was.

The other champion Bloomfield recruited was Senator Robert Kasten, Republican of Wisconsin. Kasten's interest in tax matters went back to his cosponsorship, with GOP Representative Jack Kemp of New York, of a tax-cut proposal in the early 1980s. Bloomfield approached Kasten as he did most senators—through the staff. Kasten's tax aide was Cesar Conda, who, like Mottice in Senator Mack's office, was a regular user of the American Council as a resource. Bloomfield took the additional step of inviting Kasten to one of his dinner soirees, where the two men talked about producing a broad capital-gains plan.

Conversation about the emerging plan flowed easily between the lawmakers and the lobbyists. At one point Conda faxed to Walker and lobbyist Ken Hagerty a letter that his boss had written to President Reagan in 1987. The letter, recommending that Reagan cut the capital-gains tax, was signed by seventeen GOP senators. On the cover sheet, Conda had scribbled: "In 1987, Bob [Kasten] organized a letter from 17 senators calling for 15% capgains tax. Those who signed the letter should be natural candidates for original cosponsors [of the new plan]: D'Amato, Boschwitz, Rudman, Danforth, Roth, Bond, Simpson, Humphrey, Helms, Lugar."

In response, Hagerty dispatched a plea to the capital-gains coalition. Under the heading "Major New CG Bill Planned; Cosponsors Sought," it read, in part:

> While the budget summit drags on, Senate supporters of lower capital gains taxes are preparing a major new bill to provide an "anchor to the windward" in those negotiations. By staking out an aggressive capital gains position and demonstrating solid support for it, this bill will strengthen the pro–capital gains negotiators in the summit. . . . You can make a difference

if you contact your members to ask them to urge their senators—
both Democrats and Republicans—to cosponsor the Economic
Growth and Venture Capital Act of 1990.

And so the Kasten-Mack capital-gains plan was hatched. It
certainly could not be mistaken for "weak tea." It was, in fact, a
return to the "15 percent solution" of years past. Gains on the sale
of assets held for more than a year would be taxed at a top rate of
15 percent. The President's proposal provided for a 19.6 percent
top rate, while existing law taxed capital gains at up to 33 percent.
The preferential rate would be given to the sale, by both individuals and corporations, of all types of assets, including collectibles
such as antiques and paintings, which the President's plan had
shunned as too frivolous for a tax break.

As soon as Bloomfield saw the final proposal, which was faxed
to him by the tax aides, he got on the telephone. He called Mike
Murray, Thevenot's old lobbying partner, who he knew lobbied
for some auction-house interests. Murray was glad to hear that
collectibles were part of the Kasten-Mack plan, and said he would
try to help get it passed. Bloomfield also telephoned lobbyists for
the realtors and the National Realty Committee. "This is the most
generous thing you'll get," he told them, and both groups expressed enthusiasm. Then he called a meeting of the capital-gains
coalition to ask for their help in gathering cosponsors.

At the office of Walker Associates, Walker briefed the coalition
on the details of the Kasten-Mack proposal. He even had a one-
page lobbying sheet ready; its somewhat defensive title, "Kasten-
Mack Is Fiscally Responsible," anticipated the argument that the
plan would lose oodles of revenue and do little if anything to
stimulate the economy. "Both Treasury and Joint Committee revenue estimates are unnecessarily pessimistic," the document stated,
and went on to drop the names of several economists, ranging
from Martin Feldstein to Allen Sinai, who had said some nice
things about the tax cut. (Bloomfield's American Council had even
financed a Sinai study on the subject.) The document concluded:
"If enacted, the measure will cut capital costs, stimulate additional
investment, advance the rate of economic growth, and generate
sufficient revenues to offset (probably more than offset) the cut in

rates. Therefore, no senator should be reluctant to support Kasten-Mack because of fear that it will increase the federal deficit."

Walker then turned the meeting over to Bloomfield. "We've got to move the terms of debate, and now there is a bill," Bloomfield exhorted. The pep rally continued until, as was customary, the lobbyists dutifully divided up the senators they would contact. No one raised his voice in protest, but at least two participants quietly harbored reservations. The ever-assured Mark Helmke of the venture capitalists and the ever-nervous Ed Hatcher of the electronics association eyeballed each other over the zealotry of Walker and Bloomfield, and began to talk privately about whether they had gone too far.

· · ·

If the best kind of issue for lobbyists was an unsolvable problem, the second-best was a problem too arcane for anybody to understand. The stock-versus-mutual fight did not disappoint on either count. The question was so difficult to comprehend that each side hired its own battery of legal and financial experts just to sort out the facts—so far without any consensus.

As the year progressed, each camp hired actuaries to compute the companies' taxes, and brought in high-toned economists—from ivory towers as lofty as the Brookings Institution—to explain how the two enterprises actually worked. Both also hired publicists to help spread the word about their causes. Still, almost no one but the stocks and mutuals themselves understood the issue completely.

Only one thing seemed indisputable: The two sides disagreed about everything and found it impossible to compromise. The American Council of Life Insurance—a group that included both stocks and mutuals—once hired a high-powered Cambridge, Massachusetts, team famous for the theory of negotiation detailed in the book *Getting to Yes*, to help resolve the long-simmering dispute. But after ten months and more than $100,000 in fees, the team could not get the two sides beyond no, and the exercise was suspended. Not much had changed since.

"One side says the world is flat and the other one says it's round," said John Jonas, a leading mutual lobbyist who was a partner at Patton, Boggs & Blow. Added William Harman of Davis & Harman, the lobbyist for the stocks: "It's like two eight-year-olds fighting—that's how we're viewed."

Congress had last endeavored to "fix" the insurance-taxation problem in 1984, but the result, almost everyone agreed, had been peculiar. In a twist of tax policy unique to the life-insurance industry, mutual companies were made to pay taxes on the basis not of their own earnings but of their stock-company rivals'. "It is the most bizarre provision I've ever seen," said Matthew Zinn, a lobbyist for the mutuals at the law firm of Steptoe & Johnson. "It's like GM basing its taxes on what Ford did the year before," said Henry Aaron, a senior fellow at the Brookings Institution.

The mutuals claimed that a study they had commissioned showed that mutuals were taxed just as heavily as stock companies, though at different stages in the corporate-finance process. And that opinion was not easily dismissed. The study's author was Michael Graetz, who was a Yale Law School professor when he was hired by the mutuals, and then became a deputy assistant treasury secretary in the Office of Tax Policy. "The world works in mysterious ways," mused mutual lobbyist Jonas, a former Ways and Means Committee staffer who helped write the 1984 statute.

Rational argument was sometimes only a small part of the debate. "This battle, in an emotional sense, has gone far beyond the issues at hand," said Vince Reusing, the mutual-company lobbyist and a senior vice president of Metropolitan Life Insurance Company. And surely politics would play a major role as well. There, the stock companies appeared to have an advantage. There were nearly seventeen times more stock companies (2,128) than mutual companies (126). In addition, the biggest mutuals were concentrated in the Northeast, particularly New York and Massachusetts, while the stock companies were spread throughout the country. Indeed, the greatest absurdity of the entire stock-versus-mutual contest was that the whole controversy was really over how much the U.S. government should collect in taxes from the ten biggest mutual life-insurance companies, which did 80 percent of the mutuals' business.

But since 1984, when they were perceived to have "lost" in Congress, the mutual companies had beefed up their lobbying roster. They hired Jonas, a former top aide to Representative Pete

Stark of California. That choice removed Tommy Boggs's potent lobbying firm from the ranks of the stocks, and instigated much of the open warfare of recent months. In addition to Patton, Boggs & Blow, the mutuals also hired Joe Dowley, the former Ways and Means Committee aide, Dawson Mathis, a former Democratic congressman from Georgia, and Walker Associates. For expertise in the Senate, the Mutual Company Political Committee retained Wayne Thevenot and Bill Boardman, and for help in the House, it hired Jim Rock. For expertise against the big mutuals, the small mutuals hired Timmons & Company.

The stocks had an equally formidable roster. Bill Harman was the master of insurance taxation. His partner, Tad Davis, was one of the most effective tax lobbyists in the city, successfully defending dubious tax breaks for a range of rich interests ranging from horse breeders to commodity traders. Helping them at the Stock Company Information Group were former Republican Representative Thomas Railsback of Michigan, and Anne Wexler. Stocks also hired up-and-comers: William Wilkins, James Gould, and Ken Kies of cellular-telephone fame. For one of their Democratic specialists, the stocks reached out to Robert Juliano, whose specialty for them was Ways and Means and his fellow Chicagoans on that committee, Rostenkowski and Marty Russo.

So many lobbyists were hired by both sides that odd connections developed. There were all-stock marriages, such as that of William Wilkins and his wife, Gail, who worked at Davis & Harman. Thevenot created an all-mutual couple when, late in 1989, he married Laura Ison, who lobbied for the Principal Insurance Group. There also were mixed marriages, as between William Maddox of the Equitable, a mutual, and Barbara Grove Maddox of Davis & Harman. Some were public-private marriages, like that of Michael Pate, who worked for Massachusetts Mutual, and Barbara Pate, the tax aide to Representative Jake Pickle. Pickle was considered a stock ally—albeit a slightly cockeyed one, having once referred to the two sides as "the stocks and the bonds."

With so much at stake, the stocks and mutuals made for a very antsy crowd. A Ways and Means Committee hearing on the subject was filled to overflowing with lobbyists. On the dais, Representatives Mike Andrews and Tom Downey were busily chatting about this and that when Andrews was struck with a mischievous thought. Downey was the chief backer of the mutuals, and Andrews was uncommitted. "Let's stand up and shake hands," Andrews told Downey, which they did, creating a stir in the audience. "I got four or five phone calls that afternoon," Andrews recalled with evident glee. "We didn't agree on anything but where we were going to dinner that night."

This time the renewed combat threatened to prove perilous. With at least the possibility that the year's deficit-reduction plan might call for a major tax increase, life-insurance companies were fearful that they might become a target to raise at least some of that amount. In fact, their spat made it all the more likely that one side or the other—and perhaps both—would get whacked with additional taxes. "If they can't solve it themselves, wait till we finish with them," Andrews warned. "You're asking for trouble when your industry is divided."

. . .

Mark Helmke of Robinson, Lake, Lerer & Montgomery believed that the capital-gains lobby was also asking for trouble with its "anchor windward" strategy. On Father's Day, Sunday, June 17, he took time out to write a memo that warned officers and lobbyists for the venture capitalists that the entire exercise was moving off base. On that day, Kevin Phillips, a Republican strategist, had published an essay in *The New York Times Magazine* about the rising tide of populism he saw in the country. Helmke agreed with the analysis, and was concerned that the Walker maneuver was too greedy an approach.

"Instead of winking at Walker as part of the coalition . . . we should consider opposing it," Helmke wrote. "We could separate ourselves from the 'capitalist excess' side of the debate, firm up our position on the populist side, and continue to hold up our leadership role in this debate. I admit this is a radical idea, but at least one we should debate. After attending Walker's last coalition meeting, his tactics have been worrying me. It may no longer just be a question of him using one set of tactics and us another to attain the same goal, it could be that his tactics could undercut our entire strategy."

Helmke and the venture capitalists were not alone in taking a serious look at their lobbying strategies. The tobacco lobby, for one, started quietly negotiating a settlement with the revenue-hungry lawmakers on Capitol Hill. Experienced lobbyists like those who worked for the tobacco industry understood that if there was a possibility that their clients were going to suffer a tax increase it was almost always better to play along—and cut a deal—than to allow the damage to be done randomly.

But the prospect that the tobacco industry might devise its own settlement divided the anti-excise-tax lobby. Any restraint in raising tobacco taxes would surely put pressure on lawmakers to raise other excise taxes instead, particularly those on fuel. So during one of their many hallway conversations, Jim Rock, who lobbied for a utility company, told John Winburn, who lobbied for cigarette maker Philip Morris, "You're hoping for the biggest fucking energy tax and I'm hoping for the biggest tobacco tax."

In fact, Winburn was way ahead of his younger friend. Tobacco interests had already floated a deal with key lawmakers: There would be a tobacco-tax increase, but a smaller one than Rostenkowski and others had suggested. The deal was a 50 percent increase in the sixteen-cent-a-pack cigarette tax, phased in over four years. In exchange, tobacco-state lawmakers would promise not to filibuster the budget agreement in the Senate; a filibuster could kill the entire effort.

In the meantime, the budget talks, begun with such promise in May, were getting nowhere fast. Bush continued to refuse even to say the word "taxes," and Democrats continued to insist that he do so before they would get down to serious negotiating. But finally, on Tuesday, June 26, just before the Congress was scheduled to go on a holiday recess, Bush blinked.

After a White House meeting of his top aides and the bipartisan leadership of Congress, Bush released the following statement: "It is clear to me that both the size of the deficit problem and the need for a package that can be enacted require all of the following: entitlement and mandatory program reform; tax revenue increases; growth incentives; discretionary spending reductions; orderly reductions in defense expenditures; and budget process reform—to assure that any bipartisan agreement is enforceable and that the deficit problem is brought under responsible control. The bipartisan leadership agree with me on these points."

The reaction was swift, especially over the "tax revenue" part.

Democrats were gleeful that they had gotten Bush to rescind his most fervent election-year promise. Senate Majority Leader George Mitchell kept a solemn face, but his words betrayed a secret elation. "The President has concluded that tax increases are necessary," he said. "We share the President's view." Democrats who were not in the leadership were freer to gloat. "George Bush has announced that he is raising taxes," said Representative Bob Torricelli of New Jersey. "The charade is finally over."

Republicans had a far more mixed view. Some practiced denial. "I personally don't believe that he is talking about tax increases. I think he is talking about tax revenue increases based on continued economic growth," said Representative Gerald Solomon of New York. Others flew into a rage. More than a hundred House Republicans signed a letter to the President, saying that they were "stunned" by the announcement and that, for them, "a tax increase is unacceptable." GOP candidates for the Senate also abandoned the President in droves. Representative Claudine Schneider of Rhode Island declared his switch simply "terrible."

Lobbyists did not spend much time either praising or scolding the President for his action. They just kicked into high gear.

· · ·

On Monday, July 9, the venture-capital association set aside its disagreements with Bloomfield on strategy and dispatched an "action alert" that Sarah Hull and her compatriots at Robinson, Lake designated "urgent." "There is news on the capital-gains front from the budget summit," it said. "President Bush recently announced that any deficit reduction agreement with Congress would require 'tax revenue increases.' He also said any increase would be part of a package including cuts in both domestic and military spending, *growth incentives* and changes in the budget process. 'Growth incentives' means a capital-gains tax cut. This is a critical time to contact the budget summit negotiators to urge their support for a capital-gains tax cut. Please send your letters in the next two weeks." The letter went on to say, "The more personal your letter, the more persuasive it is," but it also included a sample letter that was completely fill-in-the-blanks.

Robinson, Lake claimed that the alert generated two hundred letters to each budget negotiator, one-third from venture capitalists and the rest from individual companies. Some of the letters, such as one to Senator Bob Dole from James Diller, president of the Sierra Semiconductor Company of San Jose, California, matched the sample letter almost exactly. Others varied only slightly more.

One entrepreneur contacted by the association declined to participate. He was Mitchell Kertzman, who had led the CEO Fly-In in February. Kertzman usually abstained from such prepackaged pleas, because he had personally lobbied the lawmakers to whom the venture capitalists wanted him to write. He also doubted that near-identical letters sent at about the same time had much effect, except perhaps a negative one. "I've never been a big believer in those 'alerts,' " he said. "I think they are discounted; it's so obviously an organized campaign."

But there was more to Kertzman's reluctance than that. In the months since his visit to Washington he had become disillusioned with the new direction the capital-gains coalition had taken. In fact, after Rostenkowski's "Challenge" came out, he had switched his personal focus away from broad-scale tax cutting to deficit reduction. He had even persuaded his association to back the Rostenkowski initiative publicly. Reducing the budget deficit, the association wrote, would do more for cutting the cost of capital than any other government action.

Kertzman also claimed to have experienced "an epiphany" about capital gains during the summer. After talking to several professional lobbyists he thought he finally understood what the capital-gains lobby was all about—at least for some of the other members of the coalition. For them, he said, the exercise had more to do with boosting profits than with any of the high-minded goals the group otherwise professed. In its broadest form, a capital-gains tax cut was merely "a smokescreen for increasing personal wealth," he bitterly concluded.

Kertzman still believed that providing a carefully targeted rate reduction for start-up businesses was a good idea. It would not cost much and, he said, would help young companies grow. But he wanted to have nothing to do with the bigger, broader capital-gains tax cut the coalition was now pushing. "It became clear to me that it [the coalition's plan] was all meant to lower the tax rates on rich people," he said. From then on, he vowed, "only the high road."

. . .

If they had not realized it already, the truckers got the message that fuel taxes were going to rise from no less a source than the Secretary of Transportation, Samuel Skinner. On Friday, the thirteenth of July, Skinner convened a meeting of transportation-industry lobbyists in his executive dining room. The ostensible purpose was for him to listen to their views about the options for raising taxes. But at least some of the participants came away realizing that, no matter what they had said, those options all pointed in the same direction—up.

Representatives of the American Automobile Association and the American Trucking Associations, among others, tried hard to make the point that they had been fighting against a gas-tax hike for years and did not wish to be defeated. But Skinner did not deceive them about the prospect of staving off such a boost. The situation was "fluid," one of the lobbyists quoted him as saying. But Skinner also made it plain that there was a strong possibility that fuel taxes would go up, one way or another. One way that some in the meeting favored was a broad-based energy tax that would spread the pain around to other industries besides transportation. "A lot of people said, 'The more you spread this out, the better,' " one participant recalled. The American Petroleum Institute lobbyist, in fact, recommended that the tax be very broad indeed: a national sales tax—a value-added tax.

The truckers' chief of government affairs, Lana Batts, came away still holding out some hope that a tax increase could be avoided, but also determined not to surrender. "Nobody offered to cut a deal," she said. "This coalition is sticking together."

. . .

For Jim Rock, the President's decision to back tax increases provided a business opportunity. In early June he and some friends in the real estate lobby had noticed a change in an obscure Internal Revenue Service regulation that, they knew, could cost land developers and home builders millions of dollars a year. Though only the most vigilant of corporate accountants would have noticed the change, it was precisely the kind of minutiae that made Rock a good living.

The rule in question sounded more like an old pop tune than anything real estate moguls might deal with. It involved something called 75–25, or more exactly, Revenue Procedure 75–25. In essence, the IRS had ruled that developers could no longer add to the taxable value of their properties the cost of improvements they intended to make. Under the old rules, developers were allowed a sleight of hand that let them reduce the size of their profits, at least on paper, and therefore reduce, too, the taxes on the profits they made when they sold their properties.

The new ruling said that if a developer sold a house for $100,000 that had cost him $80,000 to build, his taxable profit would be $20,000. The old rule would have allowed him to add to that $80,000 cost whatever improvements he expected to make to his development, such as sewage facilities or landscaping. So instead of telling the IRS that his cost was $80,000, he could have claimed instead that the cost was $80,000 plus the $10,000 or so he was going to add as improvements. The old rule, in other words, led to lower taxes, which was what all corporations most wanted from the nation's capital.

Rock thrived on that desire, too. So he dashed off a proposal to The Newland Group of La Jolla, California, a big developer that he thought would be a good prospect to bankroll a lobbying campaign. The chance that Newland would bite, he knew, was enhanced by the extra likelihood of a tax bill in 1990 now that President Bush was behind the effort. Rock also thought he had a good case. The IRS reached back to penalize developers from the beginning of 1990, even though its decision came out in midyear. From long experience, Rock knew that retroactive regulation was a pet peeve of the House tax-writing committee he had once served.

"A legislative remedy appears to be the only viable means of achieving meaningful relief for land developers," Rock wrote in his proposal to Newland. And then he pointedly added: "Legislation does not get passed on its own."

His five-page proposal explained why Concord Associates was the lobbying group for the job. Concord Associates had a "legislative strategy," which would include "coordinating the activities of the real estate groups involved, developing a specific legislative proposal and lobbying materials, obtaining effective sponsors for this legislation in both the House and the Senate [and] establishing contact between affected constituents and appropriate members of the Congress."

And who could be better to do these things than Jim Rock and his partners? Under the heading "Lobbying Treasury and Congressional Staffs," Rock boasted: "A key element in any tax legislative effort is to lobby key staff members of the Treasury Department and the Congress. At Concord, we have long standing relationships with these individuals and are well equipped to coordinate and carry out this task." Then came the clincher: "Success cannot be guaranteed; however, one thing is obvious. Doing nothing will result is [sic] significantly higher taxes to land developers who have relied on Rev. Proc. 75–25 for a rational method of income reporting. . . . Concord has the experience with and knowledge of the legislative process necessary to achieve results."

Without question, Rock said, "A lot of this business is impressing clients." And he followed that rule with Newland.

· · ·

The R&D lobby also began to specialize its efforts. Not only did Coretech want to extend the R&D credit and 861, it also wanted to make sure that the new, improved configuration of the credit was maintained. To that end, Coretech again commissioned two scholars affiliated with the Brookings Institution, Martin Baily and Robert Lawrence, to do a study of the newly minted formulation. On Thursday, July 19, Coretech trumpeted its results in a press release headlined: "Economists' Study Finds New R&D Tax Credit Increases Incentive Effect of R&D Spending Four Times That of Previous Credit."

"Based on the new R&D tax credit structure," the text stated, "a conservative estimate is that R&D spending will increase 4.2 percent between 1991 and 1995. This increase in R&D spending would amount to $18 billion. Less conservative estimates suggest that the R&D spending could be as much as $51.5 billion. [The economists] estimate that a $25.7 billion increase in spending could be expected."

The release breathlessly thanked several lawmakers, especially Rostenkowski, who was given even more credit than he was due. It asserted that he had actually "designed the new structure," which of course was the product of technicians on his staff. Despite its exaggeration, the two-page release was careful to identify Rostenkowski as the congressman from the Eighth District of Illinois. That was to make it easy for local newspapers to lift Coretech's glowing comments about him and publish them word-for-word.

But neither the press release nor the study, which was attached, stopped with happy words. Coretech wanted more. It wanted permanence. "Without a permanent tax credit the new incentive effect won't make a significant difference," Roland Schmitt, Coretech's chairman, was quoted as saying. "The most effective credit won't work if it isn't viewed as a stable public policy. We urge the Congress to take this new improved structure and make it permanent."

The study was sent to every member of the Ways and Means Committee and the Finance Committee along with a letter signed by Jenkins, Anthony, Pickle, and Matsui in the House and by Danforth, Baucus, and Chafee in the Senate. And just to make sure that word got around, the relentless Eizenstat sat at his desk for two straight days telephoning the tax aides for all seventeen of the congressional budget-summit negotiators.

But Coretech did not stop there. It also wanted to avoid another "technical" change that lawmakers had previously considered when they gave passing thought to making the credit permanent. The lobbyists contended that the change, called a base limitation, would hurt small and mid-sized companies that already did a lot of research. Baily and Lawrence of Brookings agreed, asserting that "costs would be lower" to the federal government, "but incentives would be reduced" for many companies.

The type of company that would be hurt most by a base limitation was precisely the kind that belonged to the electronics association. So lobbyist Ed Hatcher took the special assignment of leading the lobbying effort against the proposed change. He recruited as the effort's chief sponsor his former employer, Bob Matsui. And on Monday, July 23, four days after the new Brookings study was unveiled, Hatcher made public a letter to Rostenkowski, signed by Matsui and twenty-four of his colleagues on the committee. It advocated keeping the limitation just where it was.

"We appreciate the work you have done with members of our committee and industry to develop a permanent research and development tax credit," the letter stated. But, it added, "given the competitive challenges facing U.S. companies and the emerging and changing global marketplace, we hope you agree that Congress should not move in this direction."

• • •

On Hatcher's other issue, capital gains, Bloomfield sensed there was dissension in the ranks. But he persisted in his militant approach. Almost every morning and every night he was on the phone to tax aides Bob Mottice and Cesar Conda. They plotted and they hoped, but so far they were getting nowhere. Their latest scheme was to attach their capital-gains proposal to a must-do bill that would raise the limit on federal borrowing. But top Bush aides did not seem thrilled at the prospect. Indeed, they were increasingly lukewarm about capital gains, given the attacks by Democrats over the "fairness" question. The hesitancy hurt, and Bloomfield confessed, "We have an administration problem."

So on Tuesday, July 31, he and Walker took the limo to the Hill for a 2 P.M. meeting with both Kasten and Mack to discuss the situation. They decided to move ahead if they could, but they recognized that the situation was out of their control. "We could have problems with Packwood, Dole, and Domenici," Bloomfield said, referring to the main Republican budget-summit negotiators from the Senate. But still, they prepared to fight. The group agreed to prepare still more "Dear Colleague" letters as a way of stirring more contacts from the grass roots. Bloomfield even proposed printing more buttons that read THE 15% SOLUTION to advertise the Kasten-Mack plan.

On top of it all, Walker sent every senator a memorandum marked "personal and urgent." Its subject was "the urgent need for a capital-gains tax cut." It cited the work of economist Allen Sinai about the economic stimulus that a 15 percent capital-gains rate would provide and declared that the estimates were neither "cooked" nor "kooky." Walker urged the senators to request their copy of the Sinai study from the American Council and use it to make the case that cutting the capital-gains tax rate "would be pro-growth, pro-jobs, and pro–capital formation."

"I loaded our cannons," Bloomfield said later, "and now we're shooting them off."

Elsewhere in the world, guns were firing—real ones. On Thursday, August 2, Iraq invaded its small, defenseless, but oil-rich neighbor, Kuwait. The attack threatened the economic stability of the Western world, and three days later President Bush declared that the takeover "will not stand." And the need to raise money to fund the government—and its war effort—became that much more imperative.

At about the same time, the insurance industry found out how deeply in trouble it was. The increased need for added revenue created by impending conflict abroad certainly was not good news. What was more, word seeped out from one of the Illinois congressional delegation's regular luncheon meetings, which Rostenkowski attended. He told the group that the Treasury was floating a proposal that would increase taxes on both stock and mutual life-insurance companies by a breathtaking $3 billion a year, an almost outrageous amount. But when Rostenkowski spoke, the lobbyists had no choice but to listen—and act. A $3-billion-a-year hike—or nearly $16 billion over five years—would have doubled the taxes the industry was paying at the time. Lobbyists reacted bitterly to the news. "Yeah, they're considering it," Rock groused, "because he [Rostenkowski] gave it to them." But, then again, the industry had only itself to blame. "Did they overlobby? Absolutely," Representative Andrews said. "Each side took the hardest position they could and were unable to coalesce behind anything that was a thoughtful approach." By beating upon each other, the stocks and mutuals were both on the verge of being defeated. So, finally, on Tuesday, August 28, the stocks and mutuals declared a truce. Their feud had placed them both in harm's way, and they decided, under some duress, to work together to stop a tax increase they would both have to shoulder.

At the urging of the association of insurance agents, called the National Association of Life Underwriters, the two sides met on neutral ground: O'Hare International Airport in Chicago. Representatives of the warring clans, including Bill Harman for the stocks and John Jonas for the mutuals, drafted and agreed to a statement that said: "The entire life insurance industry—including the American Council on Life Insurance, the National Association of Life Underwriters, the Stock Company Information Group and the Mutual Life Insurance Tax Committee—stands united in its opposition to the rumored . . . proposal, which reportedly would increase the industry's taxes by $3 billion or more a year."

The peace offering was a relief to Thevenot. "Our conclusion was there was no way to win that war," he said. "The members were saying, 'A plague on both your houses.' " But beneath the surface, tensions still seethed.

In September, the mutuals distributed a statement from Donald Schuenke, president of Northwestern Mutual of Milwaukee: "America needs a reduced federal deficit, but not at the expense of one industry and its consumers. . . . Mutual and stock companies are united in their opposition to this proposal." But Schuenke did not stop there. Despite the truce, he advocated "a rational debate about the proper tax treatment" of stock and mutual companies, as if one could really transpire. He then went on to suggest, just as the mutuals had for months, that the existing system of taxing the two types of companies be repealed to "resolve the inequity of mutual companies paying taxes based on the economic earnings of their stock counterparts."

So even under the flag of peace, the stock-versus-mutual war went on. Representative Barbara Kennelly, Democrat of Connecticut, a respected member of Ways and Means, met with insurance lobbyists and pleaded with them to desist in their disagreement. Her state was filled with insurance-company headquarters, and she foresaw only disaster if they did not lay down their arms. "Around here a lot of people sit down and try to work out their differences," she counseled. "They make themselves vulnerable by not finding a solution." So at her urging lawmakers were treated to an unusual sight in the next weeks: stock and mutual lobbyists visiting their offices together. Thevenot made a few of those runs himself. In addition, insurance agents took out a newspaper advertisement, employees and agents of the Prudential and Metropolitan life-insurance companies made telephone calls, and Prudential chairman Robert C. Winters wrote to Sununu to plead the case.

But it all came much too late. The best the companies could hope for was to reduce the multibillion-dollar tax increase that was already hanging over their heads. "We were caught offguard," said Thomas O'Hara, the head of Prudential's Washington office. "The industry expected a tax increase, but not to this extent."

Thevenot had his consolation prize, however. On Wednesday, September 5, his wife Laura gave birth to a baby girl, Casey Johanna.

· · ·

For the lawmakers negotiating the budget, it was time to get down to serious business. To help them concentrate all their efforts on their assignment, they decided to sequester themselves at Andrews Air Force Base, just outside the Washington Beltway. There, away from reporters and the distractions of daily work in Congress, the summiteers would finally be able to get down to devising a compromise package.

As an opening gambit, each side—Republican and Democratic—vowed to present a deficit-reduction package that would reduce the government's red ink by $50 billion in the first year. In separate press conferences on Thursday, September 6, negotiators from both parties said they intended to try to reach agreement on a measure that would cut the deficit by $50 billion in fiscal 1991, and $500 billion over five years.

The likelihood of actually accomplishing such an ambitious goal was increasingly remote, however. Not only had the economy begun to show signs of weakness that would make increased tax collections difficult, but Saddam Hussein's army had become entrenched in Kuwait, and energy prices had begun to surge, making it harder for the negotiators to consider new taxes on energy. As a result, both sides indicated that any final plan probably would fall short of their goals. "It's a negotiating position and we're not going to die for any part of it," said Representative Bill Frenzel, Republican of Minnesota. Still, everyone worked throughout the day in the Capitol to complete their opening offers for formal presentation the next day at Andrews.

Both plans had many things in common. Each supported increases in "sin" taxes. Democrats talked about raising excise taxes on liquor and tobacco, while Republicans were discussing higher taxes on beer and wine only. (The GOP's omission of tobacco honored a recent campaign pledge made by President Bush in

North Carolina on behalf of Senator Jesse Helms, who was running for reelection.) Meanwhile, Democrats were moving toward proposing a broad tax on energy consumption and lifting the top tax rate on the richest Americans to 33 percent from 28 percent.

Dole indicated that Republicans were also considering tax incentives for oil production, a move that would lose revenue. At least some Democrats were also suggesting a fee on imported oil as a way of helping domestic production. In addition, the Republicans decided to press for a cut in capital gains. To no one's surprise, the Democrats did not intend to support the capital-gains tax cut—at least initially. It was unclear where expiring tax provisions, such as the R&D credit, fit into the picture.

The talks began on Friday, September 7, in a converted bar in the Officers Club, where negotiators could chew over alternatives and as many steak dinners and ice cream sundaes as they could stomach. Lobbyists and reporters dined out on a steady diet of rumor and educated conjecture about the content of their talks. Indeed, nothing remained secret for long in Washington. Details of the supposedly secret conversations at the air base were readily available all around town almost every day.

Staffers on Capitol Hill, who were in constant touch with the summiteers, routinely telephoned their lobbyist allies to inform them about what they knew and to get fresh details in return. Lists of proposals and counterproposals were being compiled, and fax machines were working overtime everywhere in the city, including at Andrews. The phone numbers to the Andrews fax machines became prized tools until lobbyists like Bloomfield clogged them with so much propaganda that frustrated summiteers changed the numbers.

On the first day of the talks at Andrews, Duffy Wall & Associates faxed to other lobbyists around town a handwritten list that purported to lay out the Democrats' and Republicans' starting positions. Each side advocated the establishment of a new luxury tax, the list said, and also some increases in excise taxes. And to the horror of the life-insurance industry, both the Democrats and the Republicans were pushing to increase taxes on both stocks and mutuals—a conjecture that turned out to be essentially correct.

A stream of lists flowed out of the negotiations. Some were faxed so often that they became almost illegible. The law firm of

Skadden, Arps tried to remedy this problem, and also enhance its reputation as a valuable source of lobbying information, by retyping a "Democratic offer" dated Tuesday, September 11, in a font that made it look almost exactly like an official Joint Tax Committee document.

At least some of the leaks were purposeful efforts to gain political advantage. Early on, a Joint Tax Committee chart that showed how tough the Republicans' offer was on poor people, and how generous it was to the rich, was handed out to reporters in a Capitol Hill press gallery. The stories that followed did great damage to the capital-gains forces and bolstered the efforts of the Democrats.

One enterprising lobbyist was able to break the isolation at Andrews entirely. Frederick Graefe, a lobbyist at Ken Kies's law firm, Baker & Hostetler, was a former marine who still had friends in the military. One of them was an officer at Andrews, who, at Graefe's request, told the guards at the main gate to allow Graefe onto the base to play golf whenever he wanted. In fact, Graefe did play golf with his friend on the base's course—once. But several other times during the budget summit talks he drove his Jeep Cherokee through the gate and parked at the Officers Club, where he lay in wait for his staffer friends to come out of the "secret" meetings to consult with him.

To keep up his guise as a golfer, he always wore a polo shirt and Top-Siders and brought his clubs. "They were clearly visible in the back of my Jeep so the guard would see where I obviously was headed," Graefe said. But his real purpose was to gather intelligence about proposed Medicare changes. He was a lobbyist for hospitals, doctors, and other health care interests, all of which cared deeply about federal Medicare payments. Graefe was especially intent on helping a group of radiologists who were worried that their Medicare fees might be curtailed. When staffers on the Hill told him that Medicare was going to be discussed, he would wait patiently for their colleagues to emerge from the Officers Club and signal them to come over and talk to him in the parking lot. "I had to be very circumspect; I avoided anyone who I thought would blow the whistle on me," he said. "I couldn't stand at the door handing out cigars. The whole idea of the Andrews talks was to get away from people like me."

Not only did the members of Congress not succeed in getting away from Graefe, he succeeded in getting much of what he wanted. Despite the summit's urgent need to find budgetary savings, the radiologists' fees were left unchanged by the budget summit. He even suggested a way to protect them parliamentarily, which the negotiators eventually accepted. The savings to the radiologists amounted to a few hundred million dollars over five years, which Graefe said was not much compared with the $100-billion-a-year Medicare program. But then again, he had saved his clients hundreds of times more than they paid him to do his lobbying work.

• • •

On Monday night, September 10, Kay was awakened from a sound sleep at about ten-thirty by a telephone call from an agitated Eizenstat. The lobbyist had just gotten off the telephone with someone from the Joint Tax Committee and had learned that the R&D credit had not even been placed on the table at Andrews by either the Republicans or the Democrats.

"It's real bad news," Eizenstat concluded. "It looks like there is paper from both sides and we're not in either one." Kay did not need any more bad news. One of his two family cars, a maroon 1985 Toyota Camry, had been stolen—and then found—just the day before, and he sorely needed to rest after the experience. But by now Kay had become used to sleepless nights caused by Coretech crises. And from experience, he knew that he and Eizenstat would have to start a new round of lobbying as soon as possible. They would contact Coretech companies in the morning, and ask them to call around.

Kay was scheduled to take an eight o'clock flight the next morning to Milwaukee, where he had been asked to talk to the Society of Research Administrators about joining Coretech. Despite the problems at the budget summit, he knew he could not afford to cancel the trip. So he reconciled himself to getting just a few more hours of sleep before rushing out of town.

But it was not meant to be. At 3 A.M. Kay heard a knock at his front door. He bolted out of bed, opened the door, and found a policeman who informed him that his car had been stolen yet again—and again had been abandoned elsewhere in the city. Kay was dumbfounded. In one night he had suffered both a professional and a personal loss. His only hope was that the professional one would be as swiftly, and as happily, resolved as the personal one. He and the policeman went immediately to collect his car. He returned home with it by 4 A.M., his mind racing with thoughts of stolen cars and tax credits.

After trying unsuccessfully to fall asleep, he finally went down to his study at 6:30 A.M. and typed a note on his computer to his assistant, Michele Norman. It instructed her to inform four or five Coretech-affiliated lobbyists of the news Eizenstat had given him the night before. The lobbyists would meet again Wednesday afternoon to discuss their strategy.

By Wednesday much of the hysteria had passed. It looked as if the credit and 861 were back on the table. Still, the most active members of Coretech, including lobbyists for IBM, Hewlett-Packard, and Pfizer, met at Kay's office and agreed to get a few of their chief executives to telephone budget negotiators. They also decided to write letters to the summiteers over the signatures of Coretech's congressional sponsors and Roland Schmitt, Coretech's chairman.

With such pressure tactics, "you run a risk of getting friends angry at you," Kay said. But the lobbyists decided they would run that risk, preferring to be safe than sorry.

· · ·

Not long after the talks began at Andrews, it became increasingly clear that Bloomfield and Walker's "anchor windward" had been set too far upcurrent to make any impression on the negotiators. Any kind of capital-gains tax cut was going to be politically difficult, let alone one as big and broad as the one Bloomfield and Walker wanted. On the air base, Democrats began to talk instead about a much narrower capital-gains tax cut that was targeted to help start-up companies. This was not by coincidence: The proposal came from dissident members of the capital-gains coalition.

In late August, Mitchell Kertzman and Ed Hatcher had met with Michael Wessel, Representative Richard Gephardt's top tax aide. They gave him a copy of a plan that their electronics association had developed with the venture capitalists. Far from cutting the capital-gains tax for almost everyone, it would help just young, growing companies. It would also encourage long-term investing by withholding any tax benefit until stock had been held for at least five years.

The venture capitalists stepped up their dissident campaign for this targeted cut on Wednesday, September 12, by distributing the proposal to other congressional leaders on the Hill. Officially, the venture capitalists still supported the broader bill. But they now also advocated the targeted approach, which they termed an add-on. In fact it represented a major schism in the capital-gains fraternity, which the Democrats sought to exploit.

· · ·

The longer the budget negotiators stayed at Andrews, the louder the drumbeat in Washington got against the painful decisions they had to make. The anti-excise-tax-increase lobby was among the most vocal. On Wednesday, September 12, the Edison Electric Institute, the utility company lobby, unveiled a poll it had commissioned, which purported to show that 70 percent of the American people opposed energy-tax increases to reduce the budget deficit. The institute also tried to bolster its case by showing that groups that traditionally were its biggest enemies supported it this time in its effort to stop an energy-tax rise. Along with the poll, the institute released letters and statements from such liberal-leaning groups as the National Consumers League, the National Women's Political Caucus, and even the National Council of Jewish Women.

On Thursday, September 13, the truckers jumped into the fray when one of their affiliates, called FUEL, met at the headquarters of the American Automobile Association and agreed, according to Ken Simonson, "that it was time to go to our own members and the full Congress and say we're hearing these terrible proposals." In particular, FUEL worried that any motor-fuels tax hike would go toward deficit reduction rather than be used exclusively for the Highway Trust Fund, as it was at the moment.

FUEL put out an angry-sounding press release, and Simonson went back to the trucking associations' headquarters to insert an "action call" into the group's regular membership bulletin, which was about to go to the printer. Simonson changed the color of the border around the bulletin to red from its usual green to connote the urgency of the message, which was this: "Wire or phone your senators and representatives!"

On Tuesday, September 18, Simonson had the chance to lodge his protest directly with a member of the budget summit, Representative Frenzel. The respected lawmaker left the cloistered talks at the air base to give a noon address to the National Economists Club, of which Simonson was a member. The event was held in the Montpelier Room of the Madison Building of the Library of Congress, right on Capitol Hill. After Frenzel's speech, Simonson asked the first question. "Two hundred and forty-eight [House] members have cosponsored a resolution saying they were opposed to motor-fuel taxes for deficit reduction," he said. "And yet, reportedly both sides were recommending increasing petroleum or fuel taxes. Do you believe a majority of both parties would vote for a fuel tax?"

Frenzel paused briefly before he answered. "There is a lot in the packages that a majority would be opposed to," he conceded. "I expect to oppose most of the things in the package myself. But I also expect to vote for the agreement." He suggested that many lawmakers were, in Simonson's words later, "simply covering their rear" by cosponsoring the anti-fuels-tax resolution, and that eventually a big deficit-reducing package would pass in the House despite it.

· · ·

The day before Frenzel's remarks, Eizenstat donned his hat as Democratic party elder to deliver a luncheon address to the Woman's National Democratic Club in Washington. But, never missing an opportunity, he did not neglect his other role as lobbyist for the R&D credit. The subject of his lengthy talk was the possibility of reversing "the party's moribund state." He had many prescriptions, not the least of which was an appeal for a "progressive agenda" that included the theme "Investing in America."

"We are the party which believes government has a constructive role in supplementing the marketplace and in moderating its excesses," he stated. "We need not shrink from this role. We should strive to make industries as efficient and responsive to the market as we can, but where the market works imperfectly or where others, at home or abroad, distort it, there is an important role for government. The need for a constructive role for government, as opposed to conservative laissez-faire economics, will become increasingly evident to Americans who recognize we are in a global economic competition in which the government has to help mobilize our private-sector resources."

Eizenstat then stressed the kinds of "investment" the government needed to make. One, of course, was research. He termed it "investment in new products and processes," and specifically said Democrats should call for "incentives for basic and applied R&D."

Kay, meanwhile, was busy stirring up Coretech members to contact the summiteers. Since Fuller had been hired, Kay's pitch to Coretech was careful to include a mention of capital gains, in addition to the R&D issues. An "action alert" to Coretech members, dated Tuesday, September 25, was typical. "Now more than ever," it said, "is the time for the research community to show strong support for a growth and investment package that includes permanent R & D provisions. More importantly, now is the time to support the administration's individual capital gains reduction effort. A CEO call or telegram to Dick Darman in the next day or two could be very helpful."

Letters were quickly dispatched from, among others, Ernest Drew, CEO of Hoechst Celanese Corporation, and Maxine Sweet, a vice president of TRW Corporation. In addition, two days later, the old expiring-provisions coalition of lobbyist William Signer again got into the act. Coretech, along with the other lobbying groups concerned with soon-to-expire tax breaks, signed a letter to Speaker Tom Foley advising the Speaker how "unwise" it would be "not to include these incentives that encourage the necessary human and intellectual resources we need to be competitive as a nation."

• • •

In the meantime, the talks at Andrews had bogged down, and the negotiators left to try again at the Capitol. The talks continued there for another week. At 9 P.M. on Friday, September 28, Allen Neece, a lobbyist for the venture capitalists, was sitting in his den reading the newspaper, expecting nothing more than a peaceful weekend at home in Washington's Virginia suburbs. Then the telephone rang. Neece picked it up to hear an aide to Representative Gephardt say, "Would you hold for the majority leader?"

Gephardt came on almost immediately and identified himself to the stunned lobbyist. "I also have Nick Brady on the line," he said, and the treasury secretary also said hello. What the two men wanted was information, and they believed Neece would be able to provide it in a hurry. Besides the venture capitalists, Neece worked for a variety of small-business groups, including National Small Business United, which was part of the capital-gains coalition. In any case, Neece was known for being a small-business lobbyist, which explained Gephardt and Brady's call. They started to pepper him with questions about how big a role small businesses played in the American economy. What percentage of the work force was employed by small businesses? What percentage of the gross national product did they represent? How quickly had they been growing, compared with big businesses?

Neece stopped the questioning as soon as his expertise was exhausted. "I think you're asking some micro questions here," he said. "Look, I'm not an authority in this area, but I know people who are." In truth, Neece was not a scholar, he was a lobbyist. He might not have the information in his own head, but he could obtain detailed knowledge on most any subject, and that was what he endeavored to do. He volunteered the name of David Birch, a professor at the Massachusetts Institute of Technology, whom he described as "one of the key repositories of information about small business." Without asking why Gephardt and Brady wanted to know about small businesses, Neece said he would get in touch with Birch and get back to them as soon as possible.

Neece hung up and tried Birch's telephone numbers. There was no answer. So he tried the second-best source he could think of: Tom Gray, an economist at the federal government's own Small Business Administration. Neece found Gray at home and asked him if he would mind helping Gephardt and Brady; Gray jumped at the chance. Neece telephoned Gephardt's office and told the majority leader that he had found the perfect fellow for him. Then Neece asked if he could "take myself out of the loop," which he did. Gray worked at his home computer until after midnight to provide the information Gephardt and Brady sought.

Neece did not know for sure, but he suspected that the summit's final plan would hold a big, happy surprise for his small-business clients. And he was right. On Sunday, September 30, when the package was unveiled, it contained what the President called "important new incentives to stimulate economic growth." Aimed directly at helping small businesses were a variety of tax breaks that were even better than a simple capital-gains tax cut. Along with the package was information that Gray had given to Gephardt as justification for the extra preferences. What Neece was left thinking, he said, was why the secretary of the treasury had to ask a lobbyist for such basic data. He wondered—but did not complain.

· · ·

Except for the small-business sweeteners, the budget accord was almost all pain. Democrats had made such a nuisance of themselves about the "fairness" of the package's income distribution that a capital-gains tax cut finally had to be jettisoned. In fact, to keep the Joint Tax charts looking balanced, the negotiators had to throw in a backdoor tax-rate increase that came in the guise of limiting tax deductions taken by those with incomes above $100,000. The plan would effectively have raised marginal income-tax rates by as much as one percentage point for some taxpayers.

About three-fifths of the plan's $500 billion in projected deficit savings over five years came from increasing the federal gasoline tax, squeezing Medicare beneficiaries and their doctors, slashing farm subsidy payments, and cutting the military budget. "This is all real," Darman asserted, his eyes red from lack of sleep.

Donohue and Simonson had failed to stop the gas-tax rise. But their efforts did manage to reduce the fifteen-cent-a-gallon plan that the negotiators had begun with in the Rostenkowski Challenge. The budget accord would have increased the gasoline tax by five cents a gallon on December 1, 1990, and by another five cents a gallon on July 1, 1991. An additional two-cent-a-gallon tax on all refined petroleum products, including gasoline but not home-heating oil, would be imposed on January 1.

The excise-tax lobby in general was socked pretty hard—but not as hard as it had once feared that it would. Tobacco lobbyists managed to control their damage. Cigarette taxes were set to rise from the existing sixteen cents a pack by 50 percent, four cents a pack in 1991 and another four cents in 1993—almost exactly as the cigarette lobbyists had earlier proposed they should. In addition, beer, wine, and liquor taxes were slated to rise by $10 billion over five years. Details of that change were still to be resolved, which gave lobbyists some wiggle room.

One of the few winners in the summit effort was Coretech. The accord extended only two expiring provisions—and one was the R&D tax credit. The other was the credit that encouraged the construction of low-income housing. The housing credit was under the special protection of Senator George Mitchell, which made it a Democratic priority. In exchange, the Republicans were the champions of R&D, a fact that in some ways vindicated Coretech's decision to hire Craig Fuller.

But the budget agreement was not all good news for Coretech. There was no extension for 861, and the R&D credit extension was for only one year. Taken together, these results caused the usually ebullient Kay to fall into a terrible funk. "Those were the lowest days I've had relative to this issue," he said shortly after the agreement was announced. "That we could have worked that hard to produce a one-year extension . . ." His voice trailed off. "I had irrational thoughts."

The biggest loser was the insurance industry. Despite the belated truce, the stocks and mutuals were clobbered with a tax increase of $8 billion over five years. That was half the size of the nearly $16 billion knockout punch that the Treasury had originally suggested. But it was still the largest increase on any industry since 1986. Boardman, Thevenot, and Rock at Concord Associates did not despair, however. The Maglev funding they advocated continued to move apace, unaffected by the budget agreement. And Rock corralled The Newland Group as a client on 75–25.

The budget package was unveiled with great fanfare at a ceremony in the White House Rose Garden and soon thereafter Federal Reserve Board Chairman Alan Greenspan endorsed it all but promised that interest rates would decline if Congress enacted it. More important, President Bush began an aggressive campaign to win its passage in Congress, even dispatching Vice President Dan Quayle to the Capitol to lobby his old colleagues in the House and the Senate. "I'll be selling it to everybody I can get to listen to me," the President said. In a nationally broadcast speech on Tuesday, October 2, Bush pleaded for support for what he acknowledged was a tough budget agreement.

"This budget agreement is the result of eight months of blood, sweat, and fears—fears of the economic chaos that would follow if we fail to reduce the deficit," he said. "Of course, we cannot claim it's the best deficit-reduction plan possible; it's not. Any one of us alone might have written a better plan. But it is the best agreement that can be legislated now. It is the biggest deficit-reduction agreement ever: half a trillion dollars. It's the toughest deficit-reduction package ever. . . . This is the first time in my presidency that I've made an appeal like this to you, the American people. With your help we can at last put this budget crisis behind us and face the other challenges that lie ahead. If we do, the long-term result will be a healthier nation. And something more: We will have once again put ourselves on the path to economic growth, and we will have demonstrated that no challenge is greater than the determination of the American people."

Bush went on to ask viewers to contact their representatives and senators, and urge them to vote for the package. But he acknowledged that "the congressional leadership and I have a job to do in getting it enacted." Washington's lobbyists would try their best to make that job as hard as possible.

8

Endgame

On the night the big deal was announced, Ways and Means staffers were at work in their Longworth Building offices, happily munching on sandwiches provided by lobbyists. Tax-writing aides had a constant flow of food, compliments of the ever-eager-to-please lobbying corps, and this cool, windless night was no different. Rob Leonard, the top committee aide to Dan Rostenkowski, returned to his office from the Capitol, eager to grab a bite before going home.

But Stuart Eizenstat was on the prowl, and was lying in wait for him. Even though it was a quiet Sunday in the near-vacant Capitol, the lobbyist was dressed as formally as ever, in a two-tone shirt and a suit. He had been ducking in and out of congressional offices for some time already, seeking information and trying to make his points. His latest stop was the Ways and Means Committee, and he was ready for a fight.

"What happened?" Eizenstat asked in an exasperated tone, referring to the budget negotiators' decision to drop 861 and extend the R&D credit for only one year. "What happened?" he asked again, leaning over the counter at the entrance to the Ways and

Means Committee office, casting a stern gaze on Leonard, who was trying to remain even-tempered.

"It wasn't my decision," Leonard finally replied, shaking his head and raising a hand defensively. It had not been his choice, or Rostenkowski's, to drop Coretech's tax provisions, he said.

But Eizenstat persisted. He continued to assault the aide with questions until Leonard could not take it anymore. He stepped away from the counter and headed to a back-room office. Eizenstat was left there alone, waiting for him to return. But Leonard was determined to avoid further confrontation, and asked one of his coworkers, Charles Brain, to fetch him a sandwich so that he could eat in peace.

After a while Eizenstat departed and took his outrage to the office of Representative Jake Pickle in the nearby Cannon House Office Building. There he encountered Jim Rock, who was also canvassing for information that night. According to Rock, Eizenstat began to whine about the injustice of the budget negotiations. Why should the negotiators drop some things and take other things that are less worthy? he wondered aloud.

"It gives the members something to do," Rock said, only partly in jest. "Don't worry, they'll put all that other stuff in eventually. The one-year extension will be there, so there'll be another tax bill next year," he counseled.

"But R and D is so important!" Eizenstat opined.

"You didn't hear me," Rock said impatiently. "It has nothing to do with policy." The two lobbyists parted ways, each certain that he had the correct point of view.

．　．　．

The trucking associations did not waste a moment in alerting their four thousand members about the disaster they feared was about to befall them. As the final details were being inked on the budget agreement, Ken Simonson sat in his Alexandria, Virginia, office compiling a list of facts that could be transmitted in a "Truck Line" alert to the entire membership. The border of the bulletin once again was changed to red from green, and its message was emphatic: "Phone Congress Now." The request was faxed to about two hundred trucking-industry executives and mailed to the rest: "The timing of House and Senate floor votes remains uncertain," it began. "However, it is important to phone your senators and representatives today (at 202-224-3121) to urge them to vote against any increase in the diesel fuel tax for deficit reduction."

It went on to lay out the industry's best arguments—all of which had been penned by Simonson and put over Tom Donohue's signature. For example: "The cost of diesel fuel has risen 38% in two months from 109.8 cents a gallon to 151.6 cents a gallon, according to the Interstate Commerce Commission." The one-page statement also noted that "raising the tax on highway fuels but not other modes in the name of deficit reduction is illogical and unfair [and would] drive many motor carriers and their employees or owner-operators right off the road and into bankruptcy court." For good measure, the bulletin noted: "In 1989 the trucking industry had a profit rate of less than 2%. The annual cost of the fuel price increases that have occurred in the last two months would more than wipe out those profits for most carriers. Let your elected officials know there is no way the industry can stand a tax hike on top of these devastating cost increases."

At least for the time being, it was up to the membership to act. The lobbyists in Washington waited and watched.

· · ·

From the K Street offices of Robinson, Lake, the venture capitalists also dispatched an action alert, dated Monday, October 1. But unlike the truckers, the venture capitalists wanted their people to support the budget agreement. The "growth" package that Allen Neece had helped Richard Gephardt and Nicholas Brady justify turned out to be President Bush's consolation prize for failing to get a capital-gains tax cut. Even though the venture capitalists wanted the cut too, they were just as happy with the "growth" incentives. They were designed to help fast-growing businesses, which were the lifeblood of the venture-capital industry. So Sarah Hull dashed off a request for action from her network of entrepreneurs, along with the kind of sample letter her correspondents had gotten used to:

> A federal budget agreement has been reached. While it does not include a broad-based cut in the capital gains tax, it does include a package of capital formation tax incentives for small

growth companies. These growth incentives are specifically aimed at helping you and other small, rapidly growing, entrepreneurial businesses. . . . Thanks to your past participation we have made it this far. To ensure the capital formation tax incentives for small growth companies are enacted, contact your representatives and senators now and urge their support for this package.

Mark Bloomfield, on the other hand, was disconsolate. He publicly mourned the loss of capital gains. In anger, he labeled the pact a "banana republic proposal," a statement he would later regret having made. But he did not care. His anchor windward had helped drag down the entire capital-gains ship. And the back-channel lobbying of the venture capitalists and the electronics association had yielded big dividends at his expense. He made his way to the Hill to consult with Ed Jenkins. But the lawmaker could not give him much hope.

• • •

Like Bloomfield, professional lobbyists all over town readied themselves for a few days of intensive labor. But it soon became apparent that they did not need to work too hard. Almost from the moment it was unveiled, the budget agreement was in deep trouble. It was derided by Representative Newt Gingrich of Georgia, a key Republican budget negotiator, as a "job-killer." And the President's own pleas for support were loudly rejected by the voters and their representatives in Congress.

During his brief address that Tuesday night, Bush had asked voters to telephone their Congress members to support the deficit-cutting package. Many called, but the vast number of them were highly critical, especially about the proposed cuts in Medicare and, to the delight of the truckers, increases in the gasoline tax.

In the suburban Seattle office of Republican Representative Rod Chandler, the calls ran ten to one against the package, and the volume was so large that Chandler's wife, Joyce, came in to help answer the phones. The messages in Representative Jim Leach's office in Iowa were running three to one against the budget plan. He concluded: "The pain is real and those affected know it." The callers' biggest complaint was the five-year, $60 billion cut in

Medicare, and many of the angry callers on that subject were inspired to call by the Washington-based American Association of Retired Persons. The second biggest complaint was about the gasoline tax. Plenty of those calls were completely spontaneous—from Southerners and Westerners who thought it was unfair to raise the tax on a commodity they used just to get back and forth to work. But the truckers associations also generated thousands of calls, which added significantly to the uproar.

Other problems contributed to the reaction as well. The budget accord had been completed so hastily that the negotiators had not even bothered to wait to read the income-distribution charts. When they arrived, Democrats did not like what they saw. According to final tabulations by the Joint Tax Committee, taxpayers with average annual incomes of less than $10,000 would get a tax increase of 7.6 percent, more than quadruple the 1.7 percent average tax rise slated for those who earned $200,000 a year and over. The middle class would also face hefty tax increases. People with annual incomes of between $30,000 and $50,000 would have seen their taxes rise an average 2.9 percent, and those who earned between $20,000 and $30,000 would have had a 3.3 percent increase.

"The proposal is upside down," complained Ways and Means member Byron Dorgan. "It imposes too severe an obligation on the low- and middle-income groups and not enough on the upper-income groups." For liberals like Representative Martin Sabo, Democrat of Minnesota, this lopsidedness was simply "a fundamental flaw in the package" that would surely lead to its demise.

Even the small-business "growth" incentives were attacked as tax dodges for the rich. Depending on how the rules were written, the incentives might revive tax shelters for wealthy investors, experts said. "These could be the seeds for the tax shelters of the 1990s," said David Brockway, a former chief of staff of the Joint Tax Committee, who was then a tax lawyer at Dewey Ballantine. Indeed, Marvin Dickman, a partner at the accounting firm of Arthur Andersen in Chicago who specialized in closely held companies, was already studying the possibilities. "You will see syndications of investments like this," he predicted.

That prospect sent Rostenkowski and Senate Finance Committee Chairman Lloyd Bentsen through the roof. "What the summit

[pact] has done is to muck up the code again," Rostenkowski grumbled. And Bentsen agreed: "It has very serious flaws." So alternatives to what was supposed to be the final package began turning up everywhere. And in the wee hours of Friday morning, October 5, the House soundly rejected the plan.

After the vote, grim-faced lawmakers marched silently out of the chamber into the cool morning air, wondering what would happen next. Eight months of work had just gone down the tubes. But Representative Tom Downey was not depressed. He knew from years of experience that the battle was far from over. On his way out, he began to sing aloud a song from the Broadway musical *Annie*. "The sun will come out tomorrow . . ."

• • •

After the debacle, Bush angrily demanded that Congress try again to pass an acceptable budget of some kind. Without such a document, he threatened, he would shut down the entire government, which he could have done by vetoing a spending bill that was needed to keep the government operating beyond the next day, Saturday, October 6. And that was precisely what he did.

Over the weekend, the President began to close government services selectively. Because it was a holiday weekend—Columbus Day—the closings did little except create minor irritants for the tourists in town. But they did manage to create a little ruckus. A group of tourists cornered Representative Gephardt on his way into the Capitol to upbraid him for allowing their favorite Smithsonian Institution museums to close.

Inside the Capitol, the weekend was spent hemming and hawing about what to do. In the end, the lawmakers decided to pass a stripped-down budget plan that called for massive deficit reductions, but left plenty of room to maneuver over the details. That satisfied the President, who signed a temporary spending bill in time to open the government on Tuesday, October 9.

From that moment, the House and Senate began to sprint toward the biggest deficit-reduction package ever. The bill ultimately took less than three weeks to put together, and, despite all the furor, it was ultimately modeled, at least in broad outline, on the discredited budget accord the Congress had just defeated. The legislation moved too quickly for lobbyists to either impede or alter it in any major way. But that was perfectly in keeping with the ways of lobbying.

Lobbying is not, for the most part, a last-minute vocation, but rather relies on an accumulation of actions over time. Lobbying also rarely affects the biggest portions of any piece of legislation, but rather is content with victories on the less-noticed, though often quite lucrative, fringe. At best, lobbyists had one or two more chances to make their positions clear. And they tried to pick their opportunities carefully.

. . .

Tom Donohue took his shots right away. On the day the budget plan failed in the House, he had mailed out and faxed another Truck Line newsletter to his membership. It boasted that the defeat of the budget accord was in large measure the result of telephone calls truckers had made to their members of Congress. "YOUR outpouring of calls to Congress really had an impact!" the bulletin exclaimed, and even included two newspaper articles that said so. "NOW is the time to keep the pressure on," it continued, and then repeated the arguments that Ken Simonson had made in the earlier letter. It concluded: "CALL TODAY."

As soon as the Congress got back down to work on that Tuesday, Donohue delivered to every member of the House a letter that used America's misfortune in the Persian Gulf as yet another reason to spare America's truckers from a tax increase.

Each letter was accompanied by an eleven-by-seventeen-inch poster tied with a black ribbon. It featured the pictures of three diesel-fuel pumps: a small one marked PRE-INVASION, a larger one marked HUSSEIN HIKE and a third, even bigger pump marked FUEL TAX? Bold letters on top pleaded: DON'T MAKE IT WORSE!

That same Tuesday, Bloomfield rode a roller coaster that led to disappointment on capital gains. That day, the President first embraced and then rejected a proposal that would have raised the top income-tax rate on wealthy individuals as a trade-off for a cut in the capital-gains tax. In a nationally televised news conference that morning, Bush said that that kind of trade-off was "fine" with him. "That's on the table; that's been talked about," he said. "If it's proper, if it can be worked in proper balance between the capital-gains rate and income tax changes, fine."

But by late afternoon, after he held a meeting with seventeen anxious Senate Republicans, the President concluded that the deal was not fine at all. The lawmakers emerged from the White House to say that Bush had agreed to back away from any proposal to raise the top tax rate, because such a hike would be seen as a blatant contradiction of his no-new-taxes pledge. "Our unified position was we will not go up on the rate, not 1%, not 2%, not one penny," Senator Bob Packwood said. "We will leave the rates where they are, drop capital gains and do nothing about the rates."

Immediately after the meeting with the senators, John Sununu held a special briefing for lobbyists in the Roosevelt Room. His message to them was the same as the one given by the President to the senators: no income-tax rate increase in exchange for capital gains. Raising the top rate, Sununu implied, would fall afoul of the no-new-taxes pledge. The result: Capital gains appeared to be dead. No one was more disheartened about this than Bloomfield. He, in fact, was doubly disappointed. Not only did the turnabout destroy any hope for a meaningful capital-gains tax cut in 1990, but Bloomfield was forced to learn about the situation second-hand—from Steve Small, a lobbyist for the Securities Industry Association. Small and other capital-gains coalition lobbyists had been invited to the special White House briefing. But Bloomfield was not. The snub appeared to be punishment for his impolitic comment about the initial budget package.

That evening Bloomfield had gone up to the Longworth Building to monitor progress at the Ways and Means Committee. And at first, he was fresh with excitement because of the President's upbeat morning press conference. But after he heard Small's rendition of the Sununu meeting, Bloomfield hung his head and stepped away from the pack of lobbyists standing outside the building. He paced. He mumbled. He gestured to himself. How had it all gone so wrong?

• • •

The next day, Wednesday, October 10, the Ways and Means Committee answered the truckers' pleas and officially rejected capital gains. By voice vote it approved a "bare bones" budget package that followed the broadest outlines of the budget deal, but moderated its most unpopular components, including the motor-fuels tax. In a small victory for the truckers, it reduced the gas-tax increase slightly, to eleven cents a gallon, down by a penny from the rise proposed in the budget agreement. It also contained fewer Medicare cuts. The "growth" incentives were left out entirely, as were all tax cuts of any kind, including R&D, 861, and capital gains. The battered life-insurance companies were left in the cold. Their additional taxes remained unchanged from the original agreement: $8 billion over five years.

On top of their one-cent-a-gallon reprieve, the truckers also won a sweet little victory over the railroads. Before the Ways and Means Committee finished its bill, Representative Rod Chandler unveiled a surprise. Preparations for it had been laid weeks earlier, when the tall, gangly lawmaker dined with the chief executive of PACCAR Incorporated. PACCAR, the maker of Peterbilt trucks, was one of the biggest employers in Chandler's district. The congressman paid a lot of attention to the company. It was also a personal favorite of his because its lobbyist, Jack McRae, based in Bellevue, Washington, was both a good friend and occasional fishing companion.

In any case, through his many contacts with the company, especially the ones since his dinner in the CEO's home, Chandler came to see clearly that truckers passionately disliked two things: increases in motor-fuels taxes, and anything that had to do with railroads. He knew there was almost nothing he could do to stop the rise in gasoline and diesel taxes, but he did conceive a plan that could get back at the railroads a bit.

Without advance notice, Chandler proposed to the committee that any increase in the tax on diesel fuel for trucks should also be paid by the railroads. Representative Jim Moody, Democrat of Wisconsin, was the railroads' champion on the committee, but he could not move fast enough to stop the ambush. It passed with little opposition, and marked the first time that railroads would have been made subject to any federal motor-fuels tax. After the vote, Chandler telephoned McRae to gloat and consult about how best to preserve their success.

In general, though, the package was so spare and inoffensive that it was clearly more a way to move the process forward than a serious attempt to resolve major disputes. Rostenkowski promised that a more "Democratic" plan would soon be forthcoming. What the plan did illustrate, however, was how deeply confused the White House had become over whether to raise the top personal tax rate in exchange for reducing the tax on capital gains. The new plan, which would soon become known as Rosty I, simply sidestepped both sides of that equation. So Bloomfield did not get his capital-gains cut.

Bloomfield was despondent, but Donohue was energized. The trucking-industry lobbyists launched a rearguard action by enlisting the trucking associations' top executives to telephone their entire membership. In a small way the calls had started on Sunday, when Donohue's senior aides, including Simonson, met at the Capitol Hill office and began methodically telephoning all the truckers they knew to ask them to contact their senators and representatives. But by Thursday, October 11, Simonson and the others had gotten into full gear. As many as eighty people in the truckers' Alexandria headquarters were doing nothing but calling thousands of truckers around the country. Typical of these efforts, Simonson was given a computer printout of names and phone numbers, and also a checklist to denote how each person he contacted intended to act. According to Simonson's sheet, about three-quarters of the people he contacted had agreed to get in touch with their elected representatives.

After taking a break by gazing out his window at the Beltway traffic zipping by, Simonson ran a pen down the center of his computer list and found the next number he was supposed to dial. "Hi, is Mr. Moore available?" he began. "This is Ken Simonson from the American Trucking Associations."

He paused a moment, tapping the pen on the printout. "Hi, this is Ken Simonson, I'm calling motor carriers in Oklahoma today. We have been hearing reports that the Congress is thinking about raising motor-fuel taxes by between nine cents and twelve cents a gallon. We're asking motor carriers who oppose that to contact Senator Boren."

On the other end of the line was Terry Moore, a trucking-company owner from El Reno, Oklahoma. Moore told Simonson that he already had telephoned his senator after getting Donohue's most recent Truck Line plea, but he was eager to call again if it would help. "Great!" Simonson exclaimed. "It makes a difference because they really tally those calls. I appreciate your helping. We're calling carriers because it's still hot."

After that call, Lana Batts dropped by Simonson's office to deliver another printout with more names to call. "This is by the numbers," she said proudly about the phone-calling operation. Such lobbying was absolutely necessary, she argued, because policymakers often did not understand the implications of their acts. Like Steve Small of the Securities Industry Association, she had attended the recent Sununu briefing at the White House. And under questioning from her, the chief of staff had admitted that "we never looked at cross-industry competitiveness" in deciding the levels of taxation. That meant that the summiteers never even considered that they might be helping railroads—and hurting truckers—by setting motor-fuel taxes the way they did. Representative Chandler's coup, she said with a big grin, merely injected the fairness that had been lacking in earlier proposals.

But for now, the truckers continued to fight. "Everybody reads their mail and counts their phone calls," Batts asserted, and she was determined that there would be plenty of truckers on both lists. She then left Simonson to his duty: "Hi, this is Ken Simonson, chief economist of the American Trucking Associations," he said. "I'm calling motor carriers in Louisiana to encourage you to call Senator John Breaux. We hear the Congress is considering . . ."

By midafternoon, high-powered railroad lobbyists had descended on Chandler's office. The delegation even included Donohue's counterpart for the railroads, William Dempsey, the president of the Association of American Railroads. Lobbyists for the railroad unions and for major railroads such as Union Pacific and Burlington Northern, which was another big employer in Chandler's district, also came by. They were all seeking relief from the congressman's ambush of the day before, and he seemed willing to negotiate. "Obviously, none of us is happy with having constituents angry," Chandler told *The Washington Post*. "And Burlington Northern is a major constituent."

But Simonson did not want Chandler to go into those talks unarmed. At the request of Chandler's tax aide, Simonson faxed over some sheets comparing the government subsidies of trucks and trains. The congressman could use those arguments to preserve his pro-truck stance, which, in fact, he did.

• • •

On the same day that Simonson was telephoning around the country and faxing documents to Chandler, the venture capitalists sent a "new development" notice directly to Massachusetts. Having won—and then quickly lost—its "growth" incentives, the venture-capital association was once again pushing for capital gains. But this time there was no pretension of backing the broad-based plan. Senator John Kerry of Massachusetts had introduced a narrow tax cut that fit the group's wishes, and the venture capitalists wanted to encourage him to press for it in the final days of the Congress. So they tried to stir up some letter-writing from constituents. "Capital gains still has a chance," they wrote to their Massachusetts correspondents. "Senator Kerry needs to hear from you—his constituents. Please call him and say, I am a constituent from (city), Massachusetts. I support your tax incentive package for new ventures. It is one thing that Congress can do now to spur economic growth. What can I do to help you get this in the current budget proposal?" His office and fax number were provided.

For Ken Kay of Coretech this endgame period was dizzying. One day he had a temporary R&D credit extension; the next day he had nothing. How it would all work out was anybody's guess. Kay's best opportunity appeared to be a tax package that Bentsen and Packwood were putting together in the Senate. Rostenkowski had already passed a measure that ignored all of the extenders. Conversations with Jenkins and others led Kay to believe that the House was never going to approve the R&D credit and 861. So he turned the organization's full attention to the Senate.

On the afternoon of Friday, October 12, he led a delegation of Coretech lobbyists to speak to Michael Levy, Bentsen's administrative assistant. The group included lobbyists from Pfizer, Motorola, and IBM, each of which had facilities in Texas. During the meeting, the lobbyists emphasized something that Bentsen had already heard from them plenty of times before: The R&D credit and 861 were important to his state.

But Kay did not stop there. To make sure that Bentsen and Packwood did not waver, he drafted for their home-state newspapers press releases that commended them, in effusive language, for their devotion to the nation's research effort. Bentsen's press release was sent on the same day Kay visited his office. Packwood's was dated three days later. Both quoted local electronics executives. Bentsen's release included a quotation from Bill Stotesbery of the American Electronics Association's Texas Council: "Reports we are receiving from Washington, D.C., indicate that once again Lloyd Bentsen is making an extraordinary effort on behalf of the Texas high technology community. We are fortunate to be represented by a senator with the vision to recognize that the health and vitality of our industry, in Texas and around the country, depends on strong, consistent research and development policies." Packwood's release included the same quotation, except that Packwood's name substituted for Lloyd Bentsen's, Oregon replaced Texas, and a person named Phil Robinson, of the Oregon Council, replaced Bill Stotesbery.

In addition to the obviously ersatz praise, Packwood got some extra-special attention. Kay knew that the top three employers in Oregon were electronics companies: Tektronix, Intel, and Hewlett-Packard. So he called lobbyist Eben Tisdale of Hewlett-Packard and asked him to arrange some phone calls and letters to Packwood, which Tisdale gladly did. Hatcher was not happy that Coretech had manipulated the electronics executives without first asking him, but Kay was unrepentant. "It was critical that we got into that package," he said.

As a final effort, what Kay termed "reminder notes" regarding Coretech's tax proposals were mailed from big-name CEOs to almost everyone the coalition could think of. James Burke of Johnson & Johnson wrote to Richard Darman, and Sununu received letters from John Young of Hewlett-Packard, Roy Vagelos of Merck, and Robert Luciano of Schering-Plough Corporation. The lobbyists also made sure to touch base with Jenkins, but there was little more that he could do.

· · ·

Meanwhile, the pace of legislation had accelerated. Committees all over the Hill were spewing out bills so fast that the lobbyists could hardly keep track of them. On the day that Coretech lobbied Bentsen's aide, Rostenkowski made good on his promise to produce a "Democratic" budget bill in the House. Its contents proved the wisdom of Coretech's decision to turn its back on the House and focus, instead, on the Senate.

Crafted mostly by staffer Rob Leonard, the bill was a masterpiece of political compromise. In keeping with the Democrats' rhetoric, it thoroughly soaked the rich, with both a higher top tax rate—33 percent—and a 10 percent surtax on millionaires. At the same time, it tipped its hat to Jenkins and the other pro-capital-gains forces with a "middle-class" capital-gains cut that would have exempted from taxation half of a person's capital gains up to $200,000 over the span of a person's lifetime. But for Coretech, the plan, known as Rosty II, was as disastrous as Rosty I. It, too, failed to extend any of the expiring tax provisions. Other lobbies fared better, however. Efforts by the truckers and the senior citizens, for example, were rewarded. The plan neither raised gasoline taxes nor cut Medicare benefits by a single cent. Life insurers, on the other hand, remained in the hole for $8 billion.

On the next day, Saturday, October 13, it was the Finance Committee's turn. Working until late at night, it hewed much closer to the original budget deal, declining to alter either the top tax rate or the capital-gains rate. But the panel did make changes on the margins, most of which moved in the direction of the lobbyists' desires. All of the expiring tax provisions, for example, were extended through 1991, including the R&D credit and 861. The gas tax was set to rise by 9.5 cents a gallon, which was less than the rise contained in either the original summit plan or Rosty I. Life insurers continued to get hammered for $8 billion.

With all that legislation pending, it was hard to tell what would finally emerge. But at least some lobbyists were given a special treat. In the two days beginning with Wednesday, October 17, the Ways and Means Committee met in secret session to draft a bill that was almost entirely for lobbyists' consumption—and for that of almost no one else. The panel clandestinely approved more than two dozen narrow-interest tax breaks that would have benefited groups ranging from fishermen to nuclear-plant owners—as well as the Washington lobbyists who represented them.

The whole exercise was a kind of safety valve for lobbyists. Lawmakers beholden to their lobbyist friends for one reason or another were given the chance to pay them back. The most important action the lawmakers could take was to consider the issues that the lobbyists had been nagging them about. Representative Raymond McGrath said the session was "strictly for outside interest; it was so we could say, 'We got your bill considered this year.' " Other lawmakers, like Tom Downey, were less charitable. "It was Santa's workshop in October," he said snidely. It was, in effect, a House-side repeat of the feeding frenzy at the Senate Finance Committee the year before.

This time, though, it was unclear just how many of the narrow tax breaks were passed or how much they would cost the taxpayers if they were ever enacted. The committee refused to provide any details. Only the lobbyists who won the benefits for their clients knew for sure what had really been adopted, and they were not eager to gloat about the breaks publicly. "There's nothing to report," committee spokesman James Jaffe said. "There has not been a final action taken."

But as the lobbyists well knew, and no doubt reported with glee to their clients, at least twenty-eight revenue-losing amendments were approved, each deceptively labeled "relatively non-controversial" in a staff document. They included tax relief for private foundations, title-holding companies, and tax-exempt bond underwriters, as well as some old chestnuts from the Finance Committee in 1989 that dealt with rental tuxedos and crop dusters. There were also tax cuts for Guam, aviation-fuel distributors, and mutual funds, as well as a benefit, obtained by some particularly adept lobbyist, that affected "estate tax treatment of certain short-term debt obligations held by nonresident aliens"—whatever those were.

• • •

None of the secret tax breaks would emerge as final legislation. The event was for show. But Jim Rock believed his 75–25 project had a real chance, and he worked feverishly to round up support—with the help of Ken Kies, who also had been hired by real estate interests to press the issue. One of the first stops for each lobbyist was the office of his former employer. Rock went to Jenkins; Kies to Guy Vander Jagt. And after some gentle persuading, both lawmakers became lead sponsors of 75–25 legislation in the House.

The lobbyists then began to play the home-state angle. Rock

did most of the work. Using the far-flung holdings of his client The Newland Group, he approached the most pliant Ways and Means Committee members with pleas from their local Newland executives. A letter from Newland-Texas went to Representative Jake Pickle, for example. A letter from Newland-Florida went to GOP Representative Clay Shaw of that state. And Newland-Washington got in touch with Representative Chandler. Eventually, all four of the lawmakers, and fourteen other members of the Ways and Means Committee, signed a letter to Treasury Secretary Nicholas Brady expressing their "serious concern" about 75–25. The trap had been laid.

By Friday, October 19, both the House and the Senate had approved their budget plans. The heavily Democratic House had chosen the more partisan Rosty II as its plan. The Bentsen plan survived in the Senate mostly unscathed. But not before Bentsen beat back another, though this time mostly symbolic, attempt by Senator David Boren to pass a resolution advocating a capital-gains tax cut. Now it was time for the congressional leadership to reconcile the two bills and, in effect, begin again to negotiate a final budget deal.

As the lawmakers struggled to find enough revenue to meet the deficit-reduction targets, all manner of proposals were bandied about. It was almost as if the leaders were back at Andrews Air Force Base—back at square one—scurrying to find the right combination of proposals to meet their deficit-cutting goals. One of the new revenue-raising ideas discussed at the suggestion of Brady would have hurt the magazine and newspaper industry. The proposal would have pared the corporate deduction for advertising expenditures. Companies were currently able to deduct all advertising expenses immediately. The Brady plan would have disallowed part of that deduction in the first year and required the advertiser to write off the remaining part over five years.

Word of the idea floated out of the closed-door negotiations and all the way to Naples, Florida, where the nation's leading advertisers happened to be gathered for the annual convention of the Association of National Advertisers. Under the direction of their Washington lobbyists, the trade-group members quickly put together lists of the budget negotiators, and drummed up dozens of telephone calls of protest to them right on the spot. As a result the deduction-limitation idea simply withered away, and Rosten-kowski was compelled to publicly dismiss the suggestion. And Bentsen predicted, "That won't happen."

Bob Juliano caught wind of another new starter, and got up from his sickbed to do something about it. During most of the autumn, he had been in tender health. And on Tuesday, October 23, he planned to enter Sibley Memorial Hospital for an out-patient operation to relieve a urinary-tract infection. He was going to get up at 5 A.M. so he could be admitted by 7. His doctors told him to get plenty of rest and drink liquids in preparation.

Dutifully he had left the Senate at 6:30 P.M. on Monday and gone home. But soon after he had sat down for soup and a sand-wich, the phone rang. It was Jean Neal, the administrative assis-tant to Senator Richard Bryan, Democrat of Nevada.

"We're reluctant to call," she began. "But the senator said to let you know that we got a call, and the negotiators are talking again about the business-meal deduction."

"Don't worry," Juliano replied, feigning nonchalance. "I was just getting in the car to come back anyway."

Juliano had been careful to arrange for this call a few weeks earlier. He had told both Bryan and his old friend Senator Daniel Inouye of Hawaii to notify him if the travel-and-entertainment expense deduction came up for even private debate as part of the budget negotiations. At the time, Inouye had looked at Juliano and said, "Don't tell me they're bringing our issue up again." To which Juliano replied a simple "Yep." Both Inouye and Bryan said they would be happy to help Juliano; their states' economies depended on tourism to survive.

In the end, it was Bryan who provided the lobbyist with the heads-up he wanted, and despite his illness, Juliano rushed back to the Capitol to see what he could do. He parked his car near the Capitol, and made his way to the Senate Reception Room. There, beneath its three crystal chandeliers, Neal emerged from the Sen-ate chamber to greet him, and informed him that the negotiators were meeting nearby, in Bob Dole's office. She said that she and Bryan would try to keep Juliano up to date about their progress.

Hours passed. Bryan and Neal came out periodically to tell Juliano how his issue was faring. It turned out that the Bush administration was thinking about cutting back the value of the deduction as a way to raise revenue. As it was, only 80 percent of business meals could be written off for tax purposes. The administration's plan was to reduce that to 50 percent, a move that would raise a lot of money and could also be pitched as a way to increase taxes on rich people.

But ultimately the negotiators decided to turn to more direct, though no less controversial, means. They simply decided to raise the top tax rate to 31 percent from 28 percent. That decision did not come, however, until 1 A.M., just four hours before Juliano was supposed to wake up and go to the hospital. But he remained in the Reception Room until he was sure his issue was safe.

• • •

Life insurance was the one issue that negotiators did not soften on. This was not for lack of trying by the lobbyists, though. In fact, Wayne Thevenot went for help to the biggest lobbyist he knew: his old boss, Russell Long. Thevenot did not have far to go to consult with him. Long's office was located just two floors upstairs from Concord Associates in the Willard Office Building. During this latest period of peace between the stocks and mutuals, in fact, Thevenot often met Long in the company of another Willard Office Building tenant, Tad Davis of Davis & Harman, the lead stock-company lobbying firm. Thevenot and Davis were on different sides of the life-insurance issue, but they were longtime friends. They had hunted together and they met regularly at the 116 Club for honorarium luncheons with lawmakers. Thevenot even watched the Senate debate its budget bill on C-SPAN while sitting in Davis's spacious offices, which were located above Long's.

But both men had their work cut out for them when it came time to brief Long about the blindingly complicated issues involved in life-insurance taxation. It was like old times for Thevenot; he felt like he was still working as the senator's staffer. Thevenot knew Long's strengths and weaknesses well. He knew that Long was a strategist and had little patience for the complexity of the insurance debate. What he needed to know was how harmful a tax increase would be, and the best arguments there were to reduce it. "His pitch was the same as ours," Thevenot said. " 'Think hard about what you're doing. There are a lot of insurance companies that are on the brink. You might push them under. Fifty percent is a godawful hit.' Long was saying there may be more serious consequences to this than you think.

"The benefit of Russell Long," Thevenot continued, "is that he can get through to these people, and with some credibility in their eyes." When Long made a call, it was answered. And according to Thevenot, he reached Bentsen and Packwood and probably other former colleagues of his on the Finance Committee as well. Unfortunately, none of the lawmakers Long contacted could honestly give him much hope. They had a vast need for revenue, and the insurance companies had lots of money. By fighting among themselves for so long, they had become an easy target for a tax increase. Thevenot kept getting the same answer as he made his visits around the Hill, often with Davis at his side. He met with J. D. Foster, the tax aide to Republican Senator Bill Armstrong of Colorado, and with Cody Graves of Senator David Boren's staff; he even went back to see Carolyn Seely in Dole's office. "Those meetings produced some sympathy, but most of them shrugged their shoulders and wished you well," Thevenot said. "They were pretty honest about it: There wasn't much they could do."

The insurance-company lobbyists' case was not aided by the broadcast that week of an ABC News "PrimeTime Live" report. The network had secretly videotaped nine House members frolicking in Barbados over the Easter break with a group of lobbyists, including Vince Reusing, the mutual-company lobbyist from Metropolitan Life. Rostenkowski had led a delegation of lawmakers and their spouses on a taxpayer-paid trip to the island paradise over the spring recess, not knowing that ABC's cameras were waiting for them.

ABC found that the group had spent only seven hours in official meetings in Barbados over the entire Easter weekend. The rest of the time they played tennis, golf, and touch football on the beach with lobbyists from the insurance, toiletries, and computer industries. One sequence showed a cigar-smoking Dawson Mathis, a former House member who was now a lobbyist for Massachusetts Mutual, paying cash for a jet ski for Tom Downey. The Barbados leg of the twelve-day trip, which also took the group to other nearby countries, cost the taxpayers about $42,000, ABC said.

Through a spokesman, Reusing told *The Washington Post* that he had made the trip to discuss "matters of interest" to the firm with lawmakers "in an informal setting." An aide to Downey, who had attended only the Barbados leg of the trip, said Reusing was a friend and that he had allowed the lobbyist to pick up the check for dinner one night. Representatives Barbara Kennelly and Guy Vander Jagt were also on the trip, but not Sam Gibbons, the only lawmaker who by rights should have been there. He chaired the trade subcommittee, and the junket was supposed to concern trade with Caribbean nations.

• • •

The end came in a rush. After an all-night session on Saturday, October 27, the House voted 228–200 to approve the final budget bill, which, when printed and bound, weighed twenty-four pounds and was ten inches thick. The Senate followed at dusk, some eleven hours later, with its own assent, 54–45. The 101st Congress closed down only a few hours later, at 1:17 A.M. EST on Sunday, October 28.

The package of tax increases and spending restraints cut $492 billion from the projected deficit over five years; it was the largest and most ambitious bill of its kind in history. But it was still no cure for chronic budget deficits. For fiscal year 1991, which was already four weeks old, the shortfall was expected to reach $254 billion. And deficits were likely to hover in that same range for years. "We've only taken the first step," Dole said as the Congress came to an end. "And it was painful."

It was especially painful for Dole's Republican party and for President Bush. In the course of more than eight months of torturous budget negotiations, the President abandoned campaign promises to oppose new taxes and to win a significant capital-gains tax cut. He unintentionally revived the GOP's image as defender of the privileged. His own poll ratings plunged in the process, as did those of many Republican candidates who were about to face the voters. Some anti-tax Republicans were in open revolt against him. In addition, the President's once-amiable relations with the Democratic-controlled Congress were permanently scarred.

The final compromise asked for sacrifices from almost everyone. Income taxes were raised in a variety of ways, mostly hitting wealthier Americans. People who bought gasoline, cigarettes, beer, wine, liquor, airline tickets, and expensive automobiles would have to pay more taxes. Farm subsidies, student loans, federal employees, and veterans all faced cutbacks. Even mail rates were likely to go up, to reflect new burdens imposed on the Postal Service.

In the end, though, each of the lobbyists managed to win something. And that, so often, was the story of lobbying in the nation's capital.

Kay and Eizenstat eked out one-year extensions of both the R&D credit and the 861 allocation rule. And Ed Hatcher was successful in preventing the change in the credit that would have hurt small- and medium-size electronics firms. The lobbyists continued to profess to want permanent extensions, but contented themselves with another temporary victory. Predictably, Coretech expressed its thanks to lawmakers through a press release: "In light of all the competing interests and the limited resources available, we are particularly pleased that R&D remained a priority," it proclaimed. But, with a familiar caveat, it continued: "Coretech remains committed to a permanent R&D credit and permanent solution to the problems with 861–8. While we had hoped that the provision could be made permanent in the context of the deficit reduction legislation, we remain hopeful that Congress and the administration will permanently resolve these issues in the next Congress." Other, even more excruciating congratulations were extended through press releases for Pickle, Danforth, Chafee, and Andrews. And personal thank-you notes were written to Anthony, Baucus, and Jenkins.

Simonson and Donohue did not do badly in 1990—considering what could have happened. The motor-fuels tax was increased by just a nickel a gallon, a hike half the size of the one in the most prominent proposals prior to the budget summit, and one-third as large as the rise Rostenkowski had recommended in his "challenge." The truckers also managed to hurt their old nemesis, the railroads. Chandler's proposal to increase taxes on train fuel made it into the final bill, though the railroad lobbyists were able to modify it so that trains would have to pay only half the new tax imposed on trucks. The other excise taxes were also raised, but the tobacco lobby got its compromise: a hike in the cigarette tax of four cents a pack on January 1 and another four cents in 1993. The tax on liquor came back onto the table and rose by $1 to $13.50 a "proof gallon." Wine and beer taxes were raised by even more, but then again, they had not been increased in nearly thirty years.

Maglev rode smoothly through the process, remaining unscathed by any consideration of deficit reduction. The still-nascent effort got a total of $11.2 million in federal dollars, even though Senator Daniel Moynihan conceded, "This is one that we have lost to the Germans and Japanese." In the meantime, several members of Thevenot's Maglev USA coalition were able to ensnare at least some of those federal dollars for themselves. With the lobbyists' guidance, Morrison-Knudsen, Grumman, and Battelle Labs were among the U.S. entities that got government contracts to study Maglev development in the United States.

The stocks and the mutuals were clobbered with an $8 billion, five-year tax increase, the largest tax increase on any single industry. But then again, that was half of the nearly $16 billion tax increase that the Treasury had originally proposed. The intense though belated lobbying by the stocks, the mutuals, and life-insurance agents probably had some effect. But Thevenot was not impressed. "The best light you could shine on it was that the hit was substantially reduced," he said. "But a dose of poison, even half as large, would still kill you."

Concord Associates lost its retainer to the mutuals after 1990, but was still an active lobbying firm, and lawmakers knew it. At the end of the session, Thevenot was solicited to buy a $1,500 ticket to yet another Democratic gala and he was loath to refuse. The person asking him was Susan Torricelli, the ex-wife of the Torch, who was one of Maglev's congressional patrons. "It's almost like blackmail," Thevenot groused. "They ask for money from you as they're screwing you to the wall."

Juliano remained on retainer to the stocks. His information-gathering skills were still needed. And at a Halloween-night fund-raiser for Richard Gephardt at New York's Regency Hotel, Juliano got more good news. Always on duty, especially at parties, Juliano made sure that Jim Robinson of American Express got to chat with the guest of honor. Afterward, Robinson came back to have a private word with Juliano. He shook the lobbyist's hand and said, "As always I can't thank you enough and appreciate all your help on the business meal deduction and all the other issues we dealt with." Despite some troubles at Robinson's firm, Juliano stayed on retainer there as well.

Even Bloomfield did not walk away empty-handed. Though he ended 1990 with his coalition divided, he was able to see the capital-gains rate reduced slightly. The final bill kept the maximum rate on long-term capital gains at 28 percent, but it boosted the top personal rate to 31 percent. That meant there was a differential between the two, and that was what Bloomfield had sought. No one in the investing community believed that such a small gap mattered. But it was something. And Bloomfield believed he would soon be able to build on it, since President Bush still backed his plan.

In his report to the American Council's board of directors, Bloomfield wrote: "As we reflect on the past year, two conclusions come to mind; first, capital formation fared poorly in the tax . . . arena in 1990; second, capital formation will fare better in 1991 and the years ahead." His goal, he wrote, was to press "the business and investment community" to do "a much better job of framing the fundamental terms of the U.S. economic policy debate." As always, he was Mr. Capital Gains.

Even Rock and Kies made out in the end. As the House was passing the budget package, Rostenkowski rose on the floor to make "a few additional points unrelated to this bill." One of them had been brought to his attention by Jenkins. It was about 75–25. He said: "It has also come to my attention that the Internal Revenue Service has issued proposed regulations pursuant to section 451 (h) of the Internal Revenue Code, which would reverse a revenue procedure allowing real estate developers to include in the basis of property, for purposes of determining taxable gain, costs which they are contractually liable to incur in the future. The proposed regulations would be effective for tax years beginning after December 31, 1989. The Congress intends to review the service's proposed action to determine whether it is consistent with legislative intent. To permit such review, the Congress encourages the service to make any such regulations prospective." Rock had written a draft of those words. Soon thereafter the IRS heeded the warning. It announced that it would not require any changes in 75–25 for 1990 tax returns, and implied that any future changes would not be retroactive. Developers around the country had just saved millions of dollars in taxes. And it had all been the handiwork of Rock and Kies. "I sometimes wish," Rock said, "that you couldn't make such a good living in Washington."

But he knew he did not mean it.

Epilogue

All of the lobbyists—and most of their issues—stayed active following the enactment of the big budget bill in 1990. The Surface Transportation Act of 1991, which authorized billions of dollars in new highway and railway construction, provided a major opportunity for lobbying. Kenneth Simonson and Thomas Donohue fought against a motor-fuels tax increase in that bill, and won—with the help of President Bush, who had returned with renewed vigor to his no-tax stance. Senator Daniel Patrick Moynihan played a major role in drafting the legislation, which meant that Maglev won the promise of much more money in the years to come. But Wayne Thevenot was far from out of a job. He still had to work hard to make those Maglev promises come true with the help of his friends on the appropriations committees.

In 1992, Thevenot and the other lobbyists also had plenty of work. With the economy mired in recession and the elections looming, the President and the Congress rushed to find ways to cut taxes as a way to "stimulate growth." The fact that the annual budget deficit loomed in the $300 billion range did not seem to faze anyone. The President put together a package of proposals that included a real estate tax break allowing developers to write off their "passive" losses, a provision that Thevenot had been pushing since the Greenbrier retreat in 1989. Kenneth Kay and Stuart Eizenstat also liked the President's package because it, once again, called for a permanent R&D tax credit. But the President's favorite break remained a cut in capital-gains taxes and, to loud cheers from Mark Bloomfield and Charls Walker, he made it the centerpiece of his plan.

The mere possibility of a fiscal stimulus package brought clients to many lobbyists in 1992. Thanks to his connections with Thevenot's Maglev USA, James Rock got a contract to lobby for tax-free bonds that would pay for a Maglev system in Texas. And Robert Juliano labored to insert a provision into the Senate's tax bill that would have helped the ailing health plan of a branch of the United Mine Workers of America.

But most of this was wheel-spinning. President Bush did not want any fiscal legislation that raised taxes, even on the wealthy. And the Democrats refused to send him anything else. The 1990 budget bill, which Bush had hailed at the time, proved to be a political liability of enormous proportions. And even his great victory in the Persian Gulf war was unable to overcome the anger that many voters harbored against him for failing to reverse the slide of the national economy. The result: The bill that could most have helped the clients of Thevenot, Bloomfield, Walker, Rock, and Juliano fell prey to the President's veto pen in 1992. Even the R&D tax credit—that always hardy perennial—failed to be extended, leaving it, like so many other issues, open for more lobbying once again.

The election year of 1992 appeared to be a time of major transition. Scandal again rocked the Capitol. Voters were incensed when they learned that more than three hundred present and former members of the House had written bad checks at the House Bank. And to a degree not experienced since the resignations of Speaker James Wright and Majority Whip Tony Coelho in 1989, public resentment toward Congress—and all of Washington—boiled over into rage.

Large, perhaps massive changes seemed possible, and lobbyists were preparing to cope with them. Eizenstat, ever the Democratic politico, acted as an informal adviser to not one, but two presidential contenders: Senator Bob Kerrey of Nebraska and Governor Bill Clinton of Arkansas. Thevenot put his money—and much of his money-raising effort—on the charismatic Clinton. But most lobbyists were focused on the ever-worsening situation for incumbents in Congress, especially in the House.

Several favorites of the Washington lobbying corps were reported to have written large numbers of hot checks, and they faced a nervous election season as a result. Representative Robert Mrazek of New York, a major backer of Thevenot's Maglev train, was one of the worst abusers, with 920 overdrafts. This effectively killed his run for the Senate, and his political career. Also high on the list were Democratic backers of a cut in the capital-gains tax, including Representatives Beryl Anthony of Arkansas, who was defeated. Even though he was out of reach of the voters' wrath, Tony Coelho was identified as one of the worst abusers of the lenient banking arrangement, with a reported 316 overdrafts in one year.

Even those without an overdraft problem got caught in the festering anti-incumbent mood. Dozens of lawmakers felt certain that their political careers were about to end. And some of those who had once been considered entrenched were turned out of office. Juliano's friend Representative Marty Russo of Chicago was defeated in Illinois's Democratic primary in March. Because of redistricting, Russo was forced to run against another sitting congressman, Bill Lipinski, and lost partly because of his association with lobbyists, such as the trip to Barbados that was detailed by ABC News. For Juliano, Russo's bad fortune was upsetting, but he was not crippled as a lobbyist. On election night in Chicago he paid his respects to the vanquished Russo, but he was also careful to stop by—and be seen at—the victory party of another lawmaker of his acquaintance who also had faced a tough primary fight: Dan Rostenkowski, chairman of Ways and Means.

Rostenkowski had decided to stay in Congress and continue as leader of the powerful tax-writing panel. That was good news for Juliano. But it was bad news for Representative Ed Jenkins of Georgia. When Rostenkowski told Jenkins earlier in the year that he was not going to retire—as had been long rumored—Jenkins, who would turn sixty on the first day of the new Congress in 1993, decided it was his time to bow out. With Rostenkowski still in the saddle, the chance that Jenkins would one day take his place as chairman all but disappeared. So Jenkins decided to retire at year's end, much to the chagrin of Rock, his former aide. But, like Juliano, Rock was not despondent. As a lobbyist, Rock had already worked alongside another former boss on Capitol Hill: Kent Hance of Texas. He now anticipated that he and Jenkins also might lobby together in the years ahead. And the combination, he thought, could be quite lucrative.

"Our paths will most surely cross again," Rock said with a smile.

In 1993, Jenkins did become a lobbyist. And Rostenkowski continued as chairman of Ways and Means. But federal allegations about Rostenkowski's financial dealings, including at the House Post Office, put his future in doubt. That worry did not deter him, though, from shepherding yet another deficit-reduction bill through Congress.

Remarkably, President Clinton's deficit-reduction package was in many ways a replay of Bush's, right down to the lobbying. Thevenot found another futuristic industry to promote, wireless interactive video, and won an amendment that breathed new life into it. The allies of Bloomfield and Walker finally got a narrow version of their capital gains tax cut. And Ken Kay again was finally able to extend the R&D tax credit, albeit only temporarily.

A few lobbyists even gained some fame. Juliano was hailed in newspaper stories for saving the three-martini lunch deduction, only to have it drastically reduced in the end when his champion, Senator John Bryan of Nevada, decided to vote against the bill. Stuart Eizenstat fared better. He became the best example of how permanent an influence the influence peddlers are. In compensation for all his work on behalf of the Democratic party, Eizenstat was appointed U.S. ambassador to the European Community. Not surprisingly, his White House biography neglected to mention that he had been a lobbyist.

Acknowledgments and Sources

In late 1988, Peter Osnos of Random House suggested to me that there must be a book in corporate lobbying; now there is one. For that I remain deeply grateful to him. The difficult project that ensued was encouraged by my boss at *The Wall Street Journal*, Albert R. Hunt. The influence of both men pervades these pages.

The Lobbyists could not have been written without the cooperation of the lobbyists themselves. Their patience with me, and their thorough answers to my incessant questions, made this book possible. The episodes depicted herein are the result of hundreds of hours of interviews and of on-the-scene reporting over three years with these generous individuals: Mark Bloomfield, Thomas Donohue, Stuart Eizenstat, Robert Juliano, Kenneth Kay, James Rock, Kenneth Simonson, Wayne Thevenot, and Charls Walker. Dozens of other lobbyists also were extremely helpful, including Robert Barrie, Stephen Bell, William Boardman, Nicholas Calio, Maxine Champion, James Gould, David Hardee, Ed Hatcher, Kenneth Kies, Tom Korologos, Jeffrey Levey, Kenneth Levine, Lawrence

O'Brien, Bruce Thompson, Fred Wertheimer, William Wilkins, and John Winburn.

My own reporting was supplemented by several sources. The history of lobbying, in Chapter 1, relied on five books: *The Pressure Boys: The Inside Story of Lobbying in America*, by Kenneth G. Crawford; *The Lobbyists: The Art and Business of Influencing Lawmakers*, by Karl Schriftgiesser; *The Lobbyists*, by James Deakin; *The Washington Lobby*, edited by Colleen McGuiness; and the excellent book *Organized Interests and American Democracy*, by Kay Lehman Scholzman and John Tierney. In addition, the self-deprecating description of a lobbyist in the first chapter came from *Vested Interest*, by Charles B. Lipsen and Stephen Lesher. On matters of congressional history, I used the invaluable *Congressional Quarterly Almanac*, as well as *Politics in America*, edited by Phil Duncan, and *The Almanac of American Politics*, by Michael Barone and Grant Ujifusa.

Other journalists also helped provide some of the book's facts, quotations, and anecdotes. The profile of Stuart Eizenstat in Chapter 3 was aided by the work of Edward Walsh of *The Washington Post*. In the same chapter, details about Representative Tony Coelho and PACs were drawn from Brooks Jackson's *Honest Graft*. Chapter 4 relies on Dan Fesperman of *The Baltimore Sun* for part of its description of the 116 Club, and on John Yoo of *The Wall Street Journal* for its rendition of the Ways and Means Committee bicentennial celebration. The ongoing work on lobbying by Jill Abramson of *The Wall Street Journal*, Charles Babcock of *The Washington Post*, and Brooks Jackson of Cable News Network aided my description of the lobbyists' world.

I owe a great debt to the able and affable Henry Ferris of Times Books, who helped me craft the narrative. Additional assistance with the text was provided by Terence Moran of *Legal Times*, Thomas Petzinger of *The Wall Street Journal*, and Barry Toiv, one of my oldest friends in the world. I also thank Robert Barnett of Williams and Connolly for his superb advice. Special thanks to Karen Hosler and my partner in crime, Alan Murray.

The Wall Street Journal, my home for fourteen years, was enormously kind to me and my project. For that I thank the editors: Norman Pearlstine, Paul Steiger, Rich Jaroslovsky, Henry Oden, and Ronald Shafer. I also thank my colleagues and friends: Kenneth Bacon, Jackie Calmes, Tim Clark, Peter Edwards, Peter Grunwald, Brian Kelly, Mary Motta, James Perry, David Rogers, Gerald Rosen, David Shribman, and David Wessel.

More than words are needed to describe how much my family gave and forgave to bring this project to completion. To my parents, Earl and Esther Birnbaum, to my wife, Deborah, and most of all to my wonderful children, Michael and Julia: I thank you with all my heart.

Suggested Reading

Adams, Gordon. *The Iron Triangle: The Politics of Defense Contracting.* New York: Council on Economic Priorities, 1981.

Berry, Jeffrey M. *The Interest Group Society.* Glenview, Ill.: Scott, Foresman & Co., 1989.

Birnbaum, Jeffrey H., and Alan S. Murray. *Showdown at Gucci Gulch: Lawmakers, Lobbyists and the Unlikely Triumph of Tax Reform.* New York: Random House, 1987; Vintage, 1988.

Broder, David S. *Behind the Front Page.* New York: Simon & Schuster, 1987.

Choate, Pat. *Agents of Influence: How Japan's Lobbyists in the United States Manipulate America's Political and Economic System.* New York: Alfred A. Knopf, 1990.

Cigler, Allan J., and Burdett A. Loomis, editors. *Interest Group Politics.* Washington, D.C.: Congressional Quarterly Press, 1986.

Close, Arthur C., Gregory L. Bologna, and Curtis W. McCormick, editors. *Washington Representatives 1989*. Washington, D.C.: Columbia Books, 1989.

Crawford, Kenneth G. *The Pressure Boys: The Inside Story of Lobbying in America*. New York: Julian Messner, Inc., 1939.

Deakin, James. *The Lobbyists*. Washington, D.C.: Public Affairs Press, 1966.

Drew, Elizabeth. *Politics and Money: The New Road to Corruption*. New York: Macmillan, 1983.

Edsall, Thomas Byrne. *The New Politics of Inequality*. New York: W. W. Norton & Co., 1984.

———. *Power and Money: Writing About Politics, 1971–1987*. New York: W. W. Norton & Co., 1988.

Ehrenhalt, Alan. *The United States of Ambition: Politicians, Power, and the Pursuit of Office*. New York: Times Books, 1991.

Godwin, R. Kenneth. *One Billion Dollars of Influence: The Direct Marketing of Politics*. Chatham, N.J.: Chatham House Publishers, Inc., 1988.

Green, Mark J. *The Other Government: The Unseen Power of Washington Lawyers*. New York: W. W. Norton & Co., 1978.

Grieder, William. *Who Will Tell the People?* New York: Simon & Schuster, 1992.

Haas, Lawrence J. *Running on Empty: Bush, Congress and the Politics of a Bankrupt Government*. Homewood, Ill.: Business One Irwin, 1990.

Jackson, Brooks. *Honest Graft: Big Money and the American Political Process*. New York: Alfred A. Knopf, 1988.

Jacobs, Jerald, editor. *Federal Lobbying*. Washington, D.C.: BNA Books, 1989.

Levitan, Sar A., and Martha Cooper. *Business Lobbies: The Public Good and the Bottom Line*. Baltimore: Johns Hopkins University Press, 1983.

Lipsen, Charles B., and Stephen Lesher. *Vested Interest*. Garden City, N.Y.: Doubleday, 1977.

Malbin, Michael J. *Parties, Interest Groups and Campaign Finance Laws*. Washington, D.C.: American Enterprise Institute for Public Policy Research, 1980.

Matthews, Christopher. *Hardball: How Politics Is Played—Told by One Who Knows the Game*. New York: Summit Books, 1988.

McGuiness, Colleen, editor. *The Washington Lobby*. Washington, D.C.: Congressional Quarterly, Inc., 1987.

Nader, Ralph, and William Taylor. *The Big Boys: Power and Position in American Business*. New York: Pantheon Books, 1986.

Ornstein, Norman J., and Shirley Elder. *Interest Groups, Lobbying and Policymaking*. Washington, D.C.: Congressional Quarterly Press, 1978.

Phillips, Kevin. *The Politics of Rich and Poor: Wealth and the American Electorate in the Reagan Aftermath*. New York: Random House, 1990.

Rossiter, Clinton, editor. *The Federalist Papers*. New York: New American Library, 1961.

Sabato, Larry J. *PAC Power: Inside the World of Political Action Committees*. New York: W. W. Norton & Co., 1984.

Scholzman, Kay Lehman, and John Tierney. *Organized Interests and American Democracy*. New York: Harper & Row Publishers Inc., 1986.

Schriftgiesser, Karl. *The Lobbyists: The Art and Business of Influencing Lawmakers*. Boston: Little, Brown & Co., 1951.

Smith, Hedrick. *The Power Game: How Washington Works*. New York: Random House, 1988.

Stern, Philip M. *The Best Congress Money Can Buy*. New York: Pantheon Books, 1988.

Vogel, David. *Fluctuating Fortunes: The Political Power of Business in America*. New York: Basic Books, 1989.

Wolfe, Bruce C. *Lobbying Congress: How the System Works*. Washington, D.C.: Congressional Quarterly Press, 1990.

Zorack, John L. *The Lobbying Handbook: A Comprehensive Lobbying Guide*. Washington, D.C.: Professional Lobbying and Consulting Center, 1990.

Company and Organization Index

General Index

in lobbying outside Ways and
Means' meeting room, 133
lobbyist trade learned by, 39–40
on merging of lobbying firms,
209–10
popularity of, 40
Rostenkowski feted by, 120–22
skill of, 37
and taxation of insurance
companies, 133, 188, 249
traveling of, 148
Tuesday Night Group of, 39–40
VATs and, 33
and Ways and Means' two-
hundredth anniversary, 120–23
Justice Department, U.S., 41
HUD scandal and, 182
lobbyist registration with, 13

Kassebaum, Nancy Landon,
57–58
Kasten, Robert, capital-gains taxes
and, 245–47, 258
Kay, Kenneth, 19–20, 241–44
background of, 93–94
budget agreements and, 293
budget summits and, 264–65,
268, 271
campaign contributions and,
166–67
capital-gains taxes and, 243–44
on Eizenstat, 92
and R&D tax credits, 19, 82–83,
86, 89, 93–94, 98, 110, 117–19,
155–56, 175–76, 181–82, 202–4,
219, 241–43, 264–65, 268, 271,
284–85, 293, 298
Kaye, Tracy, 175, 220
Kemp, Jack, 245
Kennedy, John F., 15, 17, 149,
236
Kennedy, Robert F., 15

Kennelly, Barbara, 260, 292
and taxation of insurance
companies, 188–89
Kennon, Donald, 121
Kerr, Bob, 81
Kerry, John, 39, 299
capital-gains taxes and, 146, 173,
284
Kertzman, Mitchell, 191–99
capital-gains taxes and, 192–99,
253, 265
CEO Fly-In and, 192–99
and Rostenkowski's deficit-
reduction packages, 253
Keyserling, Jonathan, 128
Kiernan, Robert, 60
Kies, Kenneth, 182
corporate minimum-tax law and,
127, 132
75–25 legislation and, 287, 295–96
and taxation of insurance
companies, 249
Vander Jagt's relationship with,
126–27
Kilhenny, Valerie, 213
Kilroy, Richard, 167
Kingsley, Daniel, 232
Koch, Edward I., 93
Korea, South, U.S. officials bribed
by, 16
Korologos, Tom, 59, 236
Kravis, Henry, 166
Kuwait, Iraqi invasion of,
259, 261

Labor Department, U.S., 41
Landrum, Phil, 64
Lawrence, Robert, 87, 256–57
Leach, Jim, 276
Leath, Marvin, 42
Legislative Reorganization Act, 13
Lehman, William, 222–23

About the Author

JEFFREY H. BIRNBAUM, a White House reporter for *The Wall Street Journal*, has covered Washington and national politics from many angles. A native of Scranton, Pennsylvania, he graduated in 1977 from the University of Pennsylvania, where he was a Benjamin Franklin Scholar. He worked as a reporter for *The Miami Herald* in 1977 and 1978 before joining *The Wall Street Journal*'s New York bureau to cover retailing and advertising. In 1982, he moved to the Washington bureau, where his beats have included agriculture, taxes, Congress, and presidential campaigns. The book he co-authored with Alan S. Murray about the Tax Reform Act of 1986, *Showdown at Gucci Gulch*, was named the best book by a journalist in 1987 by the American Political Science Association. He lives in Silver Spring, Maryland, with his wife and two children.

'Who Owns Information' -Anne Wells Branscomb